GH00982769

Richard Belfield is an ... r/
director, author and pl... es
have won prizes on bo... A
Brief History of Hitmen and Assassinations, he is the author of
Can You Crack the Enigma Code? He is a Director of
Fulcrum TV, a well-established independent production
company in London, and has made programmes for every
British terrestrial channel as well as the National Geographic
Channel, Discovery, the Arts & Entertainment Network and
WGBH in the USA.

During the 1990s, he was the *New Statesman*'s Internet
correspondent, writing a weekly column, long before the web
had the global dominance it has today. He has been interviewed on radio and television as an expert on assassination
and has been a guest speaker for *Le Monde Diplomatique*, the
Forensic Science Society and at an international conference
organised by the National Security Agency in the USA.

A BRIEF HISTORY OF

HITMEN AND ASSASSINATIONS

Richard Belfield

RUNNING PRESS
PHILADELPHIA · LONDON

For George, Gloria and Lowell

Constable & Robinson Ltd
3 The Lanchesters
162 Fulham Palace Road
London W6 9ER
www.constablerobinson.com

Part 1 of this book first published in the UK as *Terminate with Extreme Prejudice* by
Robinson, an imprint of Constable & Robinson Ltd., 2005

This updated and revised edition published by Robinson, 2011

Copyright © Richard Belfield 2005, 2011

The right of Richard Belfield to be identified as the author of this work has been asserted by
him in accordance with the Copyright, Designs and Patents Act 1988

A copy of the British Library Cataloguing in
Publication data is available from the British Library

ISBN 978-1-84901-520-2

1 3 5 7 9 10 8 6 4 2

First published in the United States in 2011 by Running Press Book Publishers.

9 8 7 6 5 4 3 2 1

Digit on the right indicates the number of this printing

US Library of Congress Control: 2010928993
US ISBN 978-0-7624-4100-6

Running Press Book Publishers
2300 Chestnut Street
Philadelphia, PA 19103-4371
Visit us on the web!
www.runningpress.com

Typeset by TW Typesetting, Plymouth, Devon

Printed and bound in the EU

CONTENTS

Part 4: Aftermath

ACKNOWLEDGEMENTS

First of all I would like to thank my friend Jonathan Harris, who encouraged me to write this book. But for him, the manuscript would still be staring at me from the shelf along with the half-finished novels and two unfinished plays.

Several key friends have been invaluable. Colonel John Hughes Wilson has been an excellent companion and adviser throughout and I have selfishly taken something away from every meeting with him. Abdallah Homouda is a brilliant commentator on all matters Arabic and together we had an enthralling evening with General Nabawy Ismail, who was kind with his time and hospitality and explained many of the mysteries behind the Sadat assassination.

Joe Layburn, Dominic Yeatman, John Goetz and I made the two documentaries about the assassination of WPC Yvonne Fletcher for Channel 4's current affairs series *Dispatches*. They are all exceptional investigators and together we unravelled what happened that morning and in the months before and after her killing. I must also say a special thanks to David Lloyd, who commissioned the programmes and his then-deputy Dorothy Byrne who helped guide them on to the screen.

Steve Anderson at ITV commissioned the investigations into the death of Diana. I will always be grateful to him for his guidance as well as his unflinching and cheerful support. Both he and the Director of Programmes David Liddiment were model television executives, riding out the ill-informed flak from a small but noisy coterie of journalists – all of whom had no problem telling their readers exactly what had happened that night in Paris, even though many had not done any original research themselves. The second ITV programme was made with my good friend Anthony Scrivener QC, who consumed boxes of material and then asked questions which no one else had even considered. My special thanks to him, his assistant Ellen Staples and his wife Ying.

What would I have done without Colin Wallace, Dr Saul Kelly (who introduced me to the Special Operations Executive (SOE) diary and very kindly sent me the references to assassination), Ian Drury, Jan Burgess, Jim and Caroline Hougan, John Conway, John Stockwell, Mal Peachey, Michael Asher, Professor M.R.D. Foot, George Thom, Robin Robison and Stuart Benson.

Along with scores of other researchers, I owe a huge debt to the staff at the Public Records Office in London who are always smiling, helpful and prepared to go that extra mile to help find that elusive file containing the little gem which makes the trip to Kew worthwhile. On the other side of the Atlantic, the staff at the National Security Archive in Washington deserve a Congressional Medal of Honour. Any serious student of modern American politics should set aside a big chunk of time and log on to www.gwu.edu/~nsarchiv/, a huge treasure trove of original documents and percipient analysis located at the George Washington University in Washington DC. The Cold War History Project at the Woodrow Wilson Center, also in Washington DC, is another invaluable website which should be used in parallel. It can be found at the Woodrow Wilson website, www.wilsoncenter.org. In a country where traditional freedoms are slowly being chewed away by an aggressive state they are both invaluable beacons of knowledge and intelligence as to the world we actually live in.

My agent Robert Kirby at United Agents, along with his assistants, Catherine Cameron and Charlotte Knee. Pete Duncan, my editor at Constable & Robinson, has been focused and contributed some clever ideas towards structuring the final book.

I would like to thank those members of the intelligence services from different countries who have talked to me over the years and helped to refine my thinking. To all of you who cannot be named for obvious reasons, my eternal thanks. You know who you are, but hopefully your employers do not!

I am particularly grateful to the senior National Security Agency officer who showed me that this world is like three-dimensional chess, made more complex by the certain knowledge that there can be two things which are both true yet which are mutually exclusive and contradict each other. Over dinner in a restaurant in Georgetown, Washington DC, he explained how this insight had helped him reach a state of karmic bliss, allowing him to wander unharmed through the wilderness of mirrors without ever getting lost.

My children, George, Gloria and Lowell have been wonderful. Throughout the writing of this book I have discussed many aspects of it with them. They have all made excellent suggestions and asked those pertinent questions which have sent me back to the keyboard for yet another re-think.

And finally, a very special thanks to Chrissy White. Without her, this would simply never have happened.

Since this book was first published I have met and discussed the topic of assassination with many from this twilight world. I am very grateful to all of them for their candour and their willingness to open up on the topic of assassination and their knowledge of it, either directly or tangentially. Nothing I have heard or read has caused me to want to change anything from the original text. I remain neutral, preferring to stick with the known and the provable rather than the imagined. In my experience, this usually means discounting the official version of events as the implausible scenario.

I have discussed the Diana/Dodi Paris crash at great length with many since I first made two documentaries for ITV and wrote about it in the first edition of this book. Those who believe it was an accident argue that it could not have been murder as there was no time to plan it. I have raised this with practitioners from this world, all of whom have offered the same insight: if the target is difficult and elusive (as she was) then they would track them for months until the right moment arose. Patience is as important as planning.

I have learned one other thing from these conversations. Whilst journalists and academics often say, usually rather loftily, that they don't believe that conspiracy exists, the opposite view is held by those in the penumbra world of intelligence. This was best expressed to me in a bar in Whitehall one evening. A wonderful tirade from a retired SIS officer, who told me he despised journalists and historians who said they did not believe that conspiracies exist. 'How fucking naive! That's all I ever did for thirty years. That's what we are paid to do. If I hadn't conspired to do all the things I had to do I would have been fired – and quite right too. I am a conspirator. That was my fucking job!'

It was said with the passion of the exasperated; eloquent and visceral.

INTRODUCTION

Assassination is the world's oldest political act. Assassinations are the punctuation of history, predating the nation state, standing armies, kings and queens, monarchs and emperors. They provoke wars, bring on revolutions, causing seismic shifts in national and global power.

Assassinations are not just murders. To assassinate is to kill by treacherous violence, and the killing is usually – but not always – a well-known public figure. In most cases the motive is specific and the target is always a named individual or small group of related individuals, often family relatives. Assassination is political murder, where the motives, no matter how mixed, are all about power: those who do not have power assassinate to get it and those who have power assassinate to keep it.

Every great empire has flourished and declined, subject to the great cyclical shifts of power, trade, religious and commercial dominance, and assassination has underpinned the continuing imperial saga as emperors have come and gone, each trying to shape the world to their liking.

The discrete history of the great empires was one of persistent regicide, with their rise and fall often defined by the assassination of a key figure. Rulers arrived with a flourish but were frequently carried away on a river of blood and tears. Assassination was the constant, as were the weapons. Before the arrival of gunpowder, men used the dagger as their weapon of choice, women (usually the wives and mothers of great men) preferring poison.

All these ancient empires shared one characteristic, which made them uniquely vulnerable to assassination. They were highly centralized, with power focused on one person – usually a man – who had the power of life or death over his subjects. But it was this intense focus of imperial authority that made assassination such a seductive short-circuit route to imperial supremacy. Power was vested in the crown but no matter how gilded and magnificent this might have been, it had all the characteristics of a woolly hat: one size fitted all. Occupation of the throne and the right to juggle the baubles of state always had the potential to be a transitory experience. Though many leaders believed they were gods in human form, plugged directly into an ethereal, transcendent power derived directly from the deity of their choice, they soon discovered that this was no insurance against a brutal death, often at the hands of their relatives. Ultimately all these empires – and their leaders – marched to the beat of the assassin's drum, not their own. A world reduced to two classes: the movers and the shaken.

Nowadays, the most common form of assassination is that sponsored by the state and is far more common than most modern governments like to admit. It is a frequent extension of the normal diplomatic process and is cheaper than war. Before the Second Gulf War, the assassination of Saddam Hussein (as the cheapest solution to the problem of Iraq) was openly discussed at White House briefings for journalists.[1] This immediately became known as the '8 cent option', eight cents being the cost of a single bullet. Small calibre rounds are not always the weapon of choice. George Bush's predecessor, President Clinton, tried to solve the problem of Osama Bin Laden by ordering cruise missile strikes on the Afghanistan camp where the Central Intelligence Agency (CIA) believed he was meeting other Al Qaeda leaders, despite there being an Executive Order specifically prohibiting the use of the assassination tool by an American president.[2] At a million dollars a missile this was modern assassination in its deluxe version.

The assassination of Julius Caesar in 44 BCE[3] used far more primitive technology (knives and swords), but for the last 2,000 years it has been an object lesson for everyone in the assassination business. It backfired on the plotters: none came to power as a result of removing their leader and all were dead within three years of spilling Caesar's blood on the steps of the Senate. After this assassination, plausible deniability became the defining characteristic of the business and, apart from terrorist groups, few since have ever bragged of their acts. However, all that has changed recently.

We now live in the age of assassination. The George W. Bush administration and Israel (its closest Middle Eastern ally) both put assassination at the heart of their foreign policy, the first modern governments ever to announce this publicly. The last state to do this was the Hashshashin, known as the Assassins, a ruthless sect who terrorized the Middle East between 1090 and 1256 CE.

The US has been in the assassination business almost continually since 1945, mostly as a covert activity. But since the mid-1980s they have often not bothered to cover their tracks, in the very public attempted assassinations of Qaddafi, Saddam and Osama Bin Laden. The policy of using selective assassination against the Al Qaeda leadership has continued under President Obama. Unpiloted Predator drones fly from an airfield in Pakistan, but are controlled and operated from a US Air Force base in Nevada. They have been highly effective in killing the Al Qaeda senior command foolish enough to emerge from their caves.

On the ground in Afghanistan, the NATO coalition forces have used a TOP SECRET black ops unit called Task Force 373, with a target list of 2,000 names. What used to be 'executive action' is now euphemistically called, the 'joint prioritised effects list', JPEL for short. Included in the JPEL are senior Taliban and Al Qaeda leaders as well as major drug traders. Many have been assassinated, often killed in their beds in the middle of the night. Thousands more have been captured and taken away for interrogation and internment without trial. As is always the case with these types of operations, good intelligence is crucial, as is the ability to be able to assassinate the target – and only the target. This is not where US Special Forces are particularly strong and there have been several incidents where women, children and civilians have been killed, as well as an attack where they killed Afghan police officers. As every counter-insurgency commander knows, each incident like this is a public relations disaster. Meanwhile, Israel is the only modern state which has had a prime minister who was an operational assassin – Ehud Barak, who led one of the most daring murder operations in modern times. On 6 April 1973, dressed as a woman (black wig, heavy make-up, matching shoes and handbag, bra stuffed with grenades) he headed a killer team which slipped into Beirut at night and shot dead three senior members of the Palestine Liberation Organization (PLO).

Since the foundation of modern Israel, assassination has always been an instrument of public policy. But recently there has been a quantum break from the past: their politicians now crow about it. When the Israelis assassinated Sheikh Yassin, the spiritual leader of the terrorist group Hamas in March 2004, they were proud to say that the order came from the Prime Minister Ariel Sharon, though this was only after securing a majority vote in the Security Cabinet.[4] There was no attempt to disguise where the orders came from or who was responsible.

This assassination was condemned by politicians everywhere, except Washington. The British Foreign Secretary Jack Straw was typical of most international politicians, saying the killing was 'unlawful, unacceptable and unjustified'[5] but the morality of assassination is fluid. Eight months earlier, US troops assassinated Saddam Hussein's two sons, Uday and Qusay, firing an anti-tank TOW missile into the villa where they were hiding, rather than making any attempt to capture them alive and put them on trial for their crimes. This time there was no talk from the British of unlawful acts. Instead, Straw blamed the brothers, saying it was their fault for not leaving Iraq when they had the chance.[6] An American military spokeswoman was much less circumspect, saying the soldiers were 'absolutely giddy' and 'absolutely proud' and that the 101st Airborne Division, which carried out the attack, 'kicks ass'. She added, 'The 101st has a proud history of military tradition,[7] and this just adds to that tradition.' The USA subsequently vetoed a UN resolution condemning the assassination. Britain abstained. Another triumph for the world's self-acclaimed moral guardians.

In 2010 an Israeli assassination squad killed a Hamas leader, Mahmoud al-Mabhouh, in his hotel room in Dubai. They travelled on false British, Irish, French, German and Australian passports. Afterwards, there was much huffing and puffing from the countries affected. There were also a lot of clichés rattling from the Foreign Office and British politicians ('seriously jeopardising', 'a disgrace', 'a full investigation needed'), but that was it. All a far cry from 1986, when the then Prime Minister Margaret Thatcher closed down Mossad's UK operation after one of their agents lost a bag of forged British passports. This time round, the British expelled a Mossad officer from London – not much more than a gentle slap on the wrist.

Back in Israel, the Dubai assassination was celebrated and quickly embraced by popular culture. A retail chain, Mahsaney

Kimat Hinam (Almost Free Warehouses), produced a TV advert which aped the surveillance footage released by the Dubai police of the assassins wandering around a supermarket. The tag line for the advert was 'shooting down' prices.

Within weeks of the assassination it was back to business as usual, the Israelis secure in the knowledge that there seems to be an invisible clause in international law that makes them exempt.

In 1967, they attacked a US spy ship, the USS *Liberty*, killing thirty-four Americans and injuring 170 others. The *Liberty* was in international waters and clearly flying the Stars and Stripes on a bright afternoon in the eastern Mediterranean. The attack went on for over an hour, during which time they hit the ship from air and sea with cannons and torpedoes. Despite the weight of evidence showing that this was premeditated, the Israelis got away with it, claiming it was 'a mistake'. This single incident, and the continued failure of successive American governments to confront the issue, has confirmed their belief that they can attack whomever they wish.

One of the few exceptions to this was when the Israelis sent an assassination team to London in the 1990s. The Metropolitan Police warned their ambassador that he would be charged with conspiracy to murder if their planned assassination went ahead. After the usual flurry of denials, the Israeli team returned home.

This book is not an encyclopaedia and not every assassination is covered. Instead, I have looked at assassination as a political phenomenon and tried to identify the themes and undercurrents running through what started life as the world's oldest political act but is now a regular feature of the political landscape. There is barely a day when the newspapers do not carry an assassination-related story from somewhere in the world. Political leaders, government ministers, politicians, judges, police officers, journalists, trade union activists and civil rights lawyers are routinely assassinated. Their killers are rarely caught or brought to justice. Over time, some assassins have learned from the past and become accomplished technicians. There are some modern assassinations (Chandra Bose, Robert Kennedy, Jim Jones, WPC Yvonne Fletcher and Yitzhak Rabin) that were brilliantly choreographed, where the assassins killed their target, got away and (pretty effectively) covered their tracks. However, these tend to be the exception and even with these examples there are enough clues to give the game away.

Assassinations tend to split historians and writers into two crude camps: those who see conspiracy in everything and those who prefer to reduce everything to cock-up. I subscribe to neither theory. The reality is that assassination is far too complex to fit into either box and has more than its fair share of both conspiracy and cock-up, often intertwined.

The weakness of the conspiracy theory is that it depends too much on wishful linking and often confuses connection with cause. There is a wealth of evidence showing that the Italian mafia in the USA plotted with the CIA to assassinate President Kennedy, but this does not mean that they actually did it. For each assassination there are a far greater number of plots and conspiracies that lead to nothing. The key here is to separate plotting from action.

The cock-up theory is inadequate as a means of explaining what are often complex and contradictory events. It is intellectually lazy and fails as a means of competent analysis. It usually only works if the difficult questions are not addressed and large chunks of evidence are ignored. For example, the official scenario to explain Princess Diana's death – that it was because of a drunk driver, recklessly driving out of control, and that no one else was involved[8] – is the only scenario for which there is no credible evidence.

The blood test, which 'proved' the driver Henri Paul was drunk, used a discredited technique,[9] which is so inaccurate that it has not been allowed in a British court of law for nearly twenty years. It also has such serious internal contradictions as to make it valueless. If it is correct, then Henri Paul was not only very drunk when he arrived at the Ritz Hotel some two hours before driving to his death, he also had 30 per cent carbon monoxide poisoning.[10] The symptoms of carbon monoxide poisoning include dizziness, nausea, light-headedness, blurred and double vision, balancing problems, unclear thinking and problems keeping attention and finding words. If he had this combination of alcohol and carbon monoxide it would have been instantly obvious to everyone around him. Yet he very clearly had none of these symptoms. He chatted happily in English (his second language) with Diana's bodyguards, and the Ritz Hotel security footage shows him completely in control of himself and his surroundings, even bending down to tie up his shoe laces, an impossible act for someone carrying this amount of alcohol and carbon monoxide. To date, no pathologist has been able to come up with a coherent explanation. The best explanation so far is that it is 'an enigma'.[11] Meanwhile, the proponents of the cock-up theory of the crash deal with this awkward question by simply failing to address it.

This is not the only problem with the cock-up theory about the Paris crash. The key eyewitnesses do not support the notion of a driver racing away with no one near. Instead, they talk of a motorbike harassing the Mercedes as it entered the tunnel, making it very difficult for Henri Paul, the driver, to keep in a straight line. This person has never been identified. However, if his motive was simply to harass the driver he is guilty of manslaughter. If his intention was to cause a crash then he is guilty of murder.[12]

Only a small percentage of assassinations are spontaneous affairs, carried out by delusional psychopaths acting alone. In the vast majority of cases, there are two people or more involved and that, in legal terms, is a conspiracy, from the Latin *con spire*, to breathe together. In the case of Julius Caesar, there were sixty conspirators and the terms of the deal between them were that the dozen or so who assassinated him all had to stab him and be covered by his blood, binding them collectively to the murderous plot,[13] making this the quintessential assassination conspiracy.

Virtually all major modern assassinations involve the intelligence and security services in one way or another. In the last century, there has been hardly a single major political assassination which was not either carried out by them, facilitated or allowed by them or happened because they failed to adequately protect the target – a well-shaken cocktail of conspiracy and cock-up, with both ingredients often in the same incident.

There have been cases of elaborately planned assassinations, intricately woven conspiracies involving prime ministers, presidents, spymasters, highly trained assassins and the world's most exotic weapons, which have failed at the last minute, because of a cock-up which, if it were in a B-movie, would be dismissed by the audience as completely implausible.

In the movies, a highly trained assassin does not turn up on his target's doorstep, have a crisis of conscience, confess all and then hand himself over to the police, knowing that a long prison sentence will follow. No cinema audience would ever tolerate such an implausible plot but in real life this has actually happened – and what is even harder to believe, two assassins from the same intelligence service did exactly this, in back-to-back operations.

In fiction, top spymasters do not take handwritten notes saying 'do not mention the word assassination' during a meeting with their political masters. In real life they do. In the best thrillers, silencers are essential gear for any modern assassin and they always work brilliantly. In real life, one highly paid, trained killer threw his away because it burned his hands.

No Hollywood scriptwriter would construct a scene in which a group of hard-nosed killers decide to assassinate a political leader, agree that they have to cover their tracks and that no mention must be made of their plans – and then write a detailed minute of the meeting for the files and circulate it widely. But again, in actuality they did.

In films, the bomb always explodes as the hero runs away from the building. No studio boss would tolerate a script where a truckload of TNT fails to go off because the evil terrorist gang forgot to attach the detonator. But it happened.

The first example is Russian, the second and third are American, the fourth one is British and the final one is an Islamic Jihad group.

Operational incompetence is not a national characteristic as the New Zealand police discovered when they investigated the French attack on the Greenpeace boat, the *Rainbow Warrior*. The highly trained assassins left their scuba-diving air bottles behind (complete with French markings), were spotted by a night watchman who took their car number, had crudely forged Swiss passports and a notebook with direct-line phone numbers straight back to the French Defence Ministry in Paris. As one old French intelligence officer noted, short of leaving a beret, a baguette and a bottle of Beaujolais at the crime scene they could not have left more clues.

Not surprisingly, given the flood of revelations which has poured out in the last few years, it is fashionable to dismiss the world's intelligence services as bumbling fools, an image which the British have often cultivated for perfectly good operational reasons. But incompetence is not the sole issue, though it does run through the business of intelligence. The world's security and intelligence services share many of the characteristics of all large organizations: bureaucratic infighting is rife and this is accompanied by the inexorable rise of the mediocre. Like other unwieldy institutional machines, ineptitude and inertia are rampant. Heavy drinking and alcohol-fuelled paranoia are common and all the world's intelligence services have their fair share of drunks, the mentally disturbed and the obsessional – and given the work they do, it may well be that they have a disproportionate number of all of these.

Intelligence officers spend much of their lives loitering in the gutters of human emotion. Their basic trade is deceit and the manipulation of the least attractive aspects of human psychology (venality, treachery, duplicity, greed, disloyalty). It is therefore hardly surprising that in this looking-glass world little is what it seems. Morals are a chimera. Those in the assassination business short-circuit key parts of the brain, cutting the links between morality and action, ends and means. When this happens, assassination becomes the political currency of the day.

In 1957, the British Prime Minister Harold Macmillan and his American counterpart President Dwight Eisenhower approved a joint plan between MI6 (the UK's intelligence and espionage agency) and the CIA to fake a series of border incidents which would be used as cover for an invasion of Syria in which 'a special effort should be made to eliminate certain key individuals'. The three to be assassinated were: Abd al-Hamid Sarraj, the Head of Military Intelligence; Afif al-Bizri, the Chief of the General Staff and Khalid Bakdash, the Leader of the Communist Party. The plan was then to instal a pro-Western regime that 'would probably need to rely first upon repressive measures and arbitrary exercise of power,' that is, the usual diet of torture, state-sponsored assassination and a total disregard for the rule of law. A wily political operator, Macmillan kept the plan very tight, refusing even to discuss it with the Chiefs of Staff, because they were inveterate gossips who tended 'to chatter'.[14]

This was not the only foray into the world of assassination for Macmillan and Eisenhower. There are extensive records showing that throughout 1960, the British, Americans, Portuguese and Belgians all plotted to assassinate Patrice Lumumba, the charismatic and democratically elected leader of the Congo.[15] British intelligence officers, civil servants and politicians (including three prime ministers) discussed this at every level, in top-secret government meetings and with their opposite numbers in Washington, both at cabinet and presidential/prime ministerial level.

While these discussions were being held in secret, the voters on both sides of the Atlantic were being treated to one of the first doses of television spin. At the end of August 1960, President Eisenhower and British Prime Minister Harold Macmillan, the two leaders of the 'Free World', were filmed wearing dinner jackets, apparently engaging in impromptu conversation. It was a PR triumph as BBC television news-readers (and their opposite numbers across the Atlantic) told their viewers that the two great leaders had discussed every-thing from world peace to the desperate state of Britain's textile industry. The 'Ike and Mac' show was a masterstroke for Macmillan, who was re-elected with a huge majority less than six weeks later.

The BBC viewers were not told anything of their secret agenda: by this time, the Anglo-American plans for the Lumumba assassination were already well advanced. President Eisenhower, with the support and encouragement of the British, had already called for the assassination of Patrice Lumumba, several months earlier in July 1960.[16] The CIA had ordered their top chemist to prepare a deadly poison to be taken by their assassin, code name QJ/WIN, to Africa to kill Lumumba. In case there was any lack of clear thinking in Whitehall, a senior British diplomat had circulated a memo arguing that the simple way of 'ensuring Lumumba's removal from the scene' was 'killing him'.[17] However, it was the Belgians, with the connivance of the United Nations and its General Secretary Dag Hammarskjold, who got there first. They assassinated him after subjecting him to days of brutal beatings and torture.

There can be little doubt that had the Belgians failed to do so, the Americans would have assassinated him instead, as they had their own assassination team in the Congo, working closely with the British. At no point did the leaders of the free world in London or Washington seriously question the morality of assassinating a democratically elected leader who just wanted to raise the living standards of some of the poorest people on the planet[18] by using the huge mineral wealth of the country for the benefit of its people, rather than foreign investors who were already fabulously rich.[19] Lumumba, a passionate nationalist whose politics were remarkably close to America's own founding fathers in their war for independence against the British, was portrayed as a communist and a Russian stooge (by the Americans and the British) and this was used to justify his assassination.

While the British and the American leaders were plotting to assassinate Lumumba, the French disposed of another charismatic African leader, Félix Moumie, a radical politician from the Cameroon. Moumie knew he was at risk as the French were running a major assassination programme at the time, targeting and murdering African nationalists, as well as journalists and academics who supported them (or even wrote about them from anything other than the French government viewpoint). Moumie believed that while he was in Geneva he would be safe, a big mistake as Swiss neutrality meant nothing to the French. He went to meet a man he believed to be a journalist, telling his girlfriend that she would be better off not coming with him as they would be talking politics and she would only get bored. But the urbane sixty-six-year-old 'journalist' with a fascination for African politics was in fact a lifetime French intelligence officer, who slipped a deadly toxin, based on rat poison, into Moumie's aperitif. It was the first time this particular poison had been used and the French doctors who had made it were incompetent. The poison was poorly refined and did not work in the way it was supposed to. This was just the beginning of the ineptitude of the French: their assassin then administered the wrong dose. Despite these cock-ups, Moumie died in agony two weeks later, surviving long enough for a suspicious Swiss doctor to alert the local police – but this was long enough for the French government assassin to escape.[20] Though the Swiss issued warrants for his arrest he was never caught.

While the French Intelligence Service (SDECE) was quietly resettling its agent with a new identity in the south of France, the German police were interviewing a Russian assassin who had defected earlier that year, confessing to two assassinations on German soil, one in Munich and one in Frankfurt. Both victims were self-proclaimed Ukrainian nationalists, fighting for independence from the Soviet Union.[21]

These four nations – the USA, UK, France and the USSR – make up four of the five permanent members of the United Nations Security Council, the global guardians pledged to deliver peace, respect for the rule of law, tolerance and the fundamental rights of everyone to live in peace with one another as good neighbours. Yet they were all actively involved in the assassination business, with the orders coming directly from the leaders themselves: Eisenhower, Macmillan, De Gaulle and Khrushchev.

Throughout 1959 and 1960, there was extensive planning for a superpower summit, when these four colossi would stride across the international stage and meet to loftily talk of great matters affecting everyone on the planet and to make the world a safer place. The reality was that Eisenhower was involved in the squalid business of assassination to try and kill off any hopes of nationalism becoming rampant in the developing world. Macmillan and De Gaulle were in it to prop up the remains of their crumbling colonial empires, while Khrushchev was using it to impose discipline on the more unruly satellite states in the Soviet bloc. None could come to any conference table with clean hands.

The fifth member of the Security Council, China, was well into the most catastrophic social experiment of the twentieth century. The Great Leap Forward was an attempt by Chairman Mao to rapidly transform the country from a backward agricultural peasant economy to an industrialized nation. Twenty million died and all resistance was brutally eradicated through torture, concentration camps and assassination in the name of the communist party, the people and the revolution.

If any of these five self-appointed champions of international peace and security had ever possessed a moral compass, they had long since thrown away the needle.

Part I
PLANNING

The killing of Julius Caesar, in 44 BCE, sends a shock wave across the Roman empire and from there, throughout Europe. Here is the story with everything: complex plotting, savage animal violence and a clear moral, in which evil is punished – a tale with a twist, which is recounted endlessly and eventually turned into a great play by Shakespeare.

Informed above all by this single incident, the science of assassination is then endlessly refined. The practitioners study their history and – as always with any mature branch of scholarship – the experts develop a discreet internal language giving the world's oldest political act a lexicon all of its own.

Arcane terms, labels and impenetrable euphemisms are injected into everyday speech to protect the users from peering outside eyes but – given the human fascination for all matters clandestine – inevitably there is leakage.

By the early 1950s, the language is mature and opaque, a cloak to protect the guilty. But when the Cold War warriors of the CIA are putting together lists of communists to be 'disposed of' through 'executive action', they never dream that their language will become the currency of Hollywood thrillers. The laconic humour of referring to an assassination programme as the 'opening of the hunting season' or setting up a 'Health Alteration Committee' are phrases which are never meant to be shared with outsiders.

None ever imagine that their memoranda, typed by secretaries (nice girls in smart suits recruited from good families) on huge manual typewriters (with carbon copies for the files) will one day be digitally scanned and bounced round the globe on telephone wires for anyone to read . . .

1

NEVER WRITE ANYTHING DOWN

'No assassination instructions should ever be written or
recorded.'

CIA assassination training manual

The US Navy Air Base, Opa Locka, Florida, USA
Location code name: LINCOLN,[1] 1954 . . .
To the casual observer, it looks like a semi-abandoned airbase,
which the bureaucrats in Washington have either forgotten
about, or worse still, have not yet got round to closing. In
an anonymous-looking two-storey building, just above a
children's nursery, 'Rip' Robertson, a CIA paramilitary and
dirty tricks veteran from the Korean War, is in charge of a
top-secret training programme. The operation's code name is
PBSUCCESS and it has the very highest security classification.
Money is not an issue. The budget is $3 million, an enormous
sum for the early 1950s and it has been cleared at the highest
political levels, all the way to the president's desk. In the end,
the operation will cost over $20 million, but no one will

complain. The building itself is packed with telex machines, communications equipment, CIA case officers, cryptographers, analysts, secretaries and military back-office staff, everything necessary to execute a small war.[2] On the wall is a 40-foot chart, detailing every stage of what will become a fairly standard CIA *coup d'état* – economic sabotage to destabilize the regime, a propaganda onslaught to undermine its leaders, a conveyor belt of bribes to buy up anyone who might be useful and a paramilitary operation to seize control in the final stages.

For those 'whose death' (in the words of one of the CIA officers involved) 'provides positive advantages' there is an extensive assassination plan. For those who are going to do the assassinating (a stereotypical oddball bunch of mercenaries and misfits) there is an eighteen-page training manual, specially written for this operation.[3]

The manual starts with the basics for anyone who might not fully have grasped the fundamentals of the business they are in. It reminds them that 'the essential point of assassination is the death of the subject ... death must be absolutely certain. The attempt on Hitler's life failed because the conspiracy did not give this matter proper attention.' Given the high number of survivors of assassination attempts, from Queen Victoria to Adolf Hitler, this is a point the CIA instructor wants to establish right from day one of their training.

The manual takes the men through basic assassination training, noting that though it is possible to kill someone with your bare hands there are very few skilful enough to do this. The tyro assassins are warned that even a highly trained Judo expert will hesitate to risk this unless there is no alternative. The manual's advice is crisp and practical: the simplest tools are usually the most efficient means of assassination – a hammer, axe, wrench, screwdriver, fire poker, kitchen knife, lamp stand, anything 'hard, heavy and handy'. These weapons have two advantages: they are available and they have 'apparent innocence', which is very important if the assassin runs the risk of being searched 'before or after the act'.

These are the CIA trainer's favourite weapons. He notes that though firearms are frequently used in assassination, they are often very ineffective, as the average assassin usually has 'insufficient technical knowledge of the limitations of weapons and expects more range, accuracy and killing power than can be provided with reliability'. He complains that guns are 'consistently overrated', and then betrays a laconic sense of humour reminding his trainees that the 'obviously lethal machine gun failed to kill Trotsky where an item of sporting equipment (an ice pick) succeeded.'

Blunt weapons are much loved by crime writers, though he points out, they 'require some anatomical knowledge for effective use'. Their main advantage is they are universally available, 'a hammer may be picked up almost anywhere in the world. Baseball bats are very widely distributed. Even a rock or a heavy stick will do.' He counsels the would-be assassin to avoid the lower half of the face, from the eyes to the throat, as this area can withstand enormous blows without fatal consequences.

The CIA trainer likes edge weapons (knives) as they can be locally obtained, though he points out that 'a certain minimum of anatomical knowledge is needed for reliability' and he warns against abdominal wounds as modern medical treatment means there is no guarantee that these will always be fatal.

His final conclusion is that – not surprisingly – firearms are 'probably more efficient than any other means' of killing and he recommends that appropriate weapons be used. Ever practical, he advises that whatever firearms are selected, they should 'provide destructive power at least 100 per cent in excess of that thought to be necessary and ranges should be half that considered practical for the weapon'. His dream weapon would be 'a telescopically sighted, closed-action carbine, shooting a low-velocity bullet of great weight, and built for accuracy, but in 1954 no such weapon exists. However, the laws of supply and demand will apply here as everywhere and this technology will inevitably follow. Though crime writers love high-velocity rifles, the professionals do not, preferring low-velocity ones as these are much more likely to be lethal. A slow-moving bullet bounces around inside the body causing far more damage.

A gentleman of the early 1950s, the CIA's assassination trainer argues that firearms are good for female assassins because, as he notes, they are weaker than men. They are also perfect for taking out public figures or guarded officials, who can be killed with 'greater reliability and some safety'. For this he recommends establishing a firing point before an official occasion, a good time for assassination as the 'propaganda value can be very high', exactly the scenario of the best-known assassination of the twentieth century, that of President Kennedy.

Though handguns are frequently used on television and in the cinema, the CIA trainer dismisses them as being 'quite inefficient as a weapon of assassination'. He points out that while many assassinations have been carried out with pistols (Lincoln, Harding, Gandhi), such attempts fail as often as they succeed (Truman, Roosevelt, Churchill).

Silencers, he teaches, have been widely publicized but again this is not something on which he is keen. They are 'occasionally useful' but their use means that 'permissible velocity is low, effective precision range is held to be about 100 yards with rifle or carbine weapons'. For pistols, the distance is dramatically shorter, 'just beyond arm's length'. There is a further argument against silencers as 'mere possession' creates its own hazards, which counters its other advantages. Getting caught with a handgun is bad enough. Getting caught with a silencer is impossible to explain.[4]

The CIA trainer also notes that bombs have been used frequently though he does not recommend them as they often kill the assassin rather than the target: a small or moderate explosion is 'highly unreliable' while time delay or booby-trap devices are extremely prone to kill the wrong man.

The CIA's advice is therefore strict: bombs or grenades should never be thrown at the subject because the likelihood of success is low – the assassin might not get close enough, he might not throw the bomb with enough accuracy and it might not go off at the right time. Assassins who try this are dismissed as 'sloppy' and 'unreliable'. If bombs are going to be used then his advice is technical in detail: they need to be a minimum of 10lb, filled with nuts and bolts and tested beforehand so that fragments will penetrate at least one inch into seasoned pine. Military or commercial high explosives are good but home-made or improvised explosives are not and should be avoided. Though they are 'possibly powerful, they tend to be dangerous and unreliable'. However, anti-personnel explosive missiles are 'excellent', but again there is the skill factor – the assassin must be trained well enough to fuse them properly. Finally, the assassin who is going to detonate the bomb needs line of sight and needs to use a commercial or military firing device.[5]

Bombs have a further downside: morality. The trainees are reminded that the purpose of assassination is targeted killing. There are 'moral aspects of indiscriminate killing' but more importantly, the death of casual bystanders can often produce adverse reactions 'unfavourable to the cause for which the assassination was carried out'. In other words, a public relations disaster, which will backfire on the assassin.

Drugs come high on the CIA list as a weapon of choice, getting a 'very effective' rating, especially if the assassin is trained as a doctor or nurse. 'An overdose of morphine administered as a sedative will cause death without disturbance and is difficult to detect.' Dosage is critical and he recommends two grains as a dose strong enough to kill. As for targets, drunks are easy to kill as morphine or a similar narcotic can be 'injected at the passing out stage' and the cause of death put down to acute alcoholism. Specific poisons like arsenic or strychnine are not on the recommended list as possession or procurement is incriminating and accurate dosage is 'problematical' . . .

This extraordinary manual was written in 1954 for a few hundred men (Guatemalan exiles and mercenaries from the

USA and Central America) scattered in training camps in Latin America. Some were also taught sabotage and demolition at El Tamarindo, the plantation ranch of Anastasio Somoza, the psychopathic Nicaraguan dictator, while others were given weapons' training at Lake Managua. A dozen pilots were stationed at the airstrip at Puerto Cabezas.

These men were on a collective mission: to make the world safe from communism and sound for the United Fruit Company (UFCO), the world's largest banana company. UFCO's headquarters were in Bananera, Guatemala, but its major shareholders were back in the USA and, crucially, they included Allen Dulles, whose law firm represented the company and who was then the head of the recently formed CIA, and his brother John Foster Dulles, the US Secretary of State, who was fresh from serving on the company's Board of Trustees.

For the Dulles brothers – and their fellow Cold War warriors on Capitol Hill – the issue was a clear and present danger to American commercial and political interests. Jacobo Arbenz Guzman, the newly elected President of Guatemala, had nationalized a small portion of the assets of United Fruit. Bad news for the shareholders, and an affront to the USA, which regarded Latin America as its own backyard. John Foster Dulles knew for sure that the Russians had no interest in Guatemala as they did not even have an embassy in the country and privately he admitted there was no evidence to link Arbenz to Moscow.[6] But publicly, it was a different story. He condemned this tiny democracy as 'living under a Communist type of terrorism,'[7] a theme warmly echoed by the US press and politicians, then living under the lash of red-baiting McCarthyism.[8]

The view from Guatemala was very different. Arbenz was a moderate middle-class nationalist, elected with 65 per cent of the vote. His country was desperately poor[9] and much of the land held by UFCO was uncultivated, which the government had begun to nationalize. But this was no collective farming experiment as favoured by the Soviets. The land was distributed in small plots, turning previously landless peasants into homesteaders, a modern version of the American immigrant dream. United Fruit demanded $15.8 million compensation but Arbenz offered $1,185,000. The Guatemalan government did not just pluck this figure out of the air: it was the exact value United Fruit themselves had put on the land for Guatemalan tax purposes.[10] UFCO and the US State Department then made the fatuous claim that this figure did not actually represent the land's true value, that it was only for accounting purposes, though no one believed this, least of all the claimants themselves, who had been trying to foment a coup since before Arbenz was even elected.[11] More importantly, the Dulles brothers had decided long ago to bypass any legal negotiation and they now began to crank up their coup plans against the democratically elected government of Guatemala.

The operation to remove Arbenz and assassinate his supporters was given to the fledgling CIA, initially with the code name PBFORTUNE, which subsequently became PBSUCCESS.[12] Two days before Christmas 1953, and a month after the first 23,000 happy peasants had started tilling their newly acquired plots of land, the CIA set up base camp at Opa Locka, just north of Miami, Florida. The job was assigned to the CIA's finest up-and-coming stars. In charge was Frank Wisner, the CIA's Deputy Director of Plans, a former Wall Street lawyer, independently wealthy and a man with a huge range of contacts in every walk of life. Sophisticated, brilliant and a very sharp operator, he was one of the architects of the CIA, helping set up the Office of Policy Coordination, which reported not to the head of the CIA but directly to the Secretaries of State and Defense.[13] His deputy was Tracy Barnes, a stylish figure. Sharply dressed in highly polished tasselled loafers he was every inch the Ivy League blue blood out of Yale and Harvard Law School. The field commander was Colonel Albert Haney, the former CIA station chief in Korea. Also on the team was a CIA paramilitary trainer, 'Rip' Robertson, fresh from covert operations behind enemy lines in Korea.

While his brother was dapper, highly polished and patrician, the CIA boss Allen Dulles was a scruffy figure. Dressed in an old cardigan and carpet slippers, he shuffled round his makeshift office in the Navy building opposite the Reflecting Pool in Washington. Though he was happy to deliver death and destruction across the world to anyone who dared challenge US imperial interests, the closest he got to any action was crushing the rampant cockroaches which appeared every day round the water cooler. As a contemporary metaphor, it was lost on him: every day he cracked them open under his feet, but the next day they always returned.

Though the CIA team were all vastly experienced, they ignored the first and most basic rule of the assassination business: cover your tracks. The assassination manual, which was specially written for this operation, reminded them that 'all planning must be mental; no papers should ever contain evidence of the operation'. And in case anyone missed the point they were instructed that 'no assassination instructions should ever be written or recorded'.

It was a simple and obvious instruction, but one that was impossible to follow and they kept written records from day one of the operation. Although the CIA was only a few years old, it was already a bureaucracy and bureaucracies demand paperwork. Despite the desires of spy novelists and Hollywood screenwriters, the fact is that it is virtually impossible to set up a major international 'off-the-books' government-sponsored operation without there being some leakage. As well as the orders, the basic logistics (money, travel, weapons, transport, maps, hotels, passports) have to be dealt with and they always leave a paper trail. Guatemala was no exception.

A cable in early January 1954 asked for twenty silencers (exactly the sort of clue the CIA trainer had warned against leaving) to be sent to their training base in Honduras. Three days later, training for 'two assassins' was added to the programme and within three weeks these 'assassination specialists' were being discussed between the CIA and their placeman in Guatemala, Colonel Castillo Armas. By now the assassin-ation squads had a name. They were called K Groups (pre-sumably K for killing) and were formally included in the planning chart. The sabotage groups were told not to feel disappointed as they would not be excluded from the killing spree once the operation was under way.

In March 1954, the senior CIA case officers running the coup started the numbers game: how many Guatemalans should be assassinated? At a weekly planning meeting on 9 March, the figure of fifteen to twenty was suggested, a number endorsed in other meetings and informal discussions, all of which was noted for the files. The first thirty-seven paramilitaries grad-uated on 21 March 1954 and ten days later, a memo was circulated to all staff officers. Twenty was no longer regarded as a 'sufficient' number to be assassinated. The list was now nearly three times the size: fifty-eight supporters of the democratically elected regime ('high government and organiza-tional leaders') in Guatemala were listed for 'disposal' through 'executive action', the phrase routinely used by the CIA at this time for assassination. This plan was justified by the argument that their 'removal from the political scene is required for the immediate and future success of the new government'. Also included in the list were 'those individuals in key government and military positions of tactical importance whose removal for psychological, organizational or other reasons is mandatory for the success of military action.' According to the minutes of one meeting they were to be 'pulled out by the roots . . . if too many of these birds get out they will be back in about three years'.[14]

The sloppiness of this execution roll call was staggering. The names were out of date and came from old lists, compiled five years before by the Guatemalan Army, topped up by what was claimed to be 'recent intelligence available', though one CIA staff officer gave the game away, writing 'no, not done' in the margin next to this claim.

All the CIA officers were asked to make their 'deletions, additions and/or comments', adding their initials against the name of each individual who was going to be assassinated. They were asked to use 'careful consideration' when making additions or deletions, and at least one officer added what he considered to be a 'worthy target'. Bureaucratic efficiency was the key here. Tasks had to be completed so that 'a final list of disposees' could be 'approved promptly' so permitting 'planning to proceed on schedule'.[15] Blank pages were added to the memo for any enthusiastic case officer who needed extra space.

Assassination is an addictive business. Once embraced, it quickly becomes seen as the panacea for all problems. Those scheduled for elimination did not just include the CIA's enemies. Even some of those who were working for the Agency were also scheduled for assassination. One internal memo (still classified fifty years later) pointed out that some 'assets', that is people who had helped the CIA, were on yet another list. They too had been scheduled for 'eradication'.[16]

Within two months of the lists being compiled, one of the CIA case officers laid out a 'specific assassination schedule leading up to D-Day'. Less than three weeks later, the orders from Washington were delivered to the CIA task force in Opa Locka, Florida: 'Arbenz must go; how does not matter.'

The CIA also involved General Rafael Trujillo, the psychopathic dictator of the Dominican Republic, in the plot. Ironically, subsequently he too would be assassinated in a clumsy plot where once again the CIA would leave their fingerprints everywhere, supplying the guns and the bullets to the assassins. But in 1953, he was a convenient ally for them and they needed his help. Trujillo named his price for helping out: he was already staggeringly rich, having plundered his country for decades, and so all he asked for was the assassination of four of his enemies who were living in Guatemala. The CIA's appointed leader of Guatemala, Colonel Castillo Armas, agreed to this request, telling the General that special squads were being trained for that very purpose. In a spirit of bureaucratic efficacy, the names of the four were added to the list of those to be killed after the coup.[17] In the CIA's outline plan, these assassinations were scheduled for 'the sixth stage' of the coup when there would be what was euphemistically called a 'roll up' of Arbenz supporters.

Initially the CIA offered President Arbenz and his closest supporters huge bribes in the currency of their choice to leave the country at the same time as the CIA 'psyops' (political and psychological warfare) team turned up the heat. Mourning cards, death threats, wooden coffins, hangman's nooses and fake bombs were sent to those on the list. Slogans like 'You Only Have 5 Days' were painted on their houses. The para-militaries in the K Squads were desperate to use their newly acquired assassination skills but were held back by their CIA bosses, who believed this would have been counterproductive at that stage. A senior military commander was approached to see if he would lead a coup against Arbenz. To the fury of the CIA he started to haggle over his price: like Trujillo, he also wanted the CIA to assassinate several of his enemies. A frustrated CIA officer couldn't believe what he was hearing and angrily told him that if he wanted them killed he would have to do it himself. But just to cover every outcome, he then dutifully cabled Washington saying that, by sheer coincidence, he was convinced that the names mentioned should be added to the list so they too could be 'eliminated'.

The CIA then stepped up their propaganda operation. A fake radio broadcast described the movement of two heavily armoured columns on Guatemala, which the veteran CIA propaganda chief David Phillips called 'the final big lie'. This broadcast, coupled with the strategic bribing of several key military commanders, was enough. The army caved in and Arbenz was removed in an American-backed military *coup d'état*.

Though the government crumbled, things went badly for the CIA plotters. Instead of their appointed man Colonel Castillo Armas taking over, a different officer stepped into the vacancy created by Arbenz's removal: Colonel Carlos Enrique Diaz, who immediately clashed with the Americans.

The US ambassador John Peurifoy (who was installed by the CIA) waved the assassination lists at Diaz and ordered him to shoot them all within twenty-four hours.[18] Diaz refused and then announced that he was going to announce a general amnesty and release all political prisoners. The US ambassador, who had been bouncing these lists backwards and forwards with the CIA boss Allen Dulles back in Washington, sent a furious telegram to the coup headquarters in Opa Locka saying, 'We have been double crossed. BOMB!' A CIA plane then bombed the main army base and the radio station. A long-standing CIA Guatemalan asset, Colonel Monzon, marched Diaz into a room at machine-gun point and explained the nature of reality to him. Diaz emerged, ashen faced and announced that he had reconsidered his political ambitions and no longer wished to be president. The CIA finally got their way and their man. The last – and only serious – chance for progressive, democratic change in the region was snuffed out when the new president of Guatemala was announced: Colonel Castillo Armas, who promptly rounded up the opposition and packed them into overcrowded jails. He immediately concluded a deal with United Fruit and opened the country up to US investment. However, the only takers were the Italian mafia who teamed up with corrupt army officers to open gambling halls.

The official CIA history argues that though there were endless discussions about assassination, there is no evidence that anyone was actually murdered. This is not correct, though it is difficult to quantify the final number of dead as the names on the CIA assassination lists are still redacted. A cynic might question why these names are still hidden half a century later, if not to prevent anyone verifying this claim. What is known is that on 1 July 1954, while the US ambassador was effectively controlling the country by deciding its next ruler, seven key prominent labour organizers were all assassinated on the same day in Guatemala City, all of them murdered in very suspicious circumstances.[19] It is inconceivable that these names were not on the CIA's extensive assassination lists as one of the key issues for United Fruit had been labour agitation and strikes. Only the truly naïve could argue that these were anything other than what they appear to be: killings carried out by assassination squads, trained, armed and targeted by the CIA.

Had these murderers ever been brought to trial, there would have been a paper trail, thickly carpeted with memoranda, minutes of meetings and telegrams all leading from Guatemala to CIA headquarters. Not so much a smoking gun, more a small arsenal of heavily fingerprinted weaponry. Guatemala was a democratic country and the highly educated men of America's intelligence elite had put together a group of hired killers to go and kill trade unionists and politicians, whose only 'crime' was to exercise their democratic rights and try to improve the standard of living of their fellow countrymen.

The CIA's appointed leader started to deliver immediately. Castillo Armas changed the law, bringing in the death penalty for anyone exercising their previous democratic rights and being active in a trade union. Throughout the summer, US Secretary of State John Foster Dulles bombarded him with telegrams ordering him to arrest many of the seven hundred trade union leaders and Arbenz supporters, who were by now safely holed up as asylum seekers in foreign embassies all over Guatemala City. Such an action was a complete breach of international law, but then Dulles was famously quoted as saying, 'I confess to being one of those lawyers who do not regard international law as law at all.'[20] Arrest for anyone meant certain death often without even the formality of a trial, but Castillo Armas refused to obey his masters in Washington. To the fury of the Americans ('Castillo Armas double crossed us,' complained the ambassador) 120 of these activists were given safe passage out of the country. For those that remained, life expectancy was short. The moderate centre politics of Arbenz disappeared as thousands were rounded up, arbitrarily sent to prison, executed or 'disappeared'. Torture was rampant. The trade unions were smashed and the shooting of workers by the police reached epidemic proportions.

Castillo Armas himself was assassinated three years later, a cause for celebration for the thousands who had suffered under his brutality. Publicly, President Eisenhower described this as a tragedy for Guatemala and the world. Privately, it was a huge relief to the Americans who had installed him and especially the CIA, who described him internally as 'embarrassingly inept'. He was shot dead at 9 p.m. on 27 July 1957 as he was going to dinner with his wife at his official residence. Conveniently, his assassin, an army guard called Romeo Vasquez Sanchez, was also found dead, immediately afterwards. Pro-communist literature was then found at his house but few believed it was anything other than a plant by one of the most corrupt police forces anywhere on the planet.

The country was then plunged into a series of civil wars lasting thirty years and resulting in the assassination of tens of thousands of opponents of the increasingly corrupt military regimes that followed.

Arbenz and his fellow nationalists had wanted to build a nation that would be a haven of democracy and progress. Instead this was crushed and replaced with one built on dictatorship, terror, repression and fear, underpinned by state-sponsored torture and assassination. In the mid-1990s the Mayan Indians were subjected to a ruthless programme of genocide and 200,000 were slaughtered. By the turn of the twentieth century, army-led massacres and genocide were the routine business of politics in Guatemala. Currently, lawyers, journalists and politicians who attempt to limit the excesses of the military and the state risk assassination and there is no prospect of an end to the violence. Once assassination is injected into the system it is very hard to remove and once it becomes one of the instruments of state repression it becomes an indelible stain on the fabric of everyday life. Everyone suffers.

But back in the early 1950s, the CIA took all the wrong messages from their Guatemala operation and it became the template for many of their future operations throughout the developing world. The same basic plans, which included the routine assassination of the Agency's opponents, were endlessly used and reused and some were even carried out by the same people and even from the same locations.

Several of the key CIA figures in PBSUCCESS graduated to one of the greatest CIA disasters in history, when they supported a ragbag army of disaffected exiles as they attempted to invade and take over Cuba. The Bay of Pigs in 1961 was a humiliating failure. The Director Allen Dulles and his aide and later deputy director, Richard Bissell, were the architects. E. Howard Hunt, who went on to achieve ever greater glory as one of the Watergate buggers, Tracy Barnes, who had day-to-day operational control in Guatemala, and the paramilitary trainer 'Rip' Robertson all advanced from PBSUCCESS to the Bay of Pigs. Dulles, Barnes and Bissell then progressed to the numerous and often farcical attempts to assassinate the Cuban leader Fidel Castro. The Bay of Pigs operation was even run from the same two-storey barracks at Opa Locka in suburban Miami. Together, these men helped form the nucleus of the CIA's inner team. Obsessed with dirty tricks and winning at all costs, they defined much of the Agency's post-war character. Lurking round their coat-tails was a young and already unscrupulous politician, Richard Nixon.

But whereas the CIA learned nothing from Guatemala and repeated the same blunders, Castro had learnt everything from the fall of Arbenz. He politicized the Cuban army, bringing the officers into the system, and by doing so made it relatively immune from the seductive appeal of US corruption. But more importantly, instead of sulking like Arbenz, he took personal control of the military operation, leading from the front, and delivered a humiliating defeat to the White House-backed Cuban exiles.

But though the Bay of Pigs was a disastrous failure, the desire to assassinate Castro remained. Throughout the sixties and seventies, the CIA made numerous attempts on his life. As with

Guatemala, they forgot the most basic lesson of all and the paper trail was picked up years later by the Senate Committee investigating assassination plots against foreign leaders.[21] Though the language was frequently 'circumlocutionary' Senator Frank Church found evidence of CIA involvement in eight attempts to kill Castro.

Colonel J.C. King, the CIA chief of the Western Hemisphere Division within the Directorate of Plans, had been sidelined during the Guatemala operation and replaced by more gung-ho officers. It was a mistake he was not about to repeat. By 1961, he knew exactly what his bosses wanted and sent them a cable telling them that the 'possible removal top three leaders is requiring serious consideration'. One of those to be removed 'by arranging an accident' was Raul Castro, Fidel's brother. Ten thousand dollars was authorized to be paid 'after successful completion'.[22] Once again the language was as good as fingerprints.

This elliptical use of language is not confined to the US intelligence service. The former vice president, Richard Nixon (who had been present at the CIA debriefing after the fall of Arbenz), was a hot supporter of the assassination programme, describing Castro as a 'cancer' to be 'eradicated', one of those CIA euphemisms he had picked up in the early 1950s.

But while the Americans were pussyfooting around the English language trying to invent new ways of describing an old deed, the British had few (if any) qualms and certainly had no particular ethical problems about assassination.

After the end of the Second World War, many British intelligence officers transferred from the SOE (set up by Winston Churchill to 'set Europe ablaze') straight into MI6, the UK's intelligence and espionage agency. Defined in the heat of war, the SOE culture was based on a can-do mentality, 'ungentlemanly warfare' of subversion, sabotage and assassination, in which the minister back in London was often kept out of the loop. The SOE was involved in the assassination of the

SS Obergruppenführer Reinhard Heydrich in Czechoslovakia in 1942, providing planning, training, logistical support and – according to one account – may even have supplied the botulin-coated anti-tank grenades to be used in the attack. This is not so fanciful as it might first appear. The statement put out by the German doctors after his death said he had died of internal lesions 'caused by bacteria and possibly poisons carried into them by the bomb splinters'.[23]

Elsewhere the SOE was not so successful, though this was not through lack of enthusiasm. In one five-month period between 10 January and 5 June 1941, the SOE in the Middle East received orders to assassinate seven men.

The details are captured in the SOE war diary, which was updated every day or so and provides an extraordinary insight into the everyday business of running a military intelligence operation. The language is sparse (paper was rare) but visceral in its detail. The words 'assassination' and 'assassinate' are routinely used, though on other days the secretaries, who compiled these records, preferred to use words like 'liquidation' and 'removal'. The choice of targets was fascinating: four German agents, an Italian colonel, the Grand Mufti of Jerusalem and an Indian nationalist leader.

In January, the local SOE was instructed that if Baron Von Hentig, a German intelligence officer, was in Syria, 'Searight [an SOE officer] is to arrange for his assassination.' When Searight told London that it was not going to be as easy as they thought he was told that 'the highest authorities' were 'pressing for urgent action'. So serious was it that 'expense must be disregarded'.[24] Two months later, the minutes reported that as Subhas Chandra Bose, an Indian nationalist leader, was 'understood to be travelling from Afghanistan to Germany via Iran', two British officers, Bailey and Pollock, were directed 'to wire what arrangements they could make for his assassination'.[25] The following month, there was a further instruction to assassinate Bose. Publicly, the SOE propaganda vilified him as a Nazi and a fascist but privately they earmarked him for assassination as an 'Indian communist'. This time the instruction was sent to another SOE officer called Carver, who was also told in a separate telegram to 'arrange for the disposal' of Baron von Hentig's successor, a German agent called Paul Gluck.[26] A new SOE officer, D'Arcy Weatherbe, was then given the job of assassinating Hentig and another German agent, a man called Grobba, 'leaving the price to his discretion'.

Four days later, they had a much bigger target, the 'liquidation' of the Grand Mufti of Jerusalem, who was fomenting revolt against the British. Colonel Pollock was told to 'give the matter his immediate attention' and to discuss it with General Wavell.[27]

The following month, 2 May 1941, an internal report admitted that despite all the talk of assassination, there had been a complete failure to kill a single target. Syria was simply too hostile an environment for the British, who did not have a single agent in the country 'fitted for the coarser side of our work'.[28] Despite this bleak assessment of their capabilities, London was not to be thwarted. Within a few weeks, fresh assassination instructions were sent out. The SOE officers were told that Colonel Gabrielli – who had engineered the Italian coup in Albania – was now in Iran and they were instructed that 'everything possible should be done to arrange for his liquidation'. Meanwhile, the Grand Mufti had risen up the list of targets as a result of being the main cause of all the trouble the SOE and the British were having in Iraq. The minutes reminded everyone that it was 'of the first importance that he should not escape liquidation'.[29] Despite the expectations in London, the list of survivors of the SOE assassination programme was growing by the week. The minutes noted that another SOE officer called De Chastellain had 'asked whether his instructions to kill Chandra Bose still held good'. This was confirmed, though, in a touch of the bureaucratically macabre, the widely circulated minutes noted, 'he should inform nobody'.

Bose survived all the SOE plans to kill him and so by 1945 he had floated to the top of their assassination list for Asia.

General Wavell, the governor general of India, wrote a memo in 1945[30] saying 'it would be a good idea if he was disposed of' and it should therefore have been of little surprise to anyone when Bose died in a highly suspicious plane crash in August 1945. However, as soon as the news of his death came through, Wavell believed the crash had been faked and wrote in his journal, 'I wonder if the Japanese announcement of the Subhas Chandra Bose death in an air crash is true. I suspect it very much.' A month later, he wrote again that he was 'sceptical'. Wavell was not burdened by a quick brain but he remained convinced that the crash had been staged and that Bose was going to return.

Wavell was right to be suspicious as there is not a single element of the official version of events which stands up to more than a few moments' scrutiny. According to the formal version of events, Bose was in a K-21 Japanese heavy bomber (known as a Sally) leaving from the Taihoku airstrip in Taiwan. There was an explosion in the port engine immediately after take-off, the fuselage broke open and the petrol tanks burst into flames. Bose subsequently died that night in hospital of third degree burns. There was no post-mortem and the body was cremated immediately afterwards. Though the pilot was reported dead most of the other passengers survived the crash, including his aide who was sitting next to him, who only suffered minor burns and a superficial head wound. There were few witnesses and they changed their stories, making the official version of events barely credible and giving this death all the ingredients of a full-blown conspiracy. A judge who went to investigate was met by a group of witnesses at the end of the Inquiry who told him that though there was a crash at that airfield, it was a year before, but he refused to take their evidence and, reportedly, went shopping to buy a present for his wife instead.

Today, many in India simply refuse to believe Bose was killed in the crash, a view fuelled by the revelation that the CIA also still had their doubts as late as 1964 and were worried that the Soviets had Bose under their control and would try to install him as a Communist leader of India. The alternative view is that the British finally assassinated him after five years of trying and, in the confusion of the last days of the war, they then concocted the crash story so that he would not become a martyr. This was well within SOE's capability, as they had the skill and the experience to both kill him and then construct a credible cover story. Whatever happened, one thing is certain: the official version of events makes no sense at all and would not survive the crucible of a modern court room.[31]

Though the SOE was closed down in 1946, the mentality, the culture and many of the people then transferred seamlessly across to MI6 and the darker recesses of the British Foreign and Commonwealth Office, a government department whose name was then a bit of a misnomer. Many did not understand the notion of Commonwealth and still saw the world as the British Empire (pink and covering much of the globe) and its enemies.

Nearly sixty years on, it is hard to imagine the crude and simplistic world view of these managers of empire. For them, the world was simple: easily split between good and bad, English and non-English, white and non-white. In this paranoid world, even the Americans were regarded as 'uncertain allies'[32] by key players in MI6. This class of people occupied a hermetically sealed universe, where all the members knew each other intimately. Everything they knew and did reinforced them as members of an exclusive and self-selecting club: they were processed at the same very small number of public schools (Eton, Winchester, Harrow), were members of the same gentleman's clubs (Whites, Boodles, Travellers) and shared the same eighteenth-century imperialist world view. They spoke from the same limited vowel range, socialized together, married into each other's families and enjoyed the same anti-intellectual pursuits (hunting, shooting, fishing).

For this generation of post-war British intelligence officers it was still a world of freelance operations. They saw themselves as the chaps who delivered the solutions usually against the wishes of the dim-witted politicians and civil servants who they regarded as part of the problem. Cloak and dagger was their operational motto. Morality and legality did not even enter the equation. For them, it was not even a question of the ends justifying the means. The question was not even asked – and if it had been – it would not have been understood.

George Young, who rose to become Deputy Director of MI6, spoke for them all in the mid-1950s when he wrote: 'We are relatively free of the problems of status, precedence, departmental attitudes and evasions of personal responsibility, which create the official cast of mind. We do not have to develop, like the Parliamentarians conditioned by a lifetime, the ability to produce the ready phrase, the smart reply and the flashing smile. And so it is not surprising that the spy finds himself the main guardian of intellectual integrity.'

In early 1956, Young was MI6 Head for the Middle East when he met James Eichelberger, the CIA Station Chief in Egypt and an expert on the Middle East. Young, a ferocious and loud-mouthed racist with a profound hatred of Arabs and Arabic culture,[33] raised the issue of 'assassinating' President Nasser of Egypt. Eichelberger was genuinely shocked by the visceral brutality of Young's language and cabled his boss Allen Dulles to complain that 'he talked openly of assassinating Nasser, instead of using a polite euphemism like liquidating.' This was not just the kind of loose talk much loved by gung-ho British intelligence officers throughout the Cold War. At the time, Young was working closely both with Egyptian groups who were hostile to Nasser as well as French Intelligence, who had already made one attempt to assassinate the Egyptian president in 1954 and who still had an active hit squad in Egypt, code-named Rap 700. Eichelberger refused to be drawn into the British plot and instead used the information to his advantage, tipping off Nasser about the British and French assassination plans. This was nothing the Egyptian leader did not already know, but Nasser was a wily graduate of the conspiratorial cauldron of Egyptian domestic politics and he took something else away from this warning: the Americans were not allied that closely to the British and were playing their own game; intelligence which would be invaluable come the Suez invasion.

After he retired, George Young complained that though his political masters, the politicians, did not know how to do their jobs properly, he did. 'I was quite certain of my judgement to carry out the operations and to tell them afterwards, that's that.'[34] In the case of Nasser, however, he was at one with his prime minister, Anthony Eden, even though other parts of the Whitehall machine were not in synch with either of them.

In March 1956, shortly after Young first raised the issue of assassinating Nasser, the young King Hussein of Jordan sacked Sir John Glubb (widely known as Pasha Glubb) from his position as head of the Arab Legion, a desert-fighting force created by the British after the First World War.[35] Not surprisingly, Hussein, a proud and patriotic monarch who wanted to make his mark, thought the position should be held by a fellow Jordanian. The British Prime Minister Anthony Eden, by now quite ill and taking large doses of Benzedrine, decided, irrationally and without a single shred of evidence, that President Nasser of Egypt was responsible for Glubb's removal. Eden wanted more dagger and a lot less cloak from his intelligence services. The Secretary of State for Foreign Affairs and a man widely regarded as one of the brightest politicians of his generation, Anthony Nutting sent his Prime Minister Eden a memo with various suggestions for neutralizing Nasser's attacks on British interests. That night, while Nutting was hosting a dinner for an American friend from the UN he got a call from a dyspeptic Eden. What's all this poppycock you've sent me? What's all this nonsense about isolating Nasser or "neutralizing" him as you call it? I want him destroyed, can't you understand?' And just in case Nutting was in any doubt, he went on, 'I want him murdered, and if you and the Foreign Office don't agree, then you'd better come to the Cabinet and explain why!'[36]

A few days later, Eden again raised the issue of assassination, this time with the most senior civil servant in the Foreign Office, Sir Ivone Kirkpatrick, who told him, 'I don't think we have a department for that sort of thing, Prime Minister, but if we do, it certainly is not under my control.' By now Eden was not to be thwarted. He sidestepped his officials and went directly to Patrick Dean, the Chairman of the Joint Intelligence Committee (JIC), a man who once addressed a lunch for spies, which included the CIA Chief Allen Dulles, in Washington, 'Mr Chairman, gentlemen, fellow conspirators'.[37] Dean shared Eden's view of Nasser and together they brought in George Young, the man who had suggested assassinating Nasser in the first place. At the time, the British Foreign Office and MI6 were dominated by loud-mouthed racists like Julian Amery and George Young, who shared extreme right-wing views and a clear view of the Egyptians, who they regarded as 'wogs'. As the lists of Egyptians to be 'bumped off' began to get longer and longer, assassination lost its appeal as the cheap option. Quite soon, there were simply too many and the English desire to administer a corrective dose of 'wog bashing' escalated into a full-scale invasion of Egypt, Britain's greatest, self-inflicted, post-war foreign affairs disaster.

Eden was not the only British prime minister who relished clear and explicit language. When the democratically elected leader of the Congo, Patrice Lumumba, nationalized the nation's copper mines, he didn't just provoke the wrath of the incumbent colonial power, Belgium, which had previously owned both the country and its mines, but he soon had a coalition of the furious queuing up to assassinate him. As well as Belgium, there were several other countries all jostling to get their hands on the assassin's trigger. Britain and Portugal (both of whom had extensive interests in Africa) and the USA were all terrified of a precedent being set in which nationalist leaders seized control of their country's assets. Even the United Nations played a crucial role in delivering him to a Belgian-sponsored assassination squad.

On 19 September 1960, the US President Dwight Eisenhower met the British Foreign Minister Lord Home (who was

later to become prime minister) and stuck to the American style
of reasonably oblique language, expressing his view that he
hoped Lumumba might 'fall into a river full of crocodiles'.
Home picked up the theme, replying laconically that 'regret-
fully, we have lost many of the techniques of old-fashioned
democracy'. Just over a week later, Eisenhower met the British
Prime Minister Harold Macmillan with their foreign ministers
in Washington. For Eisenhower and Macmillan this was their
second joint foray into a world where they would conspire
together to commission the assassination of another.[38] As they
were no longer assassination virgins, there was no need for any
delicate dancing round the euphemisms. The British opened the
discussion getting straight to the point, with Lord Home asking
why 'aren't we getting rid of Lumumba now?'

On the other side of the Atlantic, there was yet more
diplomatic activity at the Foreign Office in London. A senior
official, career diplomat H.F.T. 'Howard' Smith, sent a memo
to a very small group of selected individuals, one of whom was
the then Lord Privy Seal Edward Heath, who would also
subsequently become a British prime minister. The memo,
dated 28 September 1960, with the word 'Secret' written by
hand was simply entitled, 'The Congo'.[39] Though the title was
innocuous, the contents were anything but. The Congo was not
strictly a major British concern, more a Belgian issue as the
mines were owned by the Société Général de Belgique, but the
Foreign Office was being encouraged to take action by their
man in Leopoldville. MI6 was also being prodded into action
by reports from their Congo station chief Daphne Park,[40] who
argued that Lumumba was going to take the Congo into the
Russian camp. In no time at all, a nationalist attempt to improve
the living standards of some of the poorest people on the planet
was spun into a huge paranoid conspiracy in which the long
shadow of the Soviet Union was seen everywhere. This was
now an epic struggle between east and west, capitalism versus
communism, good against evil.

Back in London, Howard Smith had a simple answer, 'I see

only two possible solutions to the problem. The first is the simple one of ensuring Lumumba's removal from the scene by killing him. This should in fact solve the problem, since so far as we can tell, Lumumba is not a leader of a movement within which there are potential successors of his quality and influence. His supporters are much less dangerous material.' Smith made it very clear that this was his preferred option. He wanted 'Lumumba to be removed from the scene altogether, because I fear that as long as he is about his power to do damage can only slightly be modified.' The second option was to bring in a constitution taking power away from Patrice Lumumba as prime minister and giving it to the president. Smith's memo was circulated round Whitehall. Later that day, A.W.M. Ross wrote on it. 'There is much to be said for eliminating Lumumba but unless Mobutu [the West's choice as incoming military leader] can get him arrested and executed promptly, he is likely to survive and continue to plague us all.' The following day, the memo was sent to another official, who cast doubts on the idea that Mobutu and Kasavubu (Lumumba's other rival in the Congo) could be trusted to get rid of Lumumba, adding 'Mr Smith's suggestion seems much more attractive – though I have my doubts whether Mr Lumumba will ever be held down by any constitution and still less voluntarily withdraw.' Heath argued that the UK should discreetly apply pressure on Lumumba's opponents, Mobutu and Kasavubu, concluding 'it does seem somewhat supine to stand aloof'. There is no evidence on the memo that any of the three raised any objections, moral, ethical or legal to Smith's preferred wish to kill a democratically elected prime minister of a sovereign state.

H.F.T. Smith was no loose cannon. At that time, Howard Smith was a Cambridge-educated, twenty-year career diplomat. A graduate of Britain's wartime code-breaking operation at Bletchley Park, he was a smooth Whitehall mandarin and would go on to become a major figure, both as a diplomat and as a spy. Shortly after writing the memo he went to Moscow as counsellor and was later awarded the CMG, a Companion in the Most Distinguished Order of Saint Michael and Saint George (known by civil servants as Call Me God), an honour for those who have rendered important services for the Commonwealth or foreign nations. He would ultimately rise to become Head of MI5 (the UK's domestic security agency) in the mid-1970s and finally the British ambassador in Moscow.

But back in 1960, Smith was still a humble foot soldier in the Whitehall trenches. While the British and American politicians were busy foraging round the English language in search of a workable vocabulary to describe their desire to murder a fellow country leader, the CIA dispatched an agent to the Congo armed with a deadly virus with which to kill Lumumba, but it was the Belgians who got there first, shooting him dead after days of brutal and inhumane treatment. The squad who shot him were in no doubt as to exactly what was expected of them. The crucial Belgian government telegram launching their assassination operation called for Lumumba's *élimination définitive*. Some Belgians have recently argued that this only meant his political elimination, not his death. However Colonel Marliere, the man in charge of Operation Barracuda, the code name for the plan to assassinate Lumumba, was in no doubt what it meant, saying he had been offered 'a crocodile hunter to bump off Lumumba'.[41]

Though plans may have been murky at the bureaucratic end of the audit trail, those at the killing end of the business, like Colonel Marliere of Belgium, usually have little doubt about what is being asked of them.

During the Algerian colonial war in the 1950s, the French routinely used assassination, often making it look like suicide. However, when they captured a lawyer called Ali Boumendjel they had a problem. He was well connected and any assassination would have looked suspect. General Aussaresses (then a major) had a discussion with a junior officer in which he told him to move Boumendjel to another building in order to prevent his escape. A simple order until Aussaresses decided they could not use the ground floor. His junior officer initially missed the point until Aussaresses made it clear. 'It's very simple: you go to the prisoner and in order to transfer him to the building next door you use the sixth-floor footbridge. I'll wait downstairs for you to be done. Do you understand me now?' The officer returned shortly afterwards to tell him that Ali Boumendjel was dead having fallen from the footbridge, though the blow to the back of his head from a club helped him on his way. Aussaresses then rushed to see his boss, General Massu, to tell him that he had carried out his orders and that Boumendjel could not escape as he had committed suicide. Massu grunted. The word assassinate was never used but no one was ever in doubt about what had been required.

This is not so unusual and soldiers everywhere know when to take the cue and when there will not be a paper trail. Whether it was British mercenaries and MI6 trying to kill Russian-backed Yemeni leaders in the early 1960s or the SAS going into the Iranian embassy siege in 1982, those carrying the guns usually know what is expected of them.

The recollection of one of the SAS soldiers involved in the hostage release at the Iranian Embassy was that their off-the-record verbal orders were clear – 'they didn't want anybody coming out alive. No surviving terrorists'. He believed an order was passed down from Mrs Thatcher. One did escape with the hostages and the SAS tried to drag him back into the building for summary execution only to be stopped by the police.

Even though the Soviet Union was a police state for much of the twentieth century, they too avoided the British passion for bluntness, ironically preferring the US option of oblique – but obvious – language.

In 1926, the Soviet Union had a special unit within their intelligence apparatus for hunting down, kidnapping and assassinating the enemies of the state, wherever they lived outside Russia. Given the conspiratorial obsessions of the Russian Intelligence services, this department inevitably had different names at different times, but regardless of what it was called, it grew to become a substantial organization of over two hundred people, at one time concealed in the wonderfully bureaucratic cloak of 'the Administration for Special Tasks'. Assassinations were referred to as 'special jobs,'[42] though the 1929 operation to kidnap and assassinate General Kutepov in Paris was referred to as 'the liquidation of G'.[43] Until Stalin's death, this unit was also known as the Spetsburo, or special bureau.[44] It was then called the Ninth Department and later (inevitably) the Thirteenth Department of the Foreign Intelligence Directorate, though for the insiders its nickname was *Mokryye Dela*, the Department of Wet Affairs, which also translates as 'dirty affairs' and wet in this context means 'blood wet'.

In early 1953, the Russian Ministry of State Security prepared a single-copy-only memo for Stalin, asking for his go-ahead to assassinate President Tito of Yugoslavia. These plans were then discussed by the Soviets' chosen assassin, Iosef Grigulevich (code name MAKS) and his controllers at a meeting in Vienna in February 1953. The options listed were among the most exotic ever suggested by any intelligence service. They included seeking a private audience with Tito and then giving him a dose of pulmonary plague bacteria (the assassin having been given the antidote in advance), shooting him with a concealed and silenced weapon at an embassy reception (while releasing tear gas to cause confusion) or setting up a Costa Rican diplomat to give him a jewellery gift box, which would release a poison gas instantly killing everyone the moment it was opened. The word assassination was not used anywhere in the memo. Though the methods were exotic the language was blunt. The assassination plans were called *aktivnye desitviia*, meaning active measures.

The world of assassination inevitably provokes a bleak graveyard humour. KGB assassins share the CIA's love of macabre language and the laconic. In the 1960s a KGB assassin, Bogdan Stashynsky, was debriefed by the Munich police after defecting to the West. He told them that among his fellow Russian assassins the preferred euphemism was to 'greet an acquaintance' as in 'I am sure the greeting was a success.'[45] The CIA euphemism of choice at that time was 'the magic button'.

This love of oblique language is one that is hard to break. Even post 9/11, there is still reluctance to use the A word, even among the hawks in the Pentagon.

In July 2002, the US Secretary of Defense Donald Rumsfeld sent a top-secret instruction to General Charles Holland, the Head of Special Operations, telling him to come up with a plan to deal with terrorists, the purpose being to either capture them for interrogation 'or, if necessary, kill them, not simply to arrest them in a law enforcement exercise'.[46] Five months later on 3 November 2002, the Americans assassinated their first senior Al Qaeda leader, Qaed Salim Sinan al-Harethi. In a spectacular display of technology, a Hellfire missile was fired from an unmanned reconnaissance aircraft, destroying his car as it sped along a remote desert road in Yemen. He was killed instantly along with five others.

A month later, Rumsfeld was asked about the policy to 'assassinate or to kill an Al Qaeda'. The normally loquacious Rumsfeld initially hid behind a joke, telling reporters, 'I'm working my way over to figuring how not to answer that!' He then said that the policy was what 'you all know it to be. We recruit, organize, train, equip and deploy young men and women, in uniform, to go out and serve as members of our military. They are not trained to do the word you used [assassinate] which I won't even repeat. That is not what they are trained to do. They are trained to serve the country and to contribute to peace and stability in the world.'[47]

Rumsfeld had obeyed the first law of assassination, which is to write nothing down, but this was little more than a fig leaf and everyone at the press conference knew it. It was, however, in the great tradition, being exactly the sort of 'polite euphemism' which the CIA Station Chief, James Eichelberger, had wanted nearly fifty years before, in the early days when the Americans first started dabbling in the post-war business of trying to rearrange the Middle East through assassination.

2

BE CAREFUL WHEN YOU CHOOSE
YOUR ASSASSIN

'In a word, he can rationalize all his actions.'
CIA assessment of their assassin code name QJ/WIN

'We don't need paid assassins. We're not Western intelligence!'
KGB boss in charge of assassination

10 March 1953, Moscow, USSR ...
Aleksandr Semyonovich Panyushkin, a senior Russian intelligence officer, is recalled to Moscow, the day after Stalin's funeral.[1] As he arrives back in the capital, the local morgues are stacked high with hundreds of dead bodies, some trampled to death, others choked and crushed as millions pack into Red Square, a mass display of public grief for the death of the man who has run Russia for as long as anyone can remember. Some suspect Lavrenti Beria, the malevolent head of Soviet Security, as the stage manager of this event but much of the grief is genuine, some mourners travelling for the best part of two days

to reach Moscow. Even years later, witnesses recall, in vivid shock, the horrific sound of hearing bones crack, such is the crush of bodies[2] in the snow-covered square. Even in death, the great mass murderer still manages to claim a few more Russian lives, a final footnote in a reign of staggering brutality, which has already taken the lives of twenty million Soviet citizens.

Only three men give speeches, Communist Party Secretary Georgy Malenkov, Lavrenti Beria, and Vyacheslav Molotov, a life-long Bolshevik, the only one apart from Stalin himself to survive the purges of the 1930s. No one is celebrating, but today is Molotov's birthday. He is sixty-three years old and the last major direct link to the revolutionary events of 1917, when the Tsar was removed and replaced by the self-styled dictatorship of the proletariat. Molotov is best remembered as the inventor of the hand-thrown fire bomb, dismissed contemptuously by the Finns as the 'Molotov cocktail' but loved everywhere by the disaffected.

After the speeches, the coffin, covered in black and red silk, is carried into Lenin's Mausoleum. There is no place here for the other giant of Russian revolutionary politics, Leon Trotsky. He is long dead and buried in the gardens of the house in Mexico City where he was assassinated on Stalin's orders.

Officially, the Russian people are told that 'the heart of the comrade-in-arms and continuer of the genius of Lenin's cause, of the wise leader and teacher of the Communist Party and the Soviet Union, has ceased to beat,' – death by natural causes then for the man who has run the Soviet Union since the 1920s. Two of the speakers, Malenkov and Beria, are among the last to see Stalin alive, having had dinner with him just before his heart attack.

There is, however, another highly plausible – and much more likely – explanation for his passing, but only Beria (for certain) knows whether the cerebral haemorrhage, which claimed Joseph Stalin at 9.50 p.m. on 5 March 1953, aged seventy-three, was death by natural causes or induced by rat poison. It has been argued that his slow and painful death was the result of a massive overdose of Warfarin,[3] a thesis which has many advocates in British and American intelligence circles.

Aleksandr Panyushkin, the diplomat returning to Moscow, has a glittering pedigree. Until the week before, he was the Russian ambassador to China and before that he served for five years as Ambassador Extraordinary and Plenipotentiary of the USSR in Washington. Privately, President Truman refers to him as SOB (son of a bitch) Pincushion[4] but back home he is well respected and heavily decorated, Order of Lenin, two Orders of the Red Banner, Order of the Red Star.[5] The official reason for his recall from Beijing is a 'transfer to other work,'[6] a classic bland euphemism when an intelligence officer moves from a public post back into the shadows. The real reason is sinister. A sheep-dipped, senior Russian intelligence officer, he is brought back to take charge of the Foreign Intelligence Department of the MVD (*Ministerstvo Vnutrennikh Del*, Ministry of Internal Affairs). Specifically, he is to take personal charge of a very important job: the training of a hand-picked assassin for the first major killing of the post-Stalin era. Its code name: Operation Rhine.

Stalin's desire to assassinate President Tito of Yugoslavia (code name 'Carrion Crow', downgraded from the previous 'Eagle' after he began to display a dangerous independence of thought) dies with him. Iosef Grigulevich, the man who is scheduled to assassinate Tito, is withdrawn for fear that he might be named by a pre-war Russian defector Alexander Orlov, who is spilling his load in the West in a book which is being serialized in *Life* magazine, whose readers are lapping up tales of life with Stalin. The new Soviet leader Nikita Khrushchev wants peaceful co-existence with his neighbours and seeks reconciliation with the Yugoslavians instead. The plans to assassinate Tito are shelved but that does not mean that the assassination programme is to be closed down.

Khrushchev is no great fan of assassination but he is no stranger to it either. Like Stalin before him, he views it as being a necessary part of the strategy for dealing with the homegrown opposition, whether inside the Soviet bloc or living abroad. As Party Secretary in the Ukraine, Khrushchev already has two successful assassinations to his name. The young, charismatic and popular Archbishop Romzha of the Uniate Catholic Church in the Ukraine was assassinated, but only on the second attempt.

In what appears to be a miracle delivered by God, he survives a carefully choreographed car crash in which his vehicle is hit by a Soviet Army truck[7] but then dies in hospital, his faith being no protection for the lethal dose of poison injected into his veins during an unscheduled late-night visit by the hospital's director and a nurse, an assassination method described in the CIA manual of the same period as 'very effective'. According to the Agency, 'if the assassin is trained as a doctor or nurse and the subject is under medical care, this is an easy and rare method'.[8] Poisoning is not so common in a functioning democracy, where the victim's family has the right to an independent pathology report, but this does not apply in a police state, where the authorities control everything and the cover-up is much easier to manage. Khrushchev's second assassination was the former Bolshevik and revolutionary socialist Ukrainian nationalist leader, Oleksander Shumsky, who was murdered on a train, not too long after being released following thirteen years in prison,[9] his years of suffering having failed to quell his spirit and love of his country.

Khrushchev knows that although assassination is an invisible driver of Russian foreign policy, it is neither widespread nor indiscriminate but rather used rarely, highly focused and confined to the elimination of Russian émigré leaders abroad, especially those operating too close to home in West Germany.

Within months of Stalin's death, Khrushchev organizes a coup against his arch-rival, Lavrenti Beria, the former Secret Police chief, who is charged with attempting 'to revive capitalism and restore the rule of the bourgeoisie', an absurd allegation but enough to get him locked up and killed. The announcement of his execution is slipped out – like all PR notices that the sender wants to be missed – on Christmas Eve later that year. The official announcement does not remind anyone that he is the third Soviet security chief to be shot on the orders of his political paymasters, making this statistically one of the twentieth century's most dangerous jobs.

By Christmas 1954, Khrushchev is effectively in supreme command and orders his first hit. The target: Georgi Okolovich, an anti-Kremlin social democrat living abroad and well known to the CIA as the Head of Secret Operations for the NTS,[10] an organization of émigré Ukrainians, largely based in Germany. But the NTS is not just a loose alliance of disaffected nationalists. It is a CIA–MI6 front, a frontline platoon in the Cold War.

The man in charge of the assassination on the other side of the Iron Curtain, Aleksandr Panyushkin, is not only an ambitious *apparatchik* but a highly accomplished operator, who is determined that nothing will go wrong. That means a clean shot and no adverse publicity. The choice of the assassin, the people Khrushchev calls 'trustworthy combat operatives,'[11] is crucial and Panyushkin selects a captain in Russian intelligence, Nikolai Khokhlov, who gets the very best training at an unmarked building on the corner of Metrostroyevskaya U1 and Turchaninski Pere Ulok[12] in Moscow. His mentor is Colonel Arkady Foteyev,[13] who runs a staff of specialist instructors. Army champion Lieutenant Colonel Godlevsky,[14] winner of five national pistol tournaments, turns him into an accomplished marksman. Soviet judo champion Mikhail Rubak,[15] known as the 'bone breaker', teaches him close-quarter combat and how to kill with his bare hands. Other trainers give him all the skills he will need to function as a modern assassin: encryption, radio communication, offensive and defensive driving, surveillance and photography. Much of what he is taught is standard training for soldiers (and particularly special forces) everywhere. But once he has completed his basic training he is introduced to the most exotic weapons on the planet at that time.

Like the CIA's technical services division and the various departments which have served MI6 and its related organizations, the Soviet intelligence services are obsessed with the exotic. Three weapons were developed for this assassination, two in cigarette cases (which are called 'Stingers')[16] and one which looks like a small gun.

This gun, which is about four inches high and four inches long, weighs about 23oz when loaded and comes from a top-secret laboratory near Kuchino outside Moscow, which builds specialist weapons and bespoke explosives and is straight out of James Bond. The author Ian Fleming, himself a former British intelligence officer, extensively culled this incident and others during the 1950s to inform the writing of *From Russia With Love*. Bizarrely, Fleming's fiction makes much of Khokhlov's story seem familiar.

Khokhlov is given the most sophisticated of the weapons. To a casual observer, the world's most sophisticated assassination tool looks exactly like a packet of Chesterfield cigarettes. When opened the ends of the cigarettes even have strands of tobacco in them, but they contain something even more lethal than nicotine, an electrically operated gun, complete with silencer.

One of the 'Chesterfield' guns has two .32 calibre barrels inside the cigarettes, the other has four .25 calibre bullets. Each weighs about 14oz when loaded. Any combination of barrels can be fired by applying pressure on bars opposite each barrel. Each clip contains three different kinds of bullet. The lead bullets have the greatest range and are effective at about 25 feet and are primarily intended to disable the victim who can then be shot again at closer range. The steel bullet is the most stable and will go through a 3cm plank at 27 feet. The poison bullets are unstable and can only be used at very close range. The barrels are not rifled but the bullets are grooved so they will spin in flight. Even the 1.5 volt battery is bespoke, specially made for this gun. Khokhlov is taken to the laboratory of special weapons, a place so secret he needs ministerial clearance beforehand. Here a lieutenant colonel demonstrates the gun, which is only accurate over 10 to 20 yards but very powerful. At 25 yards it has no problem ripping through four one-inch thick planks.

There are no recoiling parts in any of the weapons. Instead, all of them have a feature that makes them virtually unique at the time. When a gun is fired at less than the speed of sound, the bang is caused by the rapidly expanding hot gases escaping into the cold air around. In these weapons there are no escaping gases and therefore no bang. The Soviet technicians are very proud of the silencer, boasting, 'Its greatness is in its simplicity. A steel chamber. In it, a disc. The gunpowder explodes and pushes the disc. The disc throws out the bullet and at the same moment closes the opening. All the sound remains inside. Simpler than a steamed turnip!'[17] When fired the gun is no louder than someone clicking their fingers. It is the ultimate assassination weapon.

The bullets come from a specialist chemical laboratory at Khozyaistvo Zheleznovo,[18] which develops the designer poisons and drugs to be used in what are euphemistically called 'special action tasks'.[19] But these are no ordinary munitions. The bullets are made in two parts, an outer hollow, ribbed metal shell and an inner hollow pointed bullet containing the poison. The outer shell fragments on impact, ripping the flesh and creating an opening through which the inner bullet can penetrate and lodge the poison. The toxin used is a strange cocktail. The killing agent is potassium cyanide, one of the world's most lethal poisons and the same one used in the mass slaughter at Jonestown in Guyana in which more than nine hundred Americans die in November 1978 after drinking Kool-Aid laced with poison. The Russian scientists then mix in an anticoagulant to stop the blood clotting until the poison is well established in the blood stream and finally there is a gum binder to hold the mixture together. The Soviet technicians are addicted to overkill and each bullet contains enough poison to kill the occupants of a small street, but delivered to just one person it will guarantee death in two or three minutes.

In the numerous field trials, the Russian scientists discover a problem. The gun is too powerful: the bullet travels too fast and so there is no guarantee the poison will stick and work. Panyushkin takes personal control of the development, the ballistic punch is reduced and a gun that fires a slower bullet is produced, but this delays the assassination by a few weeks.

As part of the training, the young Captain Nikolai Khokhlov practices on different materials, glass, clothes, boards, even a leg of lamb. The weapon is devastating. He is given two assistants, Franz and Felix, both from East Germany, who are brought to Moscow and put through the same basic training course: hand-to-hand fighting, getaway driving and firearms. There is a further delay as the Russians discover the stamps they have used to forge their papers have been changed by the West Germans. New ones are obtained, new forged papers are made and together the three assassins set off for Frankfurt in early 1954, the date chosen is 13 February.

Four days before leaving, Khokhlov has a final meeting with Panyushkin who obsessively goes through every detail, right down to the new stamps on the forged papers. The budget for the operation is $55,000 (a huge sum for the early 1950s). Some is banked in Geneva in case they have to retreat via Switzerland and some in West German banks. Panyushkin tells him to spend the money wisely but to look after his two assistants. 'Don't spoil them especially. Whatever is necessary for the family – give. When they leave for the assignment, keep in touch with their families, so they won't be left alone.' And then, with no sense of irony he adds, 'Don't spoil them with presents. We don't need paid assassins. We're not Western intelligence!' As he is being briefed the minister phones to check everything is in order. This operation is sanctioned from the very highest levels of government downwards, everyone has their finger-prints on it. As he leaves, Panyushkin asks Khokhlov whether he is carrying a personal weapon for himself. When Khokhlov tells him that he is not, Panyushkin tells him that this is the right approach, adding 'to you and me a head is more important than a pistol,' a prophetic remark which will come back to haunt him. As he leaves, Panyushkin says, 'See you again,' but he never will – at least not face to face.

But though their basic military training is exceptional his Soviet handlers make one very bad mistake. They do not adequately profile their man and have obviously not read the CIA assassination manual (ironically written at the same time, early 1954), which warns that 'assassination can seldom be employed with a clear conscience. Persons who are morally squeamish should not attempt it.'

On 18 February 1954, Russia's best-trained assassin goes to the Frankfurt flat at 15 Hauptwache Square, the home of Georgi Okolovich, who is the particular target of Moscow's hatred. Khokhlov, a bespectacled man who looks like a bank manager or a college lecturer, does not attract any attention as he travels by tram and then walks to the flat. He knocks on the door and, when Okolovich answers, he says to him, 'Georgi Sergeyevitch. I've come to you from Moscow.' The news he imparts is no surprise but shocking nevertheless. 'The Central Committee of the Communist Party of the Soviet Union has ordered your assassination.' He then tells him about the assassination team in Frankfurt, reassuring him that he is not going to kill him. A shocked Okolovich listens as Khokhlov tells him that he wants to surrender himself to the West German authorities instead. Okolovich then introduces him to his paymasters from the CIA, who initially refuse to believe him, but after intense interrogation they become convinced and two months later, a man described by *The Times* newspaper as 'a terrorist agent' appears blinking before the world's press behind a fence of microphones at the United States consulate near Bonn. He tells the journalists that, 'his conscience prevented his carrying out the murder'. The Americans promise to spring his wife and child out of the Soviet Union at the same time as the press conference but they renege on the deal and his family are arrested in Moscow and disappear, presumed dead. Three years later, in September 1957, Nikolai Khokhlov survives a revenge assassination attempt when Soviet agents slip radioactive thallium into his coffee at an émigré's conference. Amazingly, he survives even though his skin turns brown, his hair falls out and his blood turns to plasma . . .[20]

For every intelligence service the choice of assassin is crucial and this was one of the worst ever. Khokhlov's defection, his press conference, his subsequent testimony to an American Senate Select Committee and his autobiography handed a huge propaganda coup to Russia's Cold War enemies, the Americans, the British and the French.

While the diminutive Khrushchev had to put up with humiliation at the hands of the Western press, his counterparts on the other side of the Iron Curtain had a relatively easy run. Khrushchev and his advisers in the KGB knew that three key Western countries were running their own assassination operations at exactly the same time: the CIA in South America, Africa and South East Asia; the British in Iran and Africa; and the French in Morocco and Algeria. The only difference was they were much better at it or just luckier. There were no significant Western defectors from the assassination business and therefore there was no firm evidence (at that time) to link the ranked capitalist forces with a number of suspiciously convenient deaths in key parts of the world. The Americans, the British and the French were, quite literally, getting away with murder.

Not only were the Western intelligence services better at assassination than the KGB, their propaganda machines were much more powerful. Thanks to Ian Fleming and the James Bond novels and early films, the Western perception of the KGB, and especially the division known as SMERSH, the internal department responsible for assassinations, was that it was run by emotionally cold, clear-thinking psychopaths. Even today, Soviet operatives are portrayed as ruthless assassins with no regard for their own or anyone else's lives. Perfect killing machines, the special forces foot soldiers of the Cold War who were just as at ease with a silenced handgun as they were with a garrotte. As with most crude propaganda, the truth was somewhat different.

Despite the international public relations disaster of three years earlier, President Khrushchev, the leader of one of the world's great superpowers and a former governor of the Ukraine, was still incensed by the activities of leaders both within the Soviet Union and abroad. He was short in stature[21] and even shorter of temper and whether he personally gave the orders or not, the special actions division of the KGB knew – subconsciously or not – exactly what the boss wanted: death without dishonour.

The following year, the KGB employed a German criminal and freelance killer, Wolfgang Wildprett, and contracted him to assassinate Vladimir Poremsky, the president of the NTS. While the Ukrainian émigrés were portrayed in the West as heroic nationalists fighting for the glory of their homeland now suffering under the Soviet yoke, there were many in the Kremlin who saw them in a different light – as devout Nazis who committed terrible crimes during the Second World War and who should not be allowed to go unpunished. Poremsky was typical of this bunch of psychopaths, all with long records for atrocities committed during the Second World War. To the West he was a nationalist hero, but to the Russians he was a war criminal once described as a '200 per cent Nazi'.

When the Second World War started, Poremsky, and other leading members of the NTS, joined the Nazis, offering themselves as puppet leaders fighting for the Germans against the Russians in the SS-occupied zones inside the Soviet Union.[22] After the war, the surviving NTS leaders were captured and expected to go on trial as collaborators but they were freed by the Americans to join a new army in a new war, the Capitalist West against the Communist East. Poremsky was on the MI6 payroll before the war, and in 1946, his former British Intelligence paymasters got him released from prison 'on health grounds' whereupon he immediately rejoined his fellow NTS members, eager foot soldiers in the new war against their old enemy Moscow.[23] Interestingly, though the Soviets regarded the NTS as a significant threat to their own security, they were increasingly regarded by their MI6 and CIA financiers as untrustworthy, factional and worse still, totally ineffective.

According to Poremsky, though this account sounded suspiciously like the incident the year before, Wildprett appeared on his doorstep, on Christmas Day 1955, carrying a newspaper photograph of his victim in one hand and a Walther P38 handgun in the other. He told the shocked exile leader: 'I'm here to kill you but I don't trust them [his Soviet handlers]. If I kill you, then they will tell me to murder someone else. Then one day the police will arrest me and put me in prison with a big pile of deutschmarks I can't spend.' Wildprett turned himself in to the West German police and was resettled with a new identity, another disaster for the Special Tasks Department of the Soviet Intelligence Services.

By now the KGB scorecard read: three attempted assassinations, three failures (including their attempt to kill one of their own assassins) and two defections.

Despite these humiliations, the Ukraine continued to be a major issue for the Kremlin, especially the continued activities of the dissidents, which were by then scattered round Europe. The Ukraine was a key frontline state in the Cold War and in the early 1950s the Ukrainians were the most powerful ethnic minority in the Soviet bloc, united by a rampant and volatile nationalism, which threatened to explode at any moment. The Ukraine was still shattered by the Nazi occupation when there had been extensive collaboration with the Germans. There was heavy fighting in the two years after the war between the communist Russians and the Ukrainian nationalists, many of whom were German collaborators with a Nazi past. This was a major Anglo–American intelligence operation. The Ukrainian nationalists were heavily supported by MI6, but undermined by Kim Philby, who betrayed them to the Russians. The Americans were led in part by Frank Wisner, whose next big operation would be the Guatemalan *coup d'état*.

The Soviets did not crush the main resistance until 1949 and even then it continued into the early 1950s, by which time the Ukrainian nationalist forces were reduced to the time-honoured terrorist tactics of assassinating government officials. For Stalin and the other the Second World War veterans, the memories of twenty million Russians dead in the Second World War were still fresh, informing their every thought. For them, the Ukraine was still unfinished business. So far, they had failed to assassinate two former Nazis, Georgi Okolovich in 1954 and Poremsky in 1955, both of whom were now working closely with the CIA and MI6 to undermine the Soviet state.

From the Russian perspective, both were still soldiers fighting in an ongoing war and therefore legitimate targets. Though the Ukraine was subdued by this time, there were still pockets of resistance abroad and, as far as the KGB was concerned, the key man was Stefan Bandera, another NTS leader who had been a virulent anti-Semite and enthusiastic Nazi early in the war. His Unit, OUN-B (B for Bandera) had worn German rather than Ukrainian uniforms and (much to the embarrassment of some of his new paymasters in MI6 and the CIA) had played a key role in the extermination of 900,000 in the Ukraine; his soldiers being used by the Nazis to do the really dirty work of torturing Jews and shooting children.[24] When the Nazis fled in 1943 the ragbag of anti-Soviet and nationalist forces coalesced to form the UPA (the Ukrainian insurgent army), which then fought a guerrilla war against the Russian army for much of the rest of the decade.

The KGB ran their assassination operations from a sealed compound within a military base at Karlshorst, a suburb in east Berlin. This was the headquarters of the Soviet High Command but at the side was a former three-storey hospital, surrounded by a solid wooden fence with armed sentries checking everyone in and out. From here they selected their next assassin, a champion marksman who toured East Germany taking part in shooting competitions. The deal was simple: if he assassinated

Bandera he could go and live in the West with his family and nine children. He went to live in Munich, under cover, and once he was settled he was given photographs of Bandera cut out from a magazine. The champion marksman located him, reporting back to his KGB controllers who had gradually been releasing his children and his wife. He kept stringing them along with more details about Bandera and his movements. The more details he supplied, the more the KGB were convinced that this time they had got the right man for the job. They supplied him with a high-powered rifle and gave him the order to assassinate Bandera. But the KGB was a bureaucracy like any other and in a classic case of the left hand and the right hand being in mutual ignorance they got their timing wrong, only giving him the order to assassinate Bandera, after they had released his last child and not before. As soon as he had his final child out of the Soviet Union and safe in the West, he immediately defected and was resettled by his CIA handlers.[25] Another triumph for the West and another failure for the Russians and all the CIA had done was keep the front door open for the latest walk-in.

The KGB scorecard now read: four attempted assassinations, four failures and three defections. But then as now, the Russians were stubborn long-term players and, despite the relentless diet of humiliation, they did not give up.

The assassination programme against the Ukrainian exiles continued and, in October 1957, the Soviets sent another homegrown, highly trained killer, Bogdan Stashynsky, to Munich to assassinate another émigré leader, Lev Rebet. This time they were successful. Rebet was found dead at the top of his stairs on his way into his flat. As far as the West German authorities were concerned, the cause of death was clear: he had died of a heart attack. For the Russians in Moscow, who knew differently, it was the perfect hit, man and machine in perfect harmony. Reputations were restored, state pensions were secured and for all those involved a safe, rather than a premature retirement looked more likely.

The KGB scorecard had suddenly improved, though it was a long way from their Ian Fleming image. It now read: five attempted assassinations, one success, four failures and three defections.

Two years later, the KGB assassins were back in business. In October 1959, they made another attempt at killing the prominent Ukrainian exile, Stefan Bandera, now living in Munich under the assumed name Stefan Popel. Again they were successful. Bandera/Popel was found dead of a heart attack, but this time, the police performed a more detailed post-mortem and found tiny cuts on his face caused by flying splinters of glass. The cause of death was prussic acid, the colourless liquid form of cyanide and one of the world's deadliest poisons, which is better known as one of the key ingredients of Xyklon B, the gas used by the Nazis to exterminate millions of Jews.

The German authorities knew it was murder but had no clue as to who or how. These two deaths would have remained as mysteries if the assassin had not then defected to the West, with an extraordinary story to tell, just before he began an eight-year prison sentence. Under interrogation, Bogdan Stashynsky described how he had first been sent to Munich in 1957 to kill Lev Rebet. But this was no everyday assassination, not least because the weapon used was so extraordinary.

Before he had gone on his mission, his KGB boss and a weapons instructor had taken him into a wood for a demonstration with a dog. He was given the weapon, which was unlike anything he had seen before, and told to use it on the dog, which died immediately. They took the collar and leash back but left the carcass behind. This new weapon was a vast improvement on the cigarette-packet gun of five years before. This had a seven-inch metal tube, with three sections screwed together. In the bottom section was a firing pin, which ignited a small powder charge, which in turn moved a small metal lever which then crushed a small glass ampoule, vapourizing a deadly poison. At a distance of half a metre it was fatal, the victim dropping dead immediately they inhaled. The device was elaborate for a very good reason. The KGB did not want to create martyrs in its satellite states and (after three defections) did not want to leave any fingerprints. The advantage of this weapon was that the gas used left no traces, but there were two disadvantages: the enthusiastic Soviet technicians had over-powered the gun which meant that fragments of glass were left behind. It was also potentially fatal for the assassin, but the KGB chemists had anticipated this. As soon as the assassin fired the gas, he had to immediately inhale two antidotes: sodium thiosulphate and amyl nitrate, which were kept in a gauze cloth he had to take with him.

Stashynsky told his astonished German and American interrogators that both assassinations had gone according to plan. He had met Rebet, shot him with the poison and then left the building, inhaling the antidotes before throwing the gun in the river. After the success of the first killing he was sent back to Germany, this time to 7 Kreittmayerstrasse in Munich, the home of Stefan Bandera, where again he was successful in assassinating his target. After the second killing, Stashynsky was summoned to Moscow, where the Chairman of the KGB, Alexander Shelepin, read out the citation which praised him 'for carrying out an extremely important government assignment' before presenting him with the Order of the Red Banner. But once again the amateur psychologist who wrote the CIA assassination manual was spot on: the assassin did not have a clear conscience and began to feel the pangs of the morally squeamish.

Stashynsky had married a young East German woman, Inge Pohl, and once their baby died they defected to the West, in the nick of time, crossing into west Berlin on 12 August 1961, the day before the Wall went up. At his trial, the West German judge condemned the Soviet government as the main, but absent, criminal because it had put extra-judicial murder at the heart of the state.

Back in Moscow, the embarrassment was palpable. The scorecard now read: six attempts, two successful assassinations but four failures and four defectors, two of whom were now star witnesses for the opposition in the great propaganda war being played out between the USA and the Soviet Union. Khrushchev's rage was off the Richter scale. At least seventeen KGB officers were sacked or demoted as the Kremlin began to have serious doubts and effectively abandoned its programme of state-sponsored assassination.

Khrushchev had been in power for just over a decade, as First Secretary of the Communist Party and then as Premier, but the assassination programme had brought nothing but disgrace and embarrassment. During his watch, the KGB had succeeded only twice out of six known attempts. As the CIA Assassination Manual noted, '... the assassin must not fall alive into enemy hands' but four Russian defectors had done exactly this,[26] going over to the other side, one of them taking his cigarette-packet gun with him, the photographs of which then informed a generation's beliefs of the Soviet Union. Though the weapons were masterpieces of engineering, execution was everything and Russian operational incompetence was humiliating and very public. The Kremlin policymakers had no choice but to abandon assassination as a weapon of foreign policy, an extraordinary climbdown for the foreign intelligence service of one of the world's only two superpowers.

The irony was that these bungled assassinations were becoming increasingly unimportant. With the withering away of the survivors of the Ukrainian struggle through death and old age, the number of targets for the 'trustworthy combat operatives' working in the department of 'wet affairs' was dwindling. By the early 1960s, these émigré groups were largely irrelevant and of no danger to what was now an impregnable Russian state machine. The groups themselves had largely fallen apart through internal dissent, the massive egos of their leaders and corruption. Even their paymasters in the CIA and MI6 had become disaffected with them. To seriously damage the Soviet Union, these groups needed more than just a drip feed of cash spiced up with liberation rhetoric from Western politicians. When the West failed to intervene to support the Hungarian uprising in 1956, the Kremlin should have read the signs. The West was simply not going to take any serious risks supporting national liberation movements within the Soviet bloc. The Kremlin's perceived need for assassination against the home-grown opposition was, in fact, negligible and simply not worth the risk of a major propaganda onslaught every time it went wrong and backfired on them. Though the lesson was obvious it would still take them several years more to learn it.

Their main problem was, as President Kennedy eloquently put it when he opened the new $50 million CIA headquarters in Langley, Virginia in 1961, that for intelligence services (especially those operating in democratic countries) their 'successes are unheralded, but failures are trumpeted'.

In retrospect, these Soviet operations all failed for the same reason. The weapons themselves were more sophisticated than anything the CIA or the Europeans had at that time. The basic physical training was as good as that of any other country and the assassins set out on their missions with all the operational skills necessary to complete their task. The weakness was the poor psychological profiling of their assassins. The Soviet assassin masters discovered with both Nikolai Khokhlov and Bogdan Stashynsky that effective assassins have to be commit-ted and unwavering believers in the cause. As the CIA officer running operations against them in Germany noted, 'The run-of-the-mill intelligence officer does not make a good hit man.'[27] Their choice of paid killer was not much better. They discovered with Wolfgang Wildprett that paying a contract killer could just as easily backfire as, ultimately, mercenaries have no loyalty to anyone other than themselves and their survival instinct is more powerful than the size of the next payment. The unnamed assassin who defected with his children simply outwitted them and they should have been more suspicious when he insisted on taking his wife and children to the West before the operation.

Khokhlov began to waver when he read and became convinced by the literature put out by the émigré group, whose leader he was targeting. In the end, neither Stashynsky nor Wildprett trusted the KGB, which is surprising as the Soviets had an excellent record of agent handling, as shown by their recruitment and running of the Cambridge Five and the conveyor belt of British and American spies who followed.[28] The persistent Russian failure went to the heart of the matter of assassination.

The CIA assassination manual drew a distinction between murder, which 'is not morally justifiable' and assassination, which, they argued, could be. Some simple arguments were used to justify it. 'Self-defense may be argued if the victim has knowledge which may destroy the resistance organization if divulged' – that is, far more lives (on your own side) would be put at risk. A second justification was the 'assassination of persons responsible for atrocities or reprisals' as this could be regarded as just punishment. The third reason was 'killing a political leader whose burgeoning career is a clear and present danger to the cause of freedom may be held necessary.'

In each case, there was a higher purpose claimed, which hoisted the act out of murder into a morally and politically justifiable act with a higher ideal attached. The persistent Soviet failures came about because two of their key assassins, both experienced intelligence officers, had a greater sense of proportion than their masters. Both began to wobble when they discussed the reality of their employment with their wives, who urged them to walk away and defect for a better life in the West. For them, this was not assassination motivated by a higher ideal, but murder, pure and simple and for the basest of motives. This was particularly clear in Khokhlov's case, as he had previously killed successfully for the Russians, when as a young soldier he had assassinated General Kommissar Wilhelm Kube, Hitler's man in Byelorussia, who had boasted to Berlin of slaughtering 55,000 Jews in ten weeks.

Khokhlov was a fluent linguist and, with another agent, had smuggled himself into Byelorussia, infiltrating himself into the Nazi camp in full German uniform. He recruited a local woman to plant a British magnetic bomb under Kube's mattress.[29] This bomb was simple in its design and required only a couple of minutes' training in its use. A TNT cube, in a small box with powerful magnets on either side, it could be attached to any metal surface. The fuse was a small brass pencil with a label which could be set at two, four or twelve hours. The pencil was inserted into the bomb, the time period set, allowing the assassin plenty of time to escape. It was devastatingly effective. Kube was blown to pieces while sleeping at 2 a.m. Khokhlov and his fellow officer had already escaped, commandeering a German truck and ordering the driver to pick up the two 'girls from the officers' dining room' and hitching a lift out of the town. Khokhlov carried out this assassination, as he says, with a 'gleam in my eyes'.[30] But the wartime assassination of an evil Nazi who was slaughtering fellow Russians was very different from the peacetime murder of a Ukrainian anti-Soviet, whose views he was growing to respect.

But as the Kremlin was largely getting out of the assassination business in 1960, the CIA was stepping up their programme, sending one of their own to the Congo to assassinate Patrice Lumumba. Mozes Maschkivitzan[31] was born in Antwerp in 1910 of Jewish parents, and by 1960 was a stateless citizen with a chequered past and an extensive criminal record. His code name was QJ/WIN and according to the case officers who worked with him he was 'not a man of many scruples'. Though he was operating under very deep cover, there was, as always, an extensive paper trail. Apart from the memo to pay him,[32] a CIA cable sent on 2 November 1960 described an operation, which 'might involve a large element of personal risk'.[33] Due to 'the extreme sensitivity' of his task, the recipient of the telegram was told to reduce the contents to 'cryptic necessary notes' and then destroy it.

The wages of death were good. He was paid an annual salary of $7,200 and a further $7,500 was approved for 'operational expenses'.[34] The upside of being a paid assassin for the CIA was that he was virtually immune from prosecution for any other criminal activity he might wish to get involved in. The downside was that the career prospects were not so good. According to the CIA Inspector General, the records show that QJ/WIN was 'terminated [deletion] on 21 April 1964,' a highly unfortunate turn of phrase. In the CIA dictionary of the early 1960s, terminated only had one meaning, death by assassination. QJ/WIN was followed by a second assassin (code name WI/ROGUE), another man with a long criminal record including convictions for forgery and bank robbery. Both men were stateless mercenaries, who came highly recommended for the job from other sections of the CIA.

The internal assessment of QJ/WIN described him as the perfect assassin with the right credentials. He 'learns quickly and carries out any assignment without regard for danger'.[35] Part of QJ/WIN's training was a course where he was taught 'medical immunization', a euphemism for administering the deadly poison which had been delivered to the CIA station for the assassination.

To disguise his identity, the CIA gave him plastic surgery before sending him to the Congo. As often with these operations, there was an inevitable element of farce: the CIA also fitted him out with a toupee as they believed that once they disguised him in this way he would not be recognized by other Europeans travelling in the Congo. By any measure, this was bizarre. What made it even stranger was that the normal operating procedure was for women CIA officers to use wigs in which they could hide micro equipment. Even these were a nightmare to use in a tropical climate as the glues rarely worked effectively. The business they were in was assassination, but high farce and irrational behaviour were only ever a blink away.

In the end, neither of the CIA's chosen assassins would get to assassinate their target, though this was not due to any lack of commitment or enthusiasm on their parts.

According to the CIA's Africa Division, QJ/WIN 'is indeed aware of the precepts of right and wrong, but if he is given an assignment which may be morally wrong in the eyes of the world, but necessary because his case officer ordered him to carry it out, then it is right, and he will dutifully undertake appropriate action for its execution without pangs of conscience. In a word, he can rationalize all actions.'[36]

As far as the CIA was concerned, he had the perfect psychological profile for an assassin on their payroll. Interestingly, while the Soviets recruited assassins who were believers in the cause, the CIA sought out assassins who were obedient psychopaths and who ultimately did not care but were just in it for the money and the buzz.

Both CIA assassins were recruited under a deep cover project, which was so secret that it was buried inside another, completely unrelated, programme within the CIA called the Department of Coded Communications in Foreign Countries. Formally, ZR/RIFLE was a highly covert operation whose ostensible function was to develop a capability for breaking into safes and kidnapping couriers. Both projects were run by CIA veteran William Harvey who used ZR/RIFLE to research assassination methods as well as using it as a vehicle to recruit 'individuals with criminal and underworld connections in Europe for possible multi-purpose use'. ZR was the digraph used by the CIA for operations involving intelligence interception. The pun on RIFLE (as in the weapon and rifle as in rifling through someone's mail) was not lost on anyone involved.

Europe was not the only assassin farm which the CIA cultivated at this time. According to the CIA files, they also had a potential asset in the Middle East who was 'the leader of a gambling syndicate' with 'an available pool of assassins'.

The CIA set up this general assassination capability, otherwise called executive action, after being prompted by the Kennedy White House in early 1961. William Harvey was the man in charge and his handwritten notes of a meeting, just five days after Kennedy made his inaugural address, leave no room for doubt. He referred to the business as 'the magic button', a 'last resort beyond last resort and a confession of weakness' but just in case he should ever forget what these elliptical phrases meant he also wrote: 'never mention word assassination'.[37]

Assassins were not just recruited in the Middle East and Europe. Inevitably the CIA looked closer to home, from among a group of criminals they had been working with since the end of the Second World War: the Cosa Nostra. The Italian mafia were furious that they had lost Cuba to Fidel Castro and the communists. Under the previous corrupt Batista regime they had turned the island into a brothel and casino, from which flowed a river of cash, offshore and tax-free. Like Kennedy, they wanted it back. Their reasons were financial, his solely political. After the Castro assassination programme was folded into ZR/RIFLE, the CIA teamed up with America's leading crime bosses: Santos Trafficante, Sam Giancana and his man on the west coast, Johnny Roselli.

Just like the KGB, the CIA quickly learned that the choice of assassin was crucial. In their eagerness to assassinate Castro they further cemented their alliance with the most dangerous criminals in America, an act of staggering stupidity, which has embarrassed the Agency ever since. The story broke in 1967 and President Johnson commissioned an investigation by the CIA's Inspector General Lyman Fitzpatrick. His report was a staggering catalogue of breathtaking incompetence, millions of American tax dollars wasted and a series of relationships that put the CIA and the Kennedy White House even further in hock to the mob. Organized crime now had a direct call on the CIA and the White House, a relationship they exploited, much to Kennedy's embarrassment. And for all the effectiveness of their operation they would have done less damage dumping the money straight into the Caribbean. This document was regarded as so sensitive by the CIA that neither President Johnson nor President Nixon was allowed to read it in its entirety though it was eventually published. The previous generation of assassin masters in the Kremlin who had suffered under the propaganda backlash from their own disasters must have allowed themselves a quiet smile as the details of the CIA's exotic weapons began to emerge: exploding ashtrays, exotic poisons and even drugs to make Castro's beard fall out. It was as if the baton of incompetence had been passed on from the KGB to the CIA in 1960.

On paper, the CIA's assassins in the Congo looked good but were never tested. When their assassins were put into action in Cuba, their choice looked little better than the KGB.

Through the mafia they first recruited a man called Juan Orta, who worked in Castro's office. When the mob had run Cuba, Orta had supplemented his wages taking backhanders but now that the corruption tap was switched off he needed the money. Six poison pills were made and three given to mafia boss Johnny Roselli, who delivered them to Cuba, but Orta got cold feet and fled to the Venezuelan embassy.[38] The CIA was lucky. Unlike the Russian assassins, Orta did not make a big media splash. He had nowhere to go: his immediate employers were the mafia and behind them was the federal government of the United States, both of whom – as he knew all too well – were heavily into the assassination business. Besides who would have believed him if he had gone to the newspapers telling them that he had been recruited by the mafia to assassinate Fidel Castro on the orders of the president of the United States, using poison pills made by the technical services division of the CIA? A classic conspiracy theory – easily dismissed – but in this case completely true.

The CIA then recruited two Cuban soldiers, Major Rolando Cubela and Major Ramon Guin, but again their choice of assassins was poor. Cubela's group was very leaky and the Agency pulled away from them – but only after supplying a Tasco telescopic sight and a 7.62 FAL rifle, fragmentation and incendiary grenades and large quantities of ammunition, all of which were then discovered by the Cuban intelligence service when they raided his house. Under pressure from Castro, the death sentence was commuted to thirty years. The story did not play in the West with any of the power of the Soviet defections, being easily dismissed as a communist show trial.

But the CIA's relationship with the mob was too public, too many knew about it and it inevitably leaked. Recruiting assassins from the ranks of organized crime was a step too far for many Americans and in 1975 President Ford signed a presidential order specifically forbidding the CIA or any other US government agent from assassinating foreign leaders. Like the KGB, the CIA had to suffer public humiliation on a grand scale not least from the various congressional committees, where politicians queued up to point the finger and get their picture in the media.

But the KGB and the CIA are both creatures of habit and after a generation had passed and the memories had started to fade, they both slid effortlessly back into the assassination business. But both had learnt the lesson of employing assassins who talked. They now both put their trust in a silent technological assassin who could deliver death from above, remote, removed, a killer with no moral qualms or questionable associations.

In 1986, the Americans tried to assassinate Colonel Qaddafi by dropping sixteen one ton laser-guided bombs on his tent. Though the assassination failed (Qaddafi was elsewhere at the time) there was little serious domestic fallout and no embarrassment for the CIA or the White House. President Reagan took the heat for the accidental bombing of a hospital and the whole affair was spun very successfully in the media as self-defence and a warning to Qaddafi.

The Russians restored their assassination programme in the mid-1990s; once again the target being dissident nationalists bucking against the Soviet yoke. Their major target area was Chechnya, a predominantly Muslim country in the north Caucasus, which had never sat well in the Soviet republic. Initially, the Russian leadership failed to remember the failures of the past and much to the delight of his supporters, the Chechen President Dzhokhar Dudayev survived numerous conventional assassination attempts. Eventually, the Russians put their faith in the cleverness of Soviet technology and their ultimate killer application. Though their plan did not rely on an assassin with wobbly nerves, there was initial failure. One of their first attempts involved the Russians giving one of Dudayev's bodyguards a commando knife, as a present. Hidden in the handle was a small transmitter, which acted as an electronic targeting device for Russian missiles, but the Chechens were too smart for this. They immediately discovered it which gave them a huge propaganda coup and a boost to their morale.

But then on 21 April 1996, the Russians got their man, when he least expected it. Dudayev was killed in a Russian rocket attack, but this was no random killing in the heat of war. He was assassinated by a Russian missile while making a telephone call from a portable satellite dish in woods in a remote village twenty miles outside the capital Grozny. No marksmanship was required. This was a case of fire and forget, the missile simply homed in on the signal from his phone, a remote killing, with no embarrassing television cameras or journalists around to ask difficult questions.

The use of missiles in this way has marked a quantum leap in assassination practice. The rich nations no longer need to worry about defectors and bad publicity. Advanced electronics means that missiles are now used to assassinate individuals, remotely and at a distance, where previously the assassin had needed to be close up. The problem of the squeamish assassin has been addressed: killing is now done at one-stage removed, neat and far less stressful for those on the frontline.

Taking their cue from the Russians, the CIA then used similar technology to assassinate six members of Al Qaeda in Yemen as they drove through the desert on 3 November 2003, including a man who was one of their major targets. Qaed Salim Senan al-Harthy, a former bodyguard of Osama Bin Laden, who the Americans believed was involved in planning the attack on the USS *Cole*, two years previously, when the US destroyer was attacked while at anchor in Aden Harbour. Two men in a small, motorized dinghy had drawn alongside and detonated a bomb, blowing a 40-foot square hole in the side of the ship, killing seventeen and injuring thirty-five. The pictures of the stricken ship, with a huge gaping hole just above the water line, were a public relations triumph for Al Qaeda, an effective recruitment poster on the front page of the world's newspapers. For the Americans, it was a disaster. Once again, they were on the wrong end of an asymmetric attack, where a small, dedicated terrorist group had struck a major blow against a much larger, better equipped and much richer opponent. They wanted – and got – their revenge.

Working closely with Arab intelligence services throughout the Middle East, but particularly the Yemenis, the CIA tracked al-Harthy for months. In 2000, the CIA had virtually no relationship with the Yemenis, but the American government began pouring aid into the country[39] as well as special forces to train the Yemeni Army. The local CIA station was also beefed up and in September 2001, the Americans installed a new ambassador, a State Department veteran, Ed Hull. But he was much more than just a diplomat. He was also a fluent Arab speaker with thirty years' experience of the Middle East, and most importantly, he was also a counter-terrorism expert and a man with a flexible definition of an ambassador's duties.

While Hull was still finding his feet, al-Harthy was moving freely round the Marib province, a lawless no-go zone for the Yemeni government, where local tribesmen protected him. The Yemenis first tried to capture him in 2001, but failed when he escaped after a ferocious gun battle in which eighteen soldiers were killed. But the US did not give up. Throughout 2002, the West continued to bring Yemen into the fold. In October that year, a $2.3 billion economic support package was agreed[40] and the following month, the CIA once again had al-Harthy in their sights, after paying out substantial bribes to local tribesmen to locate him.

As he drove through the desert in a car with five others, including a Yemeni American, he believed he was safe but he did not know that he was being remotely tracked by satellite and video camera. High above the speeding car, an unmanned plane carrying an anti-tank Hellfire[41] missile was following him at a discreet distance.

The drone – called the Predator – is a 27-foot long unmanned vehicle, which cruises at 84 mph and flies at up to 25,000 feet. The system is highly portable and moves around in a box nicknamed a 'coffin'. At forty-five million dollars each it is the ultimate assassination weapon. Stuffed with cameras and radar, the Predator transmits real-time video pictures back to base anywhere in the world.

As soon as one of the key Al Qaeda members used his mobile phone, confirming his identity, the button was pressed at a remote US base and the laser-guided anti-tank missile blew their taxi to pieces, leaving a charred black mess in the desert road.

For both the Russians and the Americans missile technology is now the perfect assassination weapon. It is high tech, very expensive and only available to members of the first world club and their closest allies. As such, it fits their self-image as global powers. But both the Kremlin and the Pentagon took their cue from the Israelis, who remain the world leaders in assassination technology.

In February 1992, the Israelis assassinated Sheikh Abbas Moussawi, a Hezbollah leader, with a Hellfire missile fired from a helicopter. Three years later, they assassinated another Hezbollah leader, Rida Yassin, again with Hellfire missiles fired from a helicopter. And then in April 2004, they murdered Sheikh Yassin, the spiritual leader of Hamas, the Palestine terrorist organization, again with a Hellfire missile, but this time carrying an adapted warhead. As the blind cleric was in a wheelchair, the Israelis reduced the amount of explosive, but stuffed it with the same weight of packing so that the laser-guided warhead would not be affected. But given its size, speed and momentum it would have killed him without any explosive. A month later, they assassinated his successor, again with a Hellfire missile fired from a helicopter.

For the rich and technologically advanced the search for the perfect assassin is now over. The Americans, the Russians and the Israelis have found the ultimate modern killer: just five foot four inches tall, the Hellfire missile is a remotely operated, 'fire and forget' missile, with guaranteed accuracy, totally obedient and with no moral qualms. Death from above, sudden and unexpected, the weapon of choice of the terrorist assassin. The next generation of technological assassins will be even more remote. The latest US technology, called the scramjet, will (when fully developed) allow the Pentagon to hit anywhere on the planet from the USA. Flying at 110,000 feet, it is the ultimate fantasy weapon for every redneck president: a remotely controlled, long-range assassin, able to deliver regime change at the push of a button.

This search for the perfect assassin had begun nearly a thousand years before, high in the mountains in what is now northern Iran, where a philosophic genius, Hasan ibn el-Sabah, refined the art of war and reinvented the world's first political act.

3

ASSASSINATE ONE, TERRIFY A THOUSAND

'By one single warrior on foot a king may be stricken with terror, though he own more than a hundred thousand horsemen'

An Ismaili poem

The Court of Philippe VI, France 1332 CE . . .

As part of his solemn vows, his sublime covenant with God, Philippe VI of France pledges to use all his powers – spiritual, temporal and monarchical – to rid the Christian Holy Lands of Islamic tyranny. Though thousands of Christians have already died over the previous two centuries of conflict, he knows that God sees into the deepest recesses of his soul – and he must therefore take his dutiful place in the divine Crusades to clear the lands where Jesus walked of pagans, heretics, the ungodly and other non-Christians. The year is 1332 CE and since 1095 CE Christian armies, big and small, ranging from well-organized battalions to ragbag bands of fanatical peasants have all made the journey attempting to establish their different versions of a

Christian god in a land where most prefer to follow the teachings of the Prophet Mohammed, rather than kneel to the authority of Rome.

Despite nearly two-and-a-half centuries of failure, the Vatican tries to put together yet another coalition of the rich, the susceptible and the willing, one of whom is Philippe VI, a genuinely religious man who wants a full-scale crusade (a *passagium*). So impressed is the Pope that he allows the French king to levy a tithe on church property[1] to help pay for yet another heavily armed pilgrimage.

As the endless negotiations drag on, the French king seeks advice[2] from a priest who has travelled throughout the Holy Lands. His warnings are bleak and chill the blood, as he describes a new breed of fanatical infidels wandering the Middle East, who he names 'the Assassins'. Leaving a trail of death wherever they go, these are the ultimate medieval weapon, soldiers who wear no uniforms or colours, cannot be recognized and mingle easily with the common crowd, 'like the devil, they transfigure themselves into angels of light, by imitating the gestures, garments, languages, customs and acts of various nations and peoples.' There is no defence against these programmed killers. Like missiles, they are single mission 'fire and forget', content to die once they have killed. Like the knives and swords they use, these men use their bodies as weapons. Without feelings, remorse or morality, they 'sell themselves, are thirsty for human blood, kill the innocent for a price and care nothing for either life or salvation'[3] ...

Back in 1332, the priest who gives this advice to Philippe VI of France does so seventy-six years after the Assassins have been wiped out. Right from the start, the Assassins cast a long shadow, their fearsome reputation – and the threat of assassination rather than the act itself – being their greatest weapon. Whatever the reasons, official or unofficial, the King never makes the trip.

* * *

No one in Europe had ever heard of anything like this before, but they are instantly recognizable to everyone today, for these are the prototype of the modern suicide bomber.

According to the priest, these men had neither politics nor religion, so his advice for the king's protection was limited. The best suggestion he could give was to adopt a massive programme of vetting, ensuring that every member of the royal household and every person who might meet the king was cleared, adding that 'none should be admitted, save those whose country, place, lineage, condition and person are certainly, fully and clearly known.'

The advice was good and though this is now common practice for every security service everywhere in the world, ultimately there were no guarantees for Philippe VI, or any world leader, before or since. As Abraham Lincoln told his bodyguard on the very day he was assassinated: 'I believe there are men who want to take my life and I have no doubt they will do it. I know no one could do it and escape alive, but if it is to be done, it is impossible to prevent it.'[4] Modern counter-terrorism specialists often argue that tribal and religious-based organizations, human thickets bound by marriage, family and generations of interlocking relationships, are the hardest to penetrate, yet even the smartest can still get caught.

Ahmed Shah Massoud, the Lion of Panjshir, was one of the smartest modern military commanders, a charismatic and brilliant military strategist who, as leader of the Mujahadeen, first defeated the Russians and then held the Taliban and Al Qaeda forces at bay high in the mountains of Afghanistan. He was assassinated two days before 9/11 by two Tunisians posing as a television crew, who had got through the defences using letters of introduction signed by Yassir al-Sirri, the head of the Islamic Observation Centre in London.[5] The bomb in the camera battery belt literally blew him away, killing the 'camera-man' and the translator.[6]

The word 'assassin' comes from the 'Hashshashin', one of the world's most secretive sects, which flourished between 1090 and 1256, high up in the Elburz Mountains in north-west Iran, just south of the Caspian Sea. Remote, inhospitable and virtually impossible for outsiders to penetrate (both then and now), their headquarters at Alamut was the perfect bolt-hole from which to manage a series of terrorist attacks against their neighbours. Being over six thousand feet above sea level and only accessible by steep paths, it was also the perfect site from which to spin a resilient historical fantasy.

Though many of their records were destroyed when the Mongols defeated them, a surprising amount is known about this mysterious sect, though our perception of them has been largely mediated by their enemies. Much that was recorded about them at the time was second-hand, anecdotal gossip. 'So execrable is their profession and so abominated by all that they conceal their names as much as they can,'[7] wrote a nearish contemporary, a judgement subsequently overlaid with the censorious judgements of later historians, for whom this sect was – and still is – the epitome of everything evil and un-Christian. The great eighteenth-century British historian Edward Gibbon described them as 'odious sectaries' arguing that 'the extirpation of the Assassins, or Ismailians of Persia, may be considered a service to mankind.'[8]

Despite the paucity of hard evidence, for nearly a thousand years now, three 'facts' have generally been agreed about them which are endlessly recycled by writers, historians, journalists and politicians: first, they virtually invented assassination, littering the neighbouring area with the corpses of their enemies; second, this was achieved under the influence of cannabis; and third, their name ('Hashshashin') means hashish (cannabis) eaters.[9]

All these claims are untrue. Unlike their enemies they were comparatively modest in their use of political murder, there is no evidence they used cannabis (or indeed any drugs at all) and the link between their name and hashish is little more than a coincidence of syllables, an unresearched cliché which is lightly dusted and endlessly recycled in much writing about assassination. However, what is true is that the myths surrounding the Assassins have been used very effectively by propagandists through the ages.

Long before their founder, Hasan ibn el-Sabah, established the secret doctrines of the Hashshashin in the declining years of the eleventh century CE, assassination was a routine political act in every ancient culture and religion. Indeed, assassination is the world's first and oldest political act.

The first dynastic struggle in Christian myth has Cain assassinating Abel. After the world's first recorded assassination in the Garden of Eden, it is one of the dominant themes of the Old Testament, which at times reads more like an assassin's training manual and score sheet, than a religious guide, expressing the wisdom and teachings of God.

Indeed Jerusalem under Roman occupation had its own terrorist group which, like many since, used assassination to try and achieve its ends. The *Sicarii* (named after the *sicae*, the daggers that they used) were a Jewish sect in Judea in the first century CE who terrorized the occupying Romans. Concealing their short daggers under their clothes, they moved freely among the general populace as they went about their everyday business, but then choosing to strike, often where the crowds were thickest. They would then join in the ensuing alarm and public grief, putting on a great show of heartbreaking lamentation. They killed both Romans and Jews, including the High Priest Jonathan, arguing that assassination was justifiable as they were fighting terror with terror. Their *modus operandi* is instantly familiar to anyone now – financing their operations through theft and kidnapping hostages to exchange for their own members when they were captured. Like many similar terrorist groups since, their exact motives were fuzzy at best: they knew that they did not want the Romans and all those Jews who supported them but were less clear about what they wanted in their place. Lacking focus and direction they failed against a Roman empire that was simply better organized and better equipped.

In early Muslim history, three of the first four Righteous Caliphs who followed the Prophet Mohammed were assassinated. The second Caliph, Omar, was assassinated by a disaffected Christian slave. Mindful of his place in history, on his deathbed he thanked God that it was not an inside job by a Muslim brother. His two successors did not enjoy this sectarian luxury, both being assassinated by Muslim Arabs, who justified their actions as tyrannicide, one of the enduring pretexts for assassination, both before and since, and a rationale which unites revolutionaries of every hue.

In ancient history, assassination was mainly used by aspiring rulers everywhere to seize power for themselves by removing the existing occupier of the throne. As the new tenants of power, the most ruthless then used assassination to stay in position by systematically murdering anyone (including their closest relatives, even their children) who might challenge their grasp on the shiny baubles of state.

It is impossible to dip into the history of any ancient empire and scroll very far through the lists of rulers without coming across a life prematurely ended by an assassin. No ruler can ever have felt very safe or secure – either in public or private, at day or night. No matter how wise, smart, cruel or ruthless they might have been, they were always outnumbered by the assassins, an anonymous community, who never wore a uniform, a badge or carried any form of identification to distinguish them from anyone else. They could – and did – come from anywhere. Only the foolish ever trusted their closest advisers, their ministers, servants, slaves, cooks and body-guards. Only the short-lived and stupid were seduced by the relentless fawning and grovelling that surrounded their every waking moment. Overblown and frequently expressed loyalty was the currency of everyday discourse but was only ever wired to the leader whose heart was beating.

Loyalty was an instant transaction, immediately transferable on death and the most dangerous of all were their nearest and dearest. The ties of blood were quite literally that – liquid, temporary and vulnerable. Whenever a leader's life was ended in suspicious circumstances, their closest relatives, especially their wives and lovers, were always top of the list of the usual suspects. Sleeping with one eye open did little for the stress levels, but it did help ensure a long life. The nursery was no safer than the bedroom. In any power grab, it was standard operating procedure for babies and small children to then be assassinated so as to prevent confusion as to who was going to occupy the throne. Family bonds meant nothing and spilling blood to seize power provoked no greater qualms than tipping over a goblet of wine.

In this context, the Assassins, otherwise known as the Nizari Ismailis, were a truly revolutionary force and their leader Hasan ibn el-Sabah a charismatic military genius, with a capacity for clear thought which had previously eluded the world's leaders for centuries.

He simply ignored existing military practice, which decreed that thousands of innocent and uninvolved bystanders (women, children, slaves, conscripts and anyone else who was in the wrong place at the wrong time) had to be sucked into the meat grinder of the medieval battlefield and then pillaged and raped by the conquering army. Instead of going to war, Hasan ibn el-Sabah and his followers only targeted leaders and decision makers, either killing them or more usually threatening them with assassination until they negotiated or complied. Most did, once they realized there was a world of difference between the 'courageous' decision to send their troops into battle and actually tossing their own lives into the scales of human conflict.

Just how revolutionary this was can be seen when comparing the Assassins with everything which had gone on before and much that has happened since.

Alexander the Great is typical of most empire builders in the ancient world. He occasionally showed magnanimity towards the vanquished, but was also capable of great barbarity, torturing adolescents and indulging in the wholesale slaughter of non-combatants. The tough resistance he met in his Indian conquest was treated with extraordinary savagery as an estimated 80,000 were massacred in cities across the country. After he was wounded at Malli in India his forces killed everyone, leaving 'neither woman nor child'. During the fall of Tyre, 8,000 were slaughtered. Once he took the city, the 2,000 young men of fighting age were crucified in one huge line, an act of staggering barbarity. The remaining 30,000 survivors were sold into slavery.

Hasan ibn el-Sabah's intellectual genius was to see that none of this was necessary. He distilled the art of war, bypassing the wasteful and inefficient slaughterhouse of battle and injecting assassination (or the fear of it) into the heart of the state. As one of the Ismaili poets put it, 'By one single warrior on foot a king may be stricken with terror, though he own more than a hundred thousand horsemen.'[10]

In the eleventh century the Seljuks created a new empire, stretching from their homeland in Turkey through much of the Middle East. While they were Sunni Muslims, the Assassins were Shia, who were easily outnumbered and out-powered – but only if they were to fight the Seljuks on conventional terms. Though the Seljuk empire was all-powerful it was similar to all the others that had been and gone before. It was hierarchical, with all the key decisions made by one person (nearly always a man) which made it brittle and therefore vulnerable to the leverage that comes from selective assassin-ation – or even the threat of it.

The Seljuks grew to tolerate the Ismailis and left them alone for much of the time, with good reason. Though the Assassins were not the world's first terrorist organization, Hasan ibn el-Sabah was the world's first great terrorist-philosopher, a revolutionary of genius, who can also make a decent claim to be the inventor of asymmetric warfare, the claimed 'modern' notion that a tiny well-disciplined force can defeat a much larger force.

In one much-heralded incident (which has been recounted in various ways) the Sultan of the Seljuks sent an army to try and recover the castles which the Assassins had seized from them. Hasan ibn el-Sabah, the first Grand Master of the Hashshashin, tried to negotiate peace, but without success. One morning (in an incident very reminiscent of the famous scene in *The Godfather*, where the movie producer awakes to find a dead horse's head in his bed) the Sultan woke to find a bejewelled dagger sticking in the floor beside his bed. Later that morning, Hasan ibn el-Sabah presented him with an offer he couldn't refuse, a warning delivered by a servant telling him that the dagger in the floor could just as easily have been in his chest, had Hasan ibn el-Sabah not been feeling well disposed towards him. The message from the Assassin's leader continued, 'Let him know that I, from this rock, guide the hands of the men who surround him.'[11] Bravely sending his troops into battle against a numerically weaker force was one thing, but risking his neck was another and the Sultan wisely opted for discretion. Personal survival came first and he negotiated peace. According to one of the Mongol historians, who had access to the Assassin's records, 'The Sultan sought to be on peaceful terms with them. In short, during his reign they enjoyed ease and tranquillity.'[12] After this incident, the Seljuks largely backed off and left them in peace.

The Hashshashin soon discovered one other benefit of their strategy. If they were captured by their neighbours, they were usually well treated, as any local leader knew that if he tortured or killed one of their number, then he could expect the same in return. Given the choice of providing a reasonable level of hospitality or face their own inevitable and sudden death they chose the former.

This formula of negotiation underpinned by certain assassination was highly effective. The Hashshashin quickly spread through Syria and towards the Mediterranean, their victims being mainly Sunni Muslims, rather than Christians or Jews, though their single most prominent assassination was a crusade leader, the Marquis Conrad of Montferrat, the King of Tyre, who was assassinated on 28 April 1192. It was a classic

Hashshashin hit, subterfuge followed by sudden and deadly force. In this case, the assassins disguised themselves as Christian monks, convincing their hosts they were devoted followers of the one and only Christian god. They began to move easily in royal circles and as soon as they had access to the King in his unguarded moments, they crept up on him and stabbed him to death. As usual, they made no attempt to escape.

Saladin, who had himself survived two attempted assassinations, quizzed his intelligence officer in Tyre as to their motive. The answer was surprising: under interrogation they said the killing was instigated by King Richard who wanted to get rid of his fellow crusade leader. Whatever the truth, this high-profile assassination was a huge boost to their reputation, for here was a bunch of ruthless and effective killers, who were not only prepared to murder and die for their cause but would also hire out their services to others, if it suited their agenda and if the price was right. As news of the assassination flashed throughout the Middle East, no one felt safe, which further enhanced their negotiating position.

After this assassination the Assassins exploited their reputation, demanding protection money from their neighbours as well as anyone who passed through their territories, a toll which everyone was willing to pay. Like later twentieth-century terrorist groups the Assassins discovered that living outside the law was expensive and required a constant flow of cash.[13]

Once they identified the fault line in the local Sunni dynasties, it was not surprising the Assassins were such a devastating force and a byword for terrorism and subterfuge. As well as assassination, both actual and threatened, they had one other weapon, which was even more powerful: subversion deep in the heart of their enemies, hitting them in the one place they felt secure. When the great military commander Saladin threatened them their response was clear. They told him to prepare for his personal disaster in one of the greatest letters of rebuttal ever written to a military commander. 'We have read the gist and details of your letter and taken note of its threats against us with words and deeds, and by God it is astonishing to find a fly buzzing in an elephant's ear and a gnat biting statues. Others before you have said these things and we destroyed them and none could help them. If your orders are to cut off my head and tear my castles from the solid mountains, these are false hopes and vain fantasies. We are oppressed not oppressors, deprived and not deprivers. You know the outward aspect of our affairs and the quality of our men, what they can accomplish in an instant and how they seek the intimacy of death. The common proverb says: 'Do you threaten a duck with the river?' Prepare means for disaster and don a garment against catastrophe, for I will defeat you from within your own ranks and take vengeance against you at your own place and you will be as one who encompasses his own destruction.'[14]

Saladin ignored these threats and marched against them but then suddenly withdrew, without ever tackling them on the battlefield, where he would have expected to be victorious. There are various explanations for his bizarre behaviour but there was one story told by the brother of Rashid al-Din, who was the leader of the Hashshashin at the time. He sent a messenger to Saladin with orders to deliver it in private. When he arrived the messenger was searched and, even though he was not carrying a weapon, Saladin refused to see him without his two bodyguards being present, saying he regarded these two men as his sons, 'They and I are as one.' The messenger then turned to the bodyguards and asked them, 'If I order you in the name of my master to kill this Sultan, will you do so?' To an astonished Saladin, they both drew their swords and confirmed that they were ready to accept the messenger's orders, telling him, 'Command us as you wish'.

As the narrator noted, 'Thereupon Saladin (God have mercy upon him) inclined to make peace with him and enter into friendly relations with him. And God knows best.'[15] Like the Sultan of the Seljuks, Saladin discovered that the Assassins could subvert and infiltrate better than anyone. In modern parlance, they could get between the wallpaper and the wall and Saladin knew that if they could recruit his closest bodyguards, then his life would always be in their hands not his. Saladin never moved against the Assassins again. Once again the threat of assassination had delivered compliance from one of the greatest soldiers the world has ever known, a man who otherwise was used to conquering all before him. As the Hashshashin had correctly predicted, his desire for military victory consisted of little more than false hopes and vain fantasies.

The Assassins did not just humble their neighbours and defeat one of the world's greatest soldiers, they were the most influential cult the world has ever known. They have informed and defined the behaviour of every modern terrorist group. Not only did Hasan ibn el-Sabah invent asymmetric warfare, he also created the parallel notion of asymmetric morality, where a group of revolutionaries can leverage themselves effectively against a mainstream society because they start from a position of zero morality. General Alistair Irwin, the former head of the British Army in Northern Ireland and a very interesting thinker in this area, calls terrorists like them the 'minimalists', for whom 'there are no rules, no uniforms, no frontline, no inhibitions or limitations, no territory to defend . . . the minimalist can choose where and when to strike; he can appear and disappear cloaking himself in the darkness of the underworld . . . The minimalist has all the advantages.'[16]

The Assassins placed subversion, surprise and shock at the top of the terrorist agenda and their influence can be seen everywhere in modern life. It is there in the behaviour of all terrorist groups and especially in the transnational criminal gangs[17] that now control an estimated 5 per cent of world trade. Much Al Qaeda material, and especially their own terrorist manual, reads like Assassins literature, as Osama Bin Laden and the rest of the high command have adopted their basic operating principles from this sect. Like the Assassins, Al

Qaeda brainwashes its foot soldiers into unquestioning obedience and a love of martyrdom, which effectively transforms them into programmable weapons. Both groups have much else in common and not only in their standard operating procedures, though the Assassins would have been horrified at the wanton attacks on the innocent, especially children. They both share a love of overblown language and Bin Laden's speeches and his public stance of innocent outrage at what is being done to his adopted people could have been written a thousand years before. Like the Assassins, Bin Laden loves using the hyperbolic language of the psychopath, though he lacks the poetic muscularity as well as the morality of his predecessors.

The Assassins refined the terrorist tactic of subversion from within, knowing that it would always have a devastating effect on larger forces, especially occupying armies, a lesson which has had to be endlessly learned and relearned.

Though the USA used an extensive assassination programme against the Viet Cong and their supporters (Operation PHOENIX) they too never felt safe. Assassination and sabotage were never far away even within their own compounds. The Americans (like other colonial occupying forces in other conflicts) were slowly crippled by their inability to identify the enemy within. Never knowing whether the smiling locals were friends or foes corroded the US sensibility and as the war dragged on, internal discipline collapsed. The grunts (the infantry, many of whom were conscripts) began assassinating officers, usually by rolling a fragmentation grenade into their tent, a practice called 'fragging'.[18] As this became more common, the officers retaliated, identifying those they held responsible and in turn assassinating them. Subversion and assassination destroyed the army from within. As with the Ismailis a thousand years before, the duck survived and the river flowed on, leaving a feeling of helplessness among the American veterans, a huge number of whom have committed suicide since the end of the war.[19]

As a master of the craft, Hasan ibn el-Sabah understood that assassination has its own internal dynamics and that assassins can quickly slip down the food chain and become victims themselves. He retreated to the most impregnable of his fortresses, where he surrounded himself with his most devoted followers, living out his natural days in his 'secret garden', from which comes the myth (peddled by Marco Polo and others) of 'The Old Man in the Mountain', an evil puppet master driven by greed, envy and vengeance, who sent his killers to remove anyone who offended him.

But the more remote and mysterious he was, the more potent were the myths that sprang up around him. No one had ever seen a cult as powerful as the Assassins before. Right from the start, their reputation started to resonate and stories soon began to appear which, like the very juiciest gossip, were then endlessly embroidered and recycled, all the time becoming more fantastic in their convincing detail. Much of the phenomenal power of the Assassins came from their insidious ability to splice themselves into the genetic structure of European and Middle East political life.

At the height of their sway, the Emperor Frederick Barbarossa sent an envoy to Egypt and Syria in 1175 CE to investigate. His report back described them as a bunch of outlaws living in an impregnable stronghold in the mountains, who were addicted to eating pork and who regularly committed incest with their mothers and sisters. Both these last details are unlikely to be true and smack of the sort of crude propaganda which is often used to describe any group that is different from the norm. According to this intelligence officer's report, the sect consisted of young men who were indoctrinated from birth by a single leader. Like many cults – before and since – the recipe for power and control was fairly standard. The followers were kept in isolation, knowing nothing of the outside world. They were programmed to be completely obedient to the One, worshipping no other god but the master, believing that only complete obedience would bring eternal salvation and a one-way ticket to paradise. Failure to comply with the master's wishes was not an option ever considered by any of his followers, who loved him unconditionally. But this cult was underpinned by murder: whenever the master wished to dispose of one of his enemies, he summoned a young assassin and asked him if he would do whatever was asked of him. Completely indoctrinated, the young man would throw himself at the master's feet, promising to carry out whatever orders he was given. The master then presented him with a gold dagger and the name of his victim. Without hesitation, the assassin would set off to complete the task, with no concern for his safety or even an escape plan.

Variations of this story appear in different forms, though the details are substantially the same – one (highly improbable) variation recounts how these young men would throw them-selves off walls, smashing their skulls on the rocks below, just to please the master. The same account, from the German historian Arnold of Lübeck, also tries to explain their behav-iour, arguing that the master used witchcraft and intoxicated them with a potion, which plunged them into 'ecstasy and oblivion'.[20] Though this is the enduring belief about the Assassins it is unlikely to be true.

Hasan ibn el-Sabah was an inspirational and charismatic visionary. Though his army was comparatively small, he had fantastic organizational, management and logistical skills. But far more importantly, he understood the transcendent power of ideology and belief, taking young men and giving them dignity, honour and self-respect, a far more powerful drug than cannabis. They believed that this earthly life was just a stepping stone to paradise in the next world.

Though cannabis was in common use throughout much of the Middle East at the time it was generally frowned upon by the clerics who regarded its users as heretics and therefore generally inferior forms of life. Hasan ibn el-Sabah did not use the drug himself and was singularly ascetic in his lifestyle. Modelled in his image, the Assassins regarded themselves as being made of a purer and higher essence and therefore did not embrace a drug with which they associated the dregs of society. In all the time Hasan ibn el-Sabah lived at Alamut, alcohol was banned. The severity of the prohibition there would have made legendary crimefighter Eliot Ness jealous. Hasan ibn el-Sabah had one of his sons executed when he discovered he was drinking wine.

This same level of fanaticism was seen in the 9/11 hijackers, who went to their deaths believing they had made their peace with god and booked their passage to paradise.[21] This single-minded devotion to the cause, interlocked with an unshakeable belief in the ultimate value of martyrdom, made them perfect assassins. But as well as being the prototype for Al Qaeda, the Assassins were the inspiration behind two major programmes by the KGB and the CIA.

Informed by the myths surrounding the Assassins, during the Cold War both the KGB and the CIA tried various brainwashing programmes to create the perfect assassin, but failed. The Americans and the Russians both developed mind-control programmes in the 1950s and 1960s to try to discover a way in which they could turn people into programmable automata, assassins who could be sent on missions and then conveniently forget all the details afterwards. Drugs, bizarre electromagnetic fields and hypnotism were tried, but they all proved to be no substitute for blind faith.

This notion of the programmable assassin spilled out into the Cold War thriller *The Manchurian Candidate*, in which the all-American hero Sergeant Raymond Shaw is captured and brainwashed by communists in Korea. He becomes a robotic assassin, worked remotely by an evil puppet master, Yen Lo, a master of Pavlovian techniques who replaces the independent thought of the democratic citizen with the conditioned reflexes of the communist, so that he can 'use words or symbols as triggers of installed automatic reactions'. In other words, Shaw is turned into a weapon which can be remotely fired by the

Soviets once he is back in the USA. In the novel, captured American airmen are conditioned to drink Chinese tea in tin cups and believe it is Coca-Cola. They play cards for strips of brown paper, believing these are dollar bills. In part, the novel was inspired by genuine fears that US pilots who had been shot down in Korea had been brainwashed – and the CIA had plenty of evidence that they were.

Throughout the 1950s American air force pilots invaded Korean air space to illuminate their radar sets and keep them on their toes, but every so often they got shot down. Many survived and were then returned to the USA. One such group of airmen sent the Pentagon and the CIA into a tailspin. When they returned to the USA they came back as different people, physically the same but psychologically transformed. When questioned, they reported no ill treatment and there were no traces of drugs in their blood samples. The Agency then plundered the Russian scientific literature to see if there was anything there which could point to a mind-control brainwashing programme using a technology or drugs they did not know about and therefore could not test for. The CIA discovered that the Russians believed it was possible to entrain brain rhythms and therefore control them using extremely low-frequency electromagnetic waves. This knowledge was then folded into their own mind-control programme, code-named MK-ULTRA, which was investigating everything from extra-sensory perception, hypnotism, drugs, charismatic orators, crowds and magic, to a vast range of psychotropic drugs. As part of this programme, the CIA scientists experimented to see if it was possible to brainwash individuals and turn them into remote-controlled brainwashed assassins.

The State Department also got in on the act, investigating the bizarre microwave signal being beamed at the US embassy in Moscow. This TOP SECRET investigation was called Project PANDORA and one of its aims was to see if this was a brain-programming weapon. But the CIA and the Pentagon were impatient and could not be bothered to wait for the answer so they set up their own deep-black operation called Project BIZARRE,[22] which assumed that the signal was a brainwashing weapon and asked whether they could build a similar one for the USA.

However, the evidence suggests that both the American and Soviet scientists abandoned these experiments. The electromagnetic boxes they developed could have devastating emotional effects leaving their subjects shattered, but the effects were random and unpredictable. The CIA scientists simply failed to grasp the inspirational power of belief. Hasan ibn el-Sabah, like his successors, Osama Bin Laden and the Hamas leaders, instinctively understood that there is a force much more powerful and reliable than drugs or complex extremely low-frequency electromagnetic waves: the ideology which reinforces the certitude of the religious fanatic. Bin Laden's followers – like the 9/11 hijackers and the Palestinian suicide bombers – made no attempt to escape, believing that their death was just like stepping through a door into the next world, which is a paradise of milk, honey and compliant virgins. This desire for martyrdom is not just confined to Muslims. The Christian abortion clinic bombers in the USA were happy to kill, secure in their certain belief that a place awaited them at God's right-hand side.

The non-Islamic writers and historians, mostly Christian, who have defined our views of the Assassins failed to understand the transcendent power of ideology and searched for an explanation which they could find more believable, and the answer they have repeatedly come back to is drugs and, in particular, cannabis. The main source that is usually quoted to support the Assassins–cannabis link is Marco Polo (1254–1324), the Venetian travel writer and self-publicist, many of whose claims are now disputed.[23]

According to the great explorer, there was a person at court, 'the Sheikh of the Mountain' often called 'the Old Man' who spotted twelve-year-old boys who he thought were naturally courageous. He kept them at court, grooming them to become killers through the use of a single drug. The particular form of brainwashing used was to send them into the garden in small groups, giving them a powerful potion to drink. While they slept for three days they would be carried into a secret and beautiful garden so that when they woke, they believed they were in paradise. Beautiful women would attend to their every wish, singing, entertaining them and giving them everything they could ever desire so they never wanted to leave. When the Old Man wanted someone assassinated, he would take one of these young men from the garden, give him his orders and send him on his mission, the assassin complying because he was promised a swift and immediate return to the greatest earthly paradise the world had ever known. This soft-porn vision of compliant and beautiful women, servicing a young man's every need, has seduced credulous historians and their followers for centuries.

All the elements of Marco Polo's account had appeared before, which must excite the suspicion that he was a skilful recycler of myth and legend, giving it the apparent gloss of the veracity which comes from being an eyewitness. But the fact is that he only set off on his epic journey in 1260, not reaching the mountain stronghold of the Hashshashin at Alamut until 1273, seventeen years after the sect had been wiped out.

Whatever the fantasies are that have come out of the stories told by Marco Polo and others, there is one enduring truth about them: the very notion of the Hashshashin – this secretive sect from deep in Northern Persia – has always had huge propaganda value.

From the start, the crusaders played the Assassins' card, terrifying anyone who would listen to their stories of drug-crazed Muslim fanatics sent out by a wicked godless puppet master to kill Christian leaders, useful fund-raising propaganda when they were trying to convince their audience back home that theirs was a just cause and a timely reminder to everyone as to just what the heroic crusaders were up against in trying to install God's will among a savage and barbaric people.

As the crusaders returned, the word assassin was quickly absorbed into many European languages, where it took on the meaning of a particularly evil murderer. In Dante's *Divine Comedy*,[24] he describes himself as being like a friar who is taking confession from an assassin,[25] the word here being used to describe a particularly brutal act, the burial alive – and face down – of a criminal.

It was not until the early nineteenth century that the link between the Assassins and cannabis was firmly established by academics, who in turn confirmed it for the world. But this connection was made on the flimsiest of evidence.

In 1798, the French invaded Egypt, a Muslim country where alcohol was in short supply and Napoleon's soldiers, who had long been fuelled on red wine, promptly discovered the seductive effects of cannabis. Within two years, the problem of cannabis use was so widespread that Napoleon banned the use of 'certain Muslim beverages made with hashish' as well as the inhalation of 'smoke from the seeds of hashish,' arguing that 'habitual drinkers and smokers of this plant lose their reason and are victims of violent delirium.' Napoleon wanted a firm basis to justify the ban and imported three French scientists to investigate. As dedicated empirical scientists they extracted the drug, analysed it and indulged in a fair degree of human self-experimentation. After several years of detailed investigation, the first paper appeared which pronounced (wrongly) that this was the drug used by Helen of Troy to make her guests become forgetful.[26]

But the results of this dedicated team did not just go up in smoke. In 1809, there was a quantum leap in scientific understanding. The celebrated French orientalist Antoine Isaac, Baron Silvestre de Sacy, announced that the mysterious potion mentioned by Marco Polo was cannabis, telling a meeting of the Institute of France, 'The intoxication produced by hashish can lead to a state of temporary insanity such that losing all knowledge of their debility, users commit the most brutal actions, so as to disturb the public peace.' And that was that, the link was established. The Assassins, also known as the Nizari Ismailis, had committed their acts of murder under the influence of cannabis, a 'fact' which then crossed over from empirical science to folklore and is now indelibly stained on the public consciousness.

What was nothing more than a coincidence of syllables had been elevated into a proven scientific fact, a 'fact' with such strong adhesive qualities that it is still trotted out nearly two hundred years later, even though there is no evidence to support it – and even though de Sacy then heavily qualified his claim by also saying 'it is not impossible that hemp or some parts of that vegetable, *mixed with substances unknown to us*, may have been sometimes employed to produce a state of frenzy and violence.'

The cannabis link is palpable nonsense. There is a vast library of pharmacological studies of the clinical effects of cannabis and mind-controlled assassination is not listed anywhere in any serious scientific journal. Indeed, it is exactly the wrong drug to use to train mind-controlled killers, as its effects are the opposite of what any assassin master would need to use to achieve a quasi-hypnotic state of programmed obedience. Cannabis impairs cognitive development (making learning much harder), it impairs psychomotor performance, making it harder to carry out simple physical tasks, it alters perception, producing slower reaction times and it can produce feelings of depression and anxiety, all of which are the exact opposite of the effects required for a focused assassin. Most significantly of all, it is an amotivational drug, meaning that users often suffer from a lack of ambition and loss of attention, as many US commanders in Vietnam discovered to their cost when they tried to order a troop of stoned grunts to go into action. On an anecdotal level, anyone who has been in the company of someone stoned on cannabis knows that the only thing they want to murder is the nearest jar of peanut butter, not some remote person about whom they know little and care about even less.

But common sense never entered the debate and none of this mattered to the Europeans who were fascinated by the

Assassins, those dark-skinned exotic killers from a mysterious faraway land – and once the magic potion of cannabis was folded into the mix, they became big literary business. Books with drug themes, classics like *The Thousand and One Nights* became bestsellers and the more the scientists warned against a drug that produced delirium, ecstasy and death, the more attractive it became. Cannabis became the drug for artists, but there was always a recurrent darker theme: cannabis was the psychological fuel driving assassins, a theme reinforced by Alexandre Dumas in *The Count of Monte Cristo*, where he reworked Marco Polo's story of the Man in the Mountain.

The Assassins–cannabis link popped up again in the USA in the 1930s where it was used to drive through an extraordinary legislative coup, the criminalization of cannabis and its classification as a dangerous drug.

As Mexican immigrant workers began to flood into the south-west states of America at the turn of the twentieth century, they brought cannabis with them as their recreational drug of choice. As cheap foreign labour, there were, inevitably, racially inspired clashes with the locals and the law, in which the Mexicans rather than the injustices of migrant labour were blamed. In the American mind the link was clear: where there were Mexicans there was violence and where there was violence there was cannabis. Local law officials forged the links and began to apply pressure to make it illegal. In 1915, the US Treasury banned its import, except for medical purposes. But then two years later, an official travelled round Texas and reported that Mexicans, 'Negroes and lower-class whites'[27] were using it for pleasure. The moral panic bandwagon was hitched up and lurched out on to the media highway.

By the 1920s the finest investigative journalists in New Orleans discovered that schoolboys and schoolgirls both from poorer families and 'of foreign parentage' were smoking 'mootas', cannabis-based cigarettes. Just like the Muslim clerics who informed the beliefs of the Hashshashin nearly 1,000 years before, the prevailing view among many American physicians was that cannabis was a drug of the lower classes. Take this gem, titled *The Marijuana Menace* from the *New Orleans Medical and Surgical Journal, 1931*, but which could just as easily have been written by the Islamic theologians behind the Assassins a thousand years before: 'The debasing and baneful influence of hashish and opium is not restricted to individuals but has manifested itself in nations and races as well. The dominant race and most enlightened countries are alcoholic, whilst the races and nations addicted to hemp and opium, some of which once attained to heights of culture and civilization have deteriorated both mentally and physically.'

Cannabis was the perfect evil to blame for society's ills. The editorial writers of the local newspapers had a conveniently foreign drug to blame for the disaffected behaviour of the poor, the dispossessed and the ruthlessly exploited (often migrant) labour, which underpinned their own wealth. Newspapers thundered on about the menace of marijuana, which, according to them, led to 'the disintegration of personality'. Most crimes of violence were blamed on cannabis, a drug described as no less vicious than hard drugs, like opium, heroin, cocaine or morphine. In 1936, a state narcotics officer named cannabis as the cause of 60 per cent of crimes committed in New Orleans that year.[28] Other accounts described marijuana users as 'muggle heads' who would 'shoot down police, bank clerks and casual bystanders' while high on a drug that gave them 'false courage and freedom from restraint'.[29]

The FBI got into the act as well. The temptation of muscling in on the cannabis-inspired panic was far too great for its director Edgar Hoover, a vain and insecure man who defined crime in terms of how it affected his image. The purple prose which defined his reign poured from FBI headquarters and the typical marijuana user became 'a fiend with savage or "cave man" tendencies. His sex desires are aroused and some of the most horrible crimes result. He hears light and sees sound. To get away from it, he suddenly becomes violent and may kill.' According to the best contemporary medical opinion, marijuana offered 'a shorter cut to complete madness than any other drug'.[30] With such a groundswell of moral panic, many southwestern states banned it and began to lobby for federal action.

Initially the Narcotics Commissioner, Harry J. Anslinger was not interested as his agents had enough to do trying to deal with all the other drugs and he was not that fussed about marijuana. But the long shadow of the Assassins changed all that. Besides, this gave him a chance to stake out some federal turf and expand his empire, which otherwise would be taken over by the FBI.

As always, there were congressional hearings, a crucial step in turning a moral panic into a national terror. For politicians, they are a wonderful platform for self-aggrandizement. For newspaper editors they can be a conveyor belt of lurid copy and for Harry Anslinger, the story of the ancient Persians was just too good to be true. He told the committee that, 'This drug is as old as civilization itself. Homer wrote about it, as a drug which made men forget their homes, and that turned them into swine.' Just like the French scientists a century before he had the wrong drug. When Homer was writing about men leaving their homes he was talking about lotus eaters not pot smokers, but getting the wrong drug didn't stop America's new drugs commissioner when he was high on a crusade. He continued, 'In Persia, a thousand years before Christ, there was a religious and military order founded which was called the Assassins, and they derived their name from the drug called hashish, which is now known in this country as marijuana. They were noted for their acts of cruelty and the word "assassin" very aptly describes the drug.'

Anslinger sought out the best contemporary medical opinion and was told by the American National Institute of Health that 'prolonged use leads to insanity'. What followed was not so much riding on the bandwagon as seizing the controls and taking over. In 1937, he attacked marijuana as an addictive drug that was 'as dangerous as a coiled rattlesnake' and, of course, there was the perfect headline just waiting. Marijuana is 'the Assassin of Youth'.

Anslinger continued to hammer home the link between the assassins and marijuana, putting out a statement saying that 'In the year 1090, there was founded in Persia the religious and military order of the Assassins, whose history is one of cruelty, barbarity, and murder, and for good reason. The members were confirmed users of hashish, or marijuana, and it is from the Arabic "Hashshashin" that we have the English word assassin.' Again, his understanding of ancient history was wrong but it made no difference. Cannabis was effectively made illegal, though, not surprisingly, it had no effect on America's homicide and violence rate, which has risen ever since.

Like the French scientists a century before, the American legislators and their advisers linked cannabis with violence and ultimately with the Assassins. It was a perfect formula, which allowed them to blame the ills of their own society on a bunch of sinister foreigners, who, worse still, were fuelled by an evil foreign drug, which was threatening to poison and corrupt their own youth. The Hashshashin had cast a long shadow, influencing events long after they had been wiped out by the Mongols in 1256 CE. Once again, it was a mistaken perception of them, which had the impact, rather than the actuality. But then they had always punched above their weight.

The desire to prove that the Assassins used a hypnotic drug was a very resilient one. From the crusades onwards, there has been a persistent failure by Western analysts to fully appreciate the power of ideology among the Islamists. There has been a constant search to find some other explanation, such as hypnotism, brainwashing or drugs, some rationalization, which conveniently discounts the power of belief. This has surfaced again in the recent claim that the Islamic assassins of Al Qaeda also take their courage from a hypnotic – though this time the drug claimed is Artane, which is normally used by sufferers of Parkinson's disease. Just like the story about cannabis, it is highly unlikely to be true: the potential side effects include nausea, constipation, dizziness, light-headedness, nervousness, drowsiness, increased sensitivity to light and blurred vision and are hardly those any assassin trainer would want in one of his pupils.

The Assassins were a fraternal order, bound by ideology, belief and codes of behaviour. Isolated and indoctrinated, the young assassins were imbued with powerful notions of brotherhood and blood, in every sense, both their own and that of everyone else. Though they were a minority in every society where they flourished, they infiltrated themselves into the body of the state, often parasitically taking on the functions of the state, enjoying the power without having any responsibility towards the general populace in the traditional contract between the rulers and the ruled.

Tempting though it is to argue that Al Qaeda are the natural heirs of the Hashshashin there is a much better candidate: the Cosa Nostra in Italy. Both groups have leveraged power by plugging into the mainstream of political life and then carrying on the business of daily politics but by different means. Though the Italian mafia sprang up nearly a thousand years later, they too are a secret society with internal rules and codes of loyalty to each other. Even the language of organization is similar. Both have members who are 'soldiers' in civilian clothing and every soldier is both a spy for the organization and, crucially, a killer. Initially, the Hashshashin (like the Cosa Nostra) began as outsiders with their heartland based deep in an impenetrable mountain range but soon became the dominant power, first in local and then in national politics. Eventually, both sects took over some of the functions of the state itself. Like the Hashshashin before them the Cosa Nostra have used the threat of assassination as effectively as the deed itself.

There is no doubt that generations of politicians, judges, police officers, bankers and civil servants, in fact the massed ranks of the Italian state, have complied with mafia wishes as an insurance policy against assassination. A lesson first learned a thousand years before in the mountains of northern Iran.

Part 2
EXECUTION

Assassins and their controllers are nothing if not cunning. Whether they are from Al Qaeda, the CIA, MI6, MI5, Mossad or the KGB they relentlessly study their history. For all of them, one assassination stands out: that of Julius Caesar, which is a disaster for the conspirators, all of whom are dead within three years. Many lessons are drawn from this: be cautious, do not brag about your deeds and where possible get someone else to do your dirty work for you.

As always, daily politics is all about juggling expectation and performance. In ancient times, assassination is route one to power. The incoming ruler, who has just stepped over the still warm corpse of the previous occupant of the throne, often wants everyone to know who is responsible. The message going out is clear: having killed once to secure power, there will be no reticence to kill again to keep it. Many new rulers then frequently go on a killing spree only stopping when they believe their enemies (or at least those who might assassinate them in turn) are all dead. Though they do so, few crow about it openly, preferring it to be known rather than formally announced. Even the hardest ruler is fearful of assassination's dark secret – it is very contagious.

As the practice develops, those who use assassination to achieve their political objectives begin to use others to do their dirty work wherever possible. But the really smart discover something else as well. Correctly staged and with a carefully laid trail of clues, an assassination can be pinned on someone else. By the twentieth century, this technique even has a name. In intelligence circles, it comes under those operations known as a false flag . . .

4

KEEP IT TIGHT

'O conspiracy!
Sham'st thou to show thy dangerous brow by night,
When evils are most free?'

William Shakespeare

In the beginning, there is the conspiracy. It starts – as it often
does – with two men so consumed with hatred that their only
thought is assassination. This carcinogenic thought grows until
they can think of little else. It infects their every waking thought
and then they discover they are not alone, there are others
plotting as well. A couple here, a small group there, little cabals
slowly fermenting in the shadows everywhere. Very soon, there
is one vast conspiracy, involving over sixty men.

*Where do you begin? After all, there is so much to hate about
the man.*

The leader has it all. He is taller than average, with a soldier's
muscular body, fair skin stretched smoothly over a broad face,
quick dark brown eyes which are difficult to read, a man who

has been born to lead. It's stamped into his DNA. This is a man who believes it is his natural right – his duty – to govern, not just the nation but the empire. A man who bends everyone to his will, simply because he can.

He never shows the stress in public but, like everyone else, the plotters know he is under nocturnal siege from evil dreams, which leave him petrified and shaking, clinging to his young wife in the middle of the night. He has twice succumbed to epileptic fits on the campaign trail, but his public relations men and his spinmeisters keep a tight lid on these stories.

Of course there are the rumours. There always are surrounding any great public figure. There are soldiers who claim he was sodomized when he was a young man, an affair with a member of royalty when he was trying to make his way and build his career. But ever since then, there are endless stories of affairs with women.

Has he really slept with the wives of all his colleagues? Or is that just well-coordinated PR spin to cover up his hidden homosexuality?

He fancies himself a great soldier, a leader of men but he is also a dandy, so self-obsessed he even plucks his body hair with tweezers, a narcissist who can never resist the lure of a reflecting surface. The wits say it is so he can fall in love with himself all over again. The cynics say it is to check that the few hairs he has are in perfect order, neatly trimmed and combed to cover his incipient baldness. Not surprisingly, he is always at his most relaxed on those glittering public occasions that require an ornamental hat, which conveniently covers his shining skull.

The plotters (like everyone else in public life) smile to his face. *What else is there to do?* Once he has passed his way through their midst, leaving behind a trailing scent of lavender, they sneer behind his back. Here is a man enraptured by his own brilliance, endlessly pleased with himself. The great leader comes from humble beginnings, runs up huge debts but has now amassed an even larger private fortune, making his name (and many enemies) prosecuting senior politicians for extortion and corruption. And then he rises on the frothing fountain of bribery, systematically robbing and plundering at home and abroad, using the proceeds to backhand his way to power. He is forever preaching the common good, arguing that the good of the people and his own aggrandizement are one and the same thing. Meanwhile, there is at least one grieving widow convinced he has had her husband poisoned when he threatens to block his smooth accumulation of power.

He ostentatiously surrounds himself with all things luxurious. His mansions are draped with fine art – *not because he loves or understands it but because it fits in with his image of himself as a well-rounded statesman*, they carp. His gardens are full of statues to compare himself favourably against and always there are his particular favourites, the gems. *Why he even fought a war hundreds of miles away, sending thousands of young men to their deaths to get his hands on the enemy's precious fresh-water pearl beds!* And here he is, rolling those pearls in his hands, measuring their value, luxuriating in their creamy richness.

He is a great man, they concede, but like all great men he is corrupted by the seductive yet corrosive nature of unlimited power. He rules the state, controlling every decision big and small and yet he still wants more. There is no limit to his global ambitions, no title grand enough to satisfy him. This is a man who, if he got to sit at the side of the gods, would elbow them aside, appointing himself the Supreme Being above them all.

The conspiracy gradually takes hold. The original conspirators cast their bait – a rumour here, a rumour there – and soon they discover there are others, who live the same nightmare but share the same dream. Each new member of the plot is profiled and carefully approached. All have good reason to hate him. He has curbed their power, seduced their wives (*if the gossip is even half true*) and stopped the flow of corrupt funds to their pockets, oblivious to their pleas about the horrific cost of living.

As each day passes they become more anxious. Given the enormity of their plan they huddle together, believing in the cliché of safety in numbers. But to succeed, they need to add more members to their cause and each new approach to another conspirator doubles the risk they will be unmasked. If they are discovered, they know they face an exceptionally slow and painful death, dying by the millimetre, under the passionless gaze of their tormentor – but still they drive on, the intoxicating scent of blood – and victory – in their nostrils.

With the sixth sense that keeps all great politicians dancing on their toes, the great leader knows his days are numbered. When he wakes in the morning his wife tells him of her bad dreams, which portray his imminent death. During the day, his advisers warn him to be extra careful in his public appointments and at night the terrifying visions, which pollute his dreams, only confirm their fears.

And finally he reaches the day he is going to die. His young wife (his third marriage, her first) pleads with him not to go out. She is still rocked by a nightmare that he is to be killed that day and she will never see him alive again. His closest adviser tells him of a specific threat for that day, a clear and present danger of assassination. But then another friend, a man he trusts, dismisses the advice. 'What do they know? You're a great man, the people love you, everything will be all right,' he tells the great leader, adding 'can you really disappoint everyone if you only go and see them when your wife doesn't have bad dreams?' The great leader recognizes all this to be true and therefore sees it as the best advice.

Believing that a coward dies a thousand deaths, a brave man only one, the great leader sets off to make his final public appearance, leaving his grieving wife behind. His smooth-talking friend goes with him, a weapon concealed under his clothes. The great leader leaves home, and so do the conspirators, each knowing what lies ahead. His wife is not the only one troubled. On the other side of town, as one of the assassins leaves home, his wife too pleads with him to stay at home that day. She suspects the plot and knows that if it fails she too will become a widow. After he leaves, she makes one last desperate attempt to turn the course of history, pretending to fall mortally ill. She sends a message to her husband, pleading with him to return home immediately as she is close to death. He ignores her and continues on his task, believing that there is a greater good which has to be served. She is not the only one trying to stop the plot. One of the conspirators breaks ranks and tries to get to see the great leader, carrying with him undeniable proof of a major assassination plot – but he cannot get through the crowd.

The minutes tick by.

The leader is late. The conspirators are convinced they are betrayed and their arrest is imminent. They wait anxiously, fearful they will suddenly be surrounded by his bodyguards and it will be they who never see a sunset again. Even those who have killed before are nervous, for this is a horrific crime they are about to commit.

But then he arrives. The crowds all want to touch his hand, ask him for that one favour which will transform their lives. The plotters push their way through the throng surrounding him.

The first blow is to his neck but, at the last moment, the would-be assassin loses his nerve and delivers a blow so faint it has little impact. Their target challenges them but suddenly they recover their collective nerve and now it is a blood rite. They all stab him in turn. He flails around like a tethered farm animal, rejecting and kicking against the slaughter. In the scrum of arms, blood and screaming they accidentally cut each other as well as him, as they flesh themselves with his blood, all the while stabbing, stabbing, stabbing until he is dead.[1]

For the last 2000 years the brutal killing of Julius Caesar has been *the* single assassination which, more than any other, defines the territory. As a story it has everything: intrigue, deception, conspiracies within conspiracies, a savage rite written in the victim's blood and a constant twist and turn of events with a series of dramatic – and unpredictable – conclusions. As a plot it defines much that happens subsequently.

If an assassin master was writing the definitive international training manual, this single killing, in all its visceral detail, would provide the opening case study in what not to do.

Caesar's fate was immortalized by Suetonius and Plutarch, both of whom wrote while memories were still fresh. According to Plutarch (a Greek scholar whose account was dramatized brilliantly by Shakespeare) each conspirator takes their turn to stab Caesar and be covered by his blood, so binding them all into the conspiracy, their guilt equally shared. After the event, the plotters immediately boast of what they have done. In all, there are sixty men involved and they guess – quite rightly – that their block vote is enough to carry the Senate. They tell everyone there will be no more killing, saying that Caesar – an unforgivable tyrant – is the only one scheduled to die. Initially, things go well for the conspirators, most politicians accepting what they have done.

The plotters are smart and persuade Brutus, a hugely popular figure, to front up for them. While they are not men of any great popularity or reputation, he is much loved and respected, a man of palpable integrity. He addresses the crowd in the market place, telling them it had to be done as Caesar wanted to become emperor, destroy the republic and focus all power into his hands. With some reservations, the crowd go along with him. But when one of the other plotters, Cinna, speaks and starts to bad mouth Caesar the crowd turn ugly and the conspirators wisely abandon the meeting and return home to their villas.

As a fitting compromise, it is agreed that though Caesar was killed because he was a tyrant, he is now to be given a full state funeral and be honoured as a god. His closest friend Mark Anthony carries Caesar's body into the market for all to see. In all there are twenty-three wounds, his toga slashed and covered in blood. The night has been consumed with frantic gossip, wildfire rumour and near riot. In the clear light of the pale spring morning, this assassination looks very different from the plotters' vision. This is no longer a heroic act committed for the good of the state but a cowardly attack in which he was outnumbered by his enemies who slaughter him in a frenzy of personal hatred.

In the market place, Caesar's will is read to a shocked crowd. He has left 300 *sestercae* to every man in Rome, as well as his gardens and woods. The mob does not see the body of a tyrant, who has been rightly removed from the body politic. Instead they see a great soldier, a magnificent commander who led from the front but was stabbed in the back. Here was a truly great man who brought prestige, enormous wealth and imperial swagger to Rome – and now he is dead, assassinated by a gang of lesser men. Anthony holds the blood-soaked toga up to the crowd, condemning the 'cruel and cursed' murderers. They cremate his body in the market place, but then, as their anger rises, they take torches from the pyre and set off to burn down the houses of the plotters, who immediately flee the city.

Within three years all of them are dead and so is their cherished idea of a republic. None of them come to power. Brutus' wife (who had tried to stop her husband that morning) kills herself by putting red-hot coals in her mouth. Brutus asks his friend Strato to hold his sword so he can fall on it and die with a single blow.

As with many other assassinations, before and since, there was a good reason for the act and a real reason, concealed in the shadows. The good reason was Caesar's perceived autocracy. In Plutarch's words this gave 'the people just cause, and next his enemies honest colour, to bear him ill-will'. The conspirators argued that Caesar wanted to be crowned king and that therefore their actions were justified as tyrannicide; deemed to be both right and proper and justifiable under the common code. But this was only the pretext. The real reasons were a cocktail of malice, jealousy and greed. Some wanted to be leader, some were angry about the war and all of them were bitter about their losses, whether it was relatives, property or position. Nicolaus of Damascus wrote, 'They concealed the fact that they were angry, and made the pretence of something more seemly, saying that they were displeased at the rule of a single man and that they were striving for a republican form of government. Different people had different reasons, all brought together by whatever pretext they happened upon.'

Brutus was a very popular figure, noble-minded, clear-thinking and upright, a man who would not tolerate injustice. But even he had strong personal reasons to murder Caesar. He stabbed him in the genitalia, a bizarre act unless the gossip was true: Caesar was both his mother's and his sister's lover. According to Suetonius, Caesar loved Brutus' mother 'beyond all others'. He lavished gifts on her, a huge pearl, and sold her estates at knockdown prices through public auction. She in turn then prostituted her daughter (Brutus' sister) to Caesar.

But Plutarch's brilliant account does not just provide the source material for Shakespeare, it changes the course of history. The conspirators make two major blunders: they do the killing themselves and they brag about it afterwards. Few will ever make either of these mistakes again.

After Caesar's death, assassins changed their behaviour in two significant ways, regardless of how powerful they were. From this date on (with very few exceptions) principals employed someone else to do their dirty work[2] and once the deed had been done, those pulling the strings generally avoided ever boasting about their deeds in public. Generally, this applied regardless of how secure they felt, from Roman emperors to Russian Tsars, Popes and even the Medicis and Borgias – two powerful Italian Renaissance families who built assassination into their everyday lives. Even fanatics are cautious. Osama Bin Laden, a man who is reconciled to dying in a cave in Afghanistan, has generally avoided owning up to Al Qaeda assassinations or atrocities, preferring to congratulate those responsible.[3]

When the CIA was training assassins in the early 1950s, the example of Julius Caesar was used as a case study.[4] Though the trainer got virtually every detail wrong he understood the basic architecture needed for a successful assassination. To prevent contagion and retaliation, there must be no traceable relationship between the principal who is paying for the assassination and the assassin. Though this might seem obvious it is a basic lesson easily forgotten by assassins, who are often not the slick thinkers and careful planners portrayed by Hollywood and thriller writers.

Consider the case of the Islamic assassins in Helwan, Cairo, who set out just before Christmas 1947 to murder a judge, Ahmad al-Khazindar, who had recently sent several of their fellow terrorists to prison for bombing offences. For them, the judge's offence was not that he had found the innocent guilty but that he had dared to give them long sentences, rather than let them walk free. Through the distorting prism of Islamic fundamentalism, he was therefore a puppet who was prepared to serve his colonial masters, the English.

The assassins were called Hasan Abdel Hafiz and Mahmoud Saied. They were both members of the Secret Apparatus, the covert paramilitary branch of the Muslim Brotherhood, a popular Islamic fundamentalist sect in Egypt. On the surface, this should have been an easy hit. The judge had no bodyguard and took the same route to work every day, usually at the same time. But this was to be their first – and last – assassination.

For several days they watched him as he went from his house to the court building by public transport. Once they had a clear idea of his movements, they waited for him one morning outside his home. Hasan Abdel Hafiz approached him and fired several times at close range, missing every time. Mahmoud Saied, who was only there as protection, watched this farce unfold in front of him. He grabbed the judge, threw him to the ground and shot him several times, killing him. The two hapless assassins then fled the scene, but one cock-up followed another.

They had given no previous thought as to how they would escape and had neither car nor motorbike or even bicycles and so they had to flee on foot. Neither did it occur to them that the police might chase after them in cars once they had shot a judge in cold blood in the street. Though they had spent several days carrying out their surveillance of the area, they failed to notice that the judge lived very close to the local police station. They ran away and went straight to *Al Muqattam* (the mountain), named after the headquarters of the Hashshashin.[5] In reality this was the home of Abdel Rahman al-Sindy, the head of the assassination wing of the Muslim Brotherhood. All three were then captured. In the words of the Al Qaeda assassination manual, going to his house was 'a fatal error' especially when it transpired that Hasan Abdel Hafiz had never fired a gun before nor received even any basic training. Hardly surprising that he lost his nerve.

The details of this assassination, plus several others, are outlined in an Al Qaeda training manual.[6] In all, there are eighteen lessons. Lesson fourteen covers kidnapping and assassinations using rifles and pistols, lesson fifteen deals with explosives and the sixteenth lesson details assassinations using 'poisons and cold steel'. Distributed among members of Al Qaeda, this training manual is remarkably similar to the assassination manual mentioned in Chapter 1, written almost fifty years before for another bunch of killers, the CIA death squads trained in South America for the Guatemala coup in 1954. Both cover the same ground, the same range of weapons and both draw very similar operational conclusions.

The authors of both manuals were acutely aware that the opportunity for the spectacular cock-up is never far away but the odds against this happening can be improved by better training and understanding the psychology of the assassin. The CIA wants them to be 'determined, courageous, intelligent, resourceful, and physically active'. If they are going to use any specialist equipment, like firearms or drugs, then the assassin 'must have outstanding skill'. The Al Qaeda manual wants assassins to have 'a calm personality' that will help them endure the psychological trauma that comes from 'bloodshed, murder, arrest and imprisonment' or even the deaths of all their comrades. Above all, and this is a statement of the obvious (though it is not the only one in assassination and terrorist manuals) 'he should be able to carry out the work'.

The Al Qaeda handbook is a deeply cynical document in which human life – that of their own members or their enemy – has no value. It works on the basis that their assassins are completely expendable and therefore not very bright. They need to be taught everything, the Al Qaeda manual even reminding the brothers that they should not work on making booby-trap bombs until they have mastered some basic electrical and mechanical skills, 'because the first mistake a brother makes could be his last mistake'. Good advice as the Al Qaeda assassins are clearly badly affected by nerves, especially with pistols ('most aiming mistakes are due to physical stress or nerves, which cause the hand to tremble and shake').

As a key element in the training, both manuals draw heavily on previous examples, both successful and unsuccessful. In the case of the CIA, the case studies range across world history. They look at well-known cases, both successful and not: Marat, Lincoln, Harding, Heydrich, Hitler, Mussolini, Truman, Roosevelt, Rasputin, Archduke Ferdinand, Gandhi and Trotsky, as well as some which are far less well known: Madero, Huey Long, Benes and Aung Sang. Like the CIA, the Al Qaeda trainers believe in learning from failure but their examples are much closer to home and there are some case histories here that border on low farce.

There is the Islamic fundamentalist attempt to kill an Egyptian Minister with 200 kilograms of TNT in a truck, an enormous bomb, guaranteed to leave a substantial crater. As he approached, the assassin tried to detonate it, but nothing happened as there was no fuse attached. Then there were the two fundamentalists who were on surveillance watching the Egyptian Minister for the Interior. When they saw him, they should have made detailed notes of his movements to use as valuable intelligence for a properly constructed ambush. Instead, they overreacted and opened fire on him even though he was surrounded by bodyguards.

In either lexicon, CIA or Al Qaeda, both operations were disasters.

Both organizations are in the killing business and assassination has its own internal dynamics. These tend to be true for any organization or government that gets into this business, regardless of what political backdrop they operate against. Both Al Qaeda and the CIA would like to have re-usable assassins but for the most part this is not such an issue. For Al Qaeda there is a ready conveyor belt of the young and gullible. The CIA (and the US government) prefers to use cut outs and these too are largely expendable. However, both would rather have their assassins dead than captured and talking. Concealment and escape is therefore important. Like the Hashshashin before them, both are in the business of the terroristic assassination, those killings that send a shock wave through the system and are designed to cow rather than provoke change. Though neither brags openly about their atrocities, they are quite happy to support and (where possible) congratulate those responsible. However, concealment is a much greater issue for the CIA (as it is for every first world government). Different rules therefore apply and an extra layer of planning is required. To help clarify everyone's thinking, they classify assassinations so that the techniques chosen will be appropriate for the operation in mind.

The first question is whether the target is aware of the imminent threat. If they are, then the next question is whether they are protected or not. In CIA parlance, assassinations are 'simple' if the subject is unaware. If they are aware but unguarded the assassination is called 'chase', but where the victim is aware and protected it is termed 'guarded'. The next question is the assassin. If they are to die during the attack, then this is called a 'lost' assassination. If they are to escape, then it is 'safe'. The CIA manual is adamant. There must be 'no compromises'. Under no circumstances must the assassin fall alive into enemy hands. There is a further range of classification. If it needs to look like death by natural causes or accident, then it is 'secret'. If this is not an issue, then it is 'open'. When the assassination needs publicity to be effective it is 'terroristic', which is the basic category which most Al Qaeda assassinations and their other acts fall into.

This is where both organizations are at one. The CIA notes that 'except in terroristic assassinations, it is desirable that the assassin be transient in the area. He should have an absolute minimum of contact with the rest of the organization and his instructions should be given orally by one person only. His safe evacuation after the act is absolutely essential, but here again contact should be as limited as possible. It is preferable that the person issuing instructions also conduct any withdrawal or covering action which may be necessary.' Very similar instructions are given to Al Qaeda members, who are advised not to draw attention to themselves. Their manual notes that the 'work will be successful if Allah grants that,' but it also gives meticulous instructions to shorten the odds against failure, noting that the better the plan the better chance there is of success, regardless of whether Allah shines on the work.

There is one area of overlap between the two manuals, where the irony is rich, given the way events have unfolded between the two organizations. The CIA notes that in a 'lost' assassination, where the assassin dies, he 'must be a fanatic of some sort. Politics, religion, and revenge are about the only feasible motives.' The upside is that if he dies he takes many secrets with him. The downside is that since fanatics are unstable psychologically, they 'must be handled with extreme care'. As a matter of operational need, they 'must not know the identities of the other members of the organization, for although it is intended that he die in the act, something may go wrong.'

This has been a major problem both for Al Qaeda and the other Islamic fundamentalist groups. The assassins know far too much operational detail and tend to spill everything they know in the first few days of interrogation. Some then compound this by keeping vast amounts of detail on computer as well. The number three in Al Qaeda, Khalid Sheik

Mohammed talked as soon as he was captured. The same has happened with assassins from both Mossad and French Intelligence as well as paramilitaries from both sides in Northern Ireland. In every case, their interrogators have been shocked that many have cracked almost instantly. One of the Mossad killers who was part of the team who mistakenly shot a Moroccan postman in the belief that he was an Arab terrorist broke down as soon as the Norwegian police shut the cell door on him. He suffered from extreme claustrophobia and confessed all he knew in return for a larger cell with a window. In the case of the *Rainbow Warrior*, the French assassins carried all the evidence with them and all they needed to do was fill in the remaining details.

Though assassins are usually portrayed as lone, often self-contained, misfits on the edge of society this is more for dramatic convenience than any reflection of the real world. In an ideal world this is what every organization dreams of having but the reality is different.

The great bulk of assassinations are carried out by teams and that is true for terrorists, criminals and governments. Logistics are complex and most successful assassinations require at least two people, often more, especially those that are going to be staged to look like an accident. Northern Ireland is typical of many of the other assassination-based operations run by Western governments since the Second World War. The various British 'shoot to kill' operations in Northern Ireland were complex affairs involving soldiers, intelligence officers and police and paramilitaries of every hue. As well as the Americans, British and the Russians, the Israelis, the Germans and the French have all used assassination squads at some point since the war. These operations all share meticulous training, which involves the extensive study of both assassination history and previous case histories to try and ensure that the mistakes of the past are not repeated. Despite all this, these squads have one thing in common: they frequently leave their fingerprints.

Assassins, like the organizations who employ them, are prone to incompetence. The cock-up, often barely believable, is never far away. They make terrible operational mistakes and many assassins find it impossible to take their secrets to the grave with them. No matter how late in their life, they often feel a compulsive and uncontrollable need to talk, as if the memory of their deeds is like a worm slowly eating away into the deepest recesses of their conscience.

The Israelis are technically brilliant and highly creative. After following a senior Hamas official for weeks they realized that his counter-surveillance was excellent. He used his mobile phone rarely and only ever indoors, preventing the Israelis from getting a clear fix on him. Outside he moved in crowds and changed his vehicle all the time. His only weakness was frequenting the same café and then using the phone box opposite to ring his boss on a direct line number. This kiosk was used constantly so the Israelis rigged an explosive charge under the shelf, wired so that it would be detonated only when he used the phone and dialled that one fatal number.

That Israel should be so technologically advanced at assassination is hardly that surprising as it is the only modern nation with two post-war prime ministers intimately involved in the assassination business as principals, Yitzhak Shamir and Ehud Barak. Two more prime ministers, Golda Meir and Ariel Sharon, have both signed assassination orders.

As Israel was being founded in 1948, Count Folke Bernadotte, a Swedish diplomat and the United Nations representative appointed to mediate in the Arab–Jewish dispute, was assassinated by members of a Jewish terrorist group called the Lechi, otherwise known as the Stern Gang. This terrorist group was founded in 1940, as a spin-off from another group, the Irgun. The Stern Gang assassinated Lord Moyne, a British representative in the Middle East, and also murdered British troops and other Jews whom they regarded as collaborators. Then in 1948, they assassinated Bernadotte as they objected to his plan to allow Palestinians to return to their homes. Many believe that the killing was organized by Yitzhak Shamir, one of the Stern Gang leaders, who went on to become prime minister of Israel. Two of the key Stern leaders were tried and sentenced to long prison sentences but then released within months under an amnesty.

Though Shamir has never admitted his role as organizer of the Bernadotte assassination, Ehud Barak was a hands-on assassin.

The Munich Olympics in 1972 was every Jew's worst nightmare. Their Olympic team was competing on German soil when they were attacked by an Arab terrorist group called Black September, wiping out the cream of Israeli athletes. In a bungled German rescue operation, the terrorists escaped, leaving a nation to grieve and then seek revenge. The Israeli Prime Minister Golda Meir signed between two to three dozen death warrants and launched Operation Wrath of God,[7] one of the largest post-war assassination operations ever to be formally sanctioned by a government. As with the CIA operation in Guatemala, terror and fear were built into the operations from the start as Mossad planted obituaries of well-known Palestinians in Arabic newspapers, even though they were still alive.

Many of the assassinations were exotic, designed to terrorize and disrupt everyday life. Before the year was out, they had assassinated Dr Mahmoud Hamshari, who they claimed was the head of Black September in France.[8] They broke into his flat and planted a small bomb under the table by his telephone. They then rang him, playing a high-pitched signal down the line, which detonated the bomb. He survived just long enough to describe his last conscious moments. As soon as the story percolated round the Middle East, terrorists everywhere thought twice before answering the phone. Black September responded by attempting to assassinate Golda Meir when she visited Rome, but this was foiled by a brilliant counter-terrorist operation by Mossad. Having failed to kill the prime minister, Black September then gunned down a young Mossad agent, Baruch Cohen, in a Madrid café. The Israeli response was to not just go after Black September, but anyone remotely connected with them and that meant the PLO.

Three senior PLO officials, Abu Youssef (The PLO number three), Kamal Nasser (the PLO official spokesman) and Kamal Adwan (the Head of Operations) all lived in fortified houses in Beirut, where they felt safe. In a strategy derived from the Hashshashin a thousand years before, the Israeli assassins knew that if they could kill them right in their own protected heartland the fear factor would kick in. No one would feel safe again and the PLO would be paralysed for months. The operation was one of the most audacious post-war assassinations, made even more extraordinary by the fact that the man who led it was dressed as a woman. After an eight-hour speedboat journey, the Israeli assassination team arrived at Beirut. Heavily made up as a woman and wearing a black wig, the team leader and his 'lover' walked arm in arm past the Beirut police. His cantilevered bra carried hand grenades, his large and fashionable handbag was stuffed with automatic weapons and more explosives. The man in the wig was Ehud Barak, the future prime minister of Israel. Also in the party was Yonni Netanyahu, the brother of another future prime minister. They sneaked into the apartment block where the three men were staying, killing them all, including one of their wives and three bodyguards. But military operations in crowded civilian areas are rarely clean and they also shot dead a seventy-year-old Italian woman. It was the first disaster in the whole operation, but not the last.

In July 1973, Mossad's finest were convinced they had located Ali Hassan Salameh, the mastermind behind the Munich attack, living in a small Norwegian town called Lillehammer. They tracked him down and a four-person Mossad team (three men and a woman) followed him and his girlfriend back from the cinema and gunned him down in the street. But the dead man was not a Palestinian terrorist. Lying in the road full of bullets was a Moroccan waiter, Ahmed Bouchiki, his pregnant girlfriend standing in shock. It was a diplomatic and professional blunder of major proportions.

Within a short time, the Norwegian police had six of the team in custody, some of whom cracked under the very lightest interrogation. They left a trail of clues, scraps of paper with the direct-line number of the Head of Security at the Israeli embassy and a key to a safe house in Paris that they gave to the French police, which led to further safe houses scattered round the capital. The Israelis could not even manage an apology to Bouchiki's girlfriend and the official inquiry – predictably – cleared everyone of blame. But for Mossad, this was humiliation on a grand scale, as Operation Wrath of God was cancelled, not to be resumed for another five years.

Though the French gloated about the Israeli embarrassment, they too would be rocked by their own scandal, where once again assassination and breathtaking incompetence would go hand in hand. As with the Israeli disaster in Norway, complacency and arrogance would underpin the events that were to follow. After years of eviscerating the Pacific with a pointless nuclear programme, the French government felt under siege from a conspiracy of long-haired environmentalists from Greenpeace, Pacific Islanders demanding independence and ecologists at home questioning the safety of the French nuclear industry.

In particular, they felt humiliated by Greenpeace in New Zealand, which had effortlessly captured the world's headlines. Prickly, arrogant and sensitive, the French overreacted. The plan put together by the French Secret Service (DGSE) was amateurish at best and the execution read like a *Pink Panther* script. Two French divers attached mines to the side of the Greenpeace campaign vessel, the *Rainbow Warrior*. After the first bomb went off, the crew left but one returned and was killed in the second blast. From this point on it reads like a very badly written French farce. Half an hour after the explosion, two French intelligence [*sic*] agents returned to collect their gear and were spotted by the night watchman who wrote down the number of their hire car. They were then picked up by the New

Zealand police when they took the car back. There was no shortage of other clues. The frogmen dumped their air bottles (with French markings) at the harbour and one of the agents was carrying a notebook full of phone numbers. When the New Zealand police rang them they discovered they were talking to the French Ministry of Defence.

The DGSE incompetence was then compounded in one of the most ludicrous cover-ups in assassination history, one which could only be attempted by a government which believes that newspapers are hymn sheets, journalists are totally compliant and that the voters are foolish enough to rally round the flag when the government plays the patriotism flag. After the *Rainbow Warrior* affair began to leak, the DGSE began a long process of disinformation through selected journalists. First, it was said that the Greenpeace boat was really a KGB front. When this failed, it was alleged that the whole affair was an 'Anglo Saxon' plot by MI6 and the CIA to discredit the French. The inquiry, chaired by Judge Bernard Tricot, was like all official inquiries and – quite predictably – he completely exonerated the DGSE. By this time the newspapers had had enough. One headline proclaimed *Tricot Washes Whiter* and when his daughter commited suicide shortly afterwards – some said from shame – the gloves were off. Mitterrand had believed the argument that the intelligence services are a key part of the nation's defence and should not therefore be questioned or analysed, would get him through. It did not, as shame was a stronger emotion.

As with the assassination of Felix Moumie, the French protected their assassins. Once incarcerated, the French applied economic sanctions, holding up New Zealand exports to France and then threatening to force the EC to raise the tariffs on the country's butter exports. Money talks and the New Zealand government caved in. The French government paid the family of the dead crew member 2.3 million francs, reimbursed Greenpeace for the loss of their boat and formally apologized to New Zealand, an empty but humiliating gesture. The assassins were then released to French custody in 1986, with an agreement that they would stay in prison on the island of Hao, a French base in the Pacific. The French immediately reneged on the deal. Within a year one of them, Major Alain Mafart, was repatriated to France with stomach ache. The husband of Dominique Prieur, the other assassin, was sent to the island with strict orders from the French government: impregnate your wife, which he duly did and the family were then returned to France. A UN tribunal saw through this charade and France was ordered to pay another two million US dollars in compensation to the New Zealand government, a small price to pay to preserve the French right to behave badly wherever they choose.

Though the government protected its assassins, the damage was done. For many in France, the crime was not the assassination itself, but the incompetence of the operation.

At the time, the French government briefed journalists that they had a right to sink the *Rainbow Warrior*, their only crime was getting caught. This was then compounded when the French Prime Minister Laurent Fabius told the New Zealand government that they should release the assassins because they were not guilty, as they were only acting under orders. This fatuous defence had been used and rejected at Nuremburg. France, as one of the five permanent members of the United Nations Security Council, should have known better. Though the French were attacked for this throughout the 'civilized' world, Fabius was only expressing what his government assumed was the invisible and assumed right of every post-war colonial power to protect their assets through assassination. Every major first world colonial power has routinely used assassination (and everything that goes with it including torture, repression and military intervention) to suppress the spark of nationalism.

This has been routinely covered up but it is hard to conceal. Assassins often leave a paper trail and they are inveterate gossips. Throughout the 1950s and early 1960s, the French brutally repressed the Algerian nationalists fighting against their colonial masters. The French denied the worst excesses, refusing even to admit there was a war, calling it instead 'operations to maintain order'. The 1965 movie *The Battle of Algiers* which graphically depicts the struggle was banned.

But then, in May 2001, one of the key French army commanders, General Paul Aussaresses, aged eighty-three, published his account of just three years of the war, 1955–7. In pungent and graphic detail, he described how the French ran death squads and how he personally tortured and killed twenty-four Algerians. He was unrepentant, 'I cannot express remorse. That implies guilt. I consider I did my difficult duty of a soldier implicated in a difficult mission.' He argued that this was 'the proper thing to do' because the jails were crowded and the military tribunals were overstretched. In all, three thousand out of twenty-four thousand Algerian prisoners were murdered by the French, one in eight, a number which the General dismisses as 'not a lot'. His only defence was that he did it 'without pleasure'. Again the French openly protected their assassins. He was not charged with war crimes or murder (there being a convenient amnesty) but with justifying war crimes.

His fine, a massive €7,500, just three hundred euros for each assassination he committed.

5

GET SOMEONE ELSE TO DO YOUR DIRTY WORK

National Security Agency (NSA) Headquarters,
Fort Meade, Maryland, USA 7.15 p.m., EST . . .
Deep in black space, an American spy satellite picks up a short burst of encrypted traffic. In England, it is just after midnight and the sender is in one of the most prestigious addresses in the heart of London's west end. The receiver is in the private office of Colonel Muammar Qaddafi in Libya, a man widely regarded by some as the world's leading terrorist. A few minutes later, there is another much shorter burst of traffic, this time from Qaddafi's office back to London. The Libyans believe that their intelligence traffic, which uses a Russian encryption system, is secure, but it is no match for the banks of Cray supercomputers at the headquarters of the American National Security Agency (NSA) in Ford Meade, Maryland. The message is decoded and translated, virtually in real time.

The first telex from the Libyan People's Bureau in St James's Square asks what to do about a group of anti-Qaddafi demonstrators who are due outside in less than twelve hours' time. There are three options presented to Tripoli: do nothing, grab some of the demonstrators and drag them inside the embassy for a good kicking, or shoot them. The reply from Tripoli is to choose option three.

Shortly after the signal is sent, a delegation of the old guard diplomats at the Libyan embassy trot round to the Foreign Office to meet the night duty officer and plead for the demonstration to be cancelled. Their concerns are duly noted and put on the file.

Back in Maryland, the NSA analysts immediately spot the significance of this and send a FLASH message to their British allies at Government Communications Headquarters (GCHQ) in Cheltenham, Wiltshire. Even though it is the middle of the night, the GCHQ analysts are wide awake and they too see the need for immediate action. The message is flashed to their London Office, a wonderfully nondescript office in Palmer Street just round the corner from Scotland Yard, but this is as close as it ever gets to the police. The GCHQ night duty staff jump into immediate action. The intercept is marked FLASH, the most urgent priority available, and fired round Whitehall to the Foreign Office, Cabinet Office, MI6 and MI5, who have the responsibility to act on it. The whole operation from intercept to circulation is measured in minutes.

FLASH signals are very rare in Whitehall.[1] Everyone jumps. Junior officers do not like taking responsibility. Cars are sent, middle-ranking bosses are dragged out of bed and they in turn fetch their bosses. This is 24/7 intelligence. But on this night, nothing happens. MI5 sit on the information and do nothing with it, subsequently briefing friendly journalists that it was just one of those cock-ups that sometimes happen. Intelligence insiders dismiss this, doubting that a signal which carries the highest priority, would somehow get lost in the bureaucratic fog of Whitehall. What adds to the suspicion is that this is not the only warning MI5 receives that night. MI6, who have also bugged the embassy and have at least one Libyan diplomat on the payroll, separately discover that a shooting is planned for later that morning.

Around four in the morning, MI6 contacts MI5 to pass on the intelligence it has received. Given the relentless turf wars and mutual loathing between the two organizations, the shock value alone of the call should have been enough to make MI5 sit up but this too is ignored.

The police are excluded from the Whitehall machine so while the security and intelligence wheels grind slowly, the police set up barriers in the square, blissfully unaware that they are walking into a shooting gallery. By 10 a.m., the stage is set.

It is a beautiful spring morning. Central London at its best, the battleship grey skies of winter are gone and the air is crisp and clean. The parks glisten, green and fresh. In St James's Square, tucked in between Pall Mall and Piccadilly, birds collect twigs for their nests and commuters scurry to work. A few miles away in north London, a coach carrying demonstrators arrives from Newcastle via Leeds. It has driven down that morning, collecting students and other Libyan exiles, gathering a few more at Swiss Cottage. Just the week before, the Libyan leader, Colonel Muammar al-Qaddafi has hanged dissident students in the capital Tripoli, the grisly event being played on Libyan television, a warning for local and international consumption.

Qaddafi has been in power for fifteen years and is one of the world's longest-surviving dictators. Ruthless, cunning and focused, he has achieved what none thought possible when he seized power in 1969, aged just twenty-seven. He has curbed the warring tribes and begun construction of a modern Islamic state. Publicly, he is everyone's hate figure but privately there are many in the British Foreign Office who are closet supporters. There is a huge amount of trade between the two countries but more importantly, the British are worried about the rise of Islamic fundamentalism in north Africa and Qaddafi has been more successful than anyone at curbing the power of the mullahs. But he has only achieved this by destroying the

Libyan opposition, both at home and abroad. On the bus, the demonstrators know their life expectancy is not as good as it was the day before. In Qaddafi's words, they are 'stray dogs' who need to be put down.

Despite this, the mood is upbeat. They are going to have their say, something denied to their comrades back home. But ever fearful of reprisals, they cover their faces with sunglasses, hats and *shamags*, the traditional Arab scarf, worn in Islamic states everywhere. It is a fairly pointless precaution as their movement is heavily penetrated by Qaddafi's intelligence, but it makes a strong rhetorical point. But they too have good intelligence on the opposition. On the bus, they are given an astonishing warning: there is to be shooting that day from the embassy.[2] But as their coach negotiates the crowded streets, it is hard to take this threat seriously, after all this is England, it is a sensationally beautiful spring morning and these things do not happen, not in London and not in broad daylight. So they are more exhilarated than frightened and full of revolutionary fervour.

Shortly after 10 a.m., the coach drops them off, just round the corner from the Libyan People's Bureau (the embassy) nestling in the corner of the square, between the headquarters of RTZ (Rio Tinto Zinc, a mining conglomerate) at number six and the government's Employment Appeals Tribunal at number four. In eighteenth-century London, this was the smartest of smart addresses. In 1721, St James's Square provided homes for six dukes, seven earls, a countess and a baronet. For its creator, Henry Jermyn, this was an earthly paradise. He lived at number thirty-one, surrounded by his aristocratic chums. By 1984, the square housed a bank, the London Library (used by Dr Watson when he was researching Chinese pottery for his friend Sherlock Holmes), the Army and Navy Club (which serves one of the best curries in the area) and Chatham House, once home to three different British prime ministers[3] but now home to one of the world's most influential foreign affairs think-tanks, the Royal Institute for International Affairs.

St James's Square is the heart of British imperial swagger, a crucible of power lubricated by old money from land and new money from international commerce. But there in the corner, in one of London's finest buildings, is what the US White House believes is the heart of a worldwide terrorist network – the Libyan People's Bureau. A network financed by the sudden transfer of wealth to oil-rich countries like Libya.

By the time the demonstrators arrive the police are already in position, having put barriers in place that morning, one on each side of the street to keep the two factions apart. British fair play at its best but it has already upset some at the Bureau. One diplomat, the Press Secretary, Omar Sodani, was arrested earlier that morning after a scuffle. Despite this the atmosphere is low-key, relaxed and friendly. The police, all from West End Central, situated in the heart of embassy land, are familiar with this kind of event and chat with the demonstrators, a mature democracy in action. Two British freelance film crews are on hand, having been booked the day before by a Libyan TV producer. A third video camera, hired that morning by one of the demonstrators is also recording events, though he stands some distance away, down the street from the embassy.

A group of pro-Qaddafi supporters come out of the embassy and hurl insults at the demonstrators. Unmasked, they know the pictures will play well back home in Tripoli and their relatives can expect a reciprocal gesture of Qaddafi's generosity. Standing among Qaddafi's team is an incongruous figure, a British intelligence officer, mid-thirties, thinning ginger hair, dressed in a double-breasted fawn overcoat (called a 'warm'), complete with epaulettes. Further round the square are other watchers, though none of them blend in easily with the crowd. Just for good measure, the building is heavily bugged by both MI5 and MI6, though neither know of each other's listening devices.

Just after 10.15 a.m., WPC Yvonne Fletcher strolls across to the film crew standing in the doorway by number three, asking them where they are from. Satisfied, she strolls back across the road to rejoin the cordon of police standing between the two sets of demonstrators. At five foot three inches, she is the smallest officer in the Metropolitan Police. Just above her, a large sash window in the ambassador's office on the first floor opens a foot or so. A short barrel pokes out, a Mark II Sterling sub-machine gun.

Few witnesses agree on what happens next. There is gunfire, some say a single burst, others say more. One witness says a group of three or four men stand on the balcony and spray the crowd with bullets. The police recover just twelve bullets. Some are found in the road in front of the embassy, others fly across the square, one going through a plate-glass window, bouncing off a filing cabinet and hitting a secretary on the head, just at the point it runs out of energy. But much closer to the embassy, Yvonne Fletcher is not so lucky. A single bullet rips through her liver. In the chaos immediately after the shooting, police and demonstrators run in every direction. Two of her colleagues grab her and carry her to safety round the corner. An ambulance takes her to hospital but the wound is fatal and she is pronounced dead at midday.

The square is sealed off. For the next ten days, the building is watched by MI5, MI6 and the Police Special Branch. At an RAF base just outside London, a group of SAS soldiers map out a plan of the building in a hangar, using a map secured from a local estate agent. Bricks are used for walls. But there is to be no repeat of the Iranian embassy siege where the SAS stormed the building, killing all but one of the hostage takers. After ten days watching, the SAS are given operational control and tell their political masters that they will go in the following morning at 5 a.m., some in from the roof, others in a frontal assault using Land Rovers and short ladders. An hour beforehand, they are stood down and returned to barracks at Hereford, with no explanation, though they have their suspicions as to why . . .

Just over a week later, the Libyan diplomats are taken to Gatwick Airport and interviewed before they leave. It is hot in the airport and the air conditioning is not working so each is offered a glass of water, a small act of generosity by the British. By the time they leave, the police have a full set of fingerprints. Back in Libya they are given a hero's welcome, in public at least, but as far as the world's press is concerned this is an open and shut case of Libyan terrorism. There is an attempted coup against Qaddafi three weeks later but despite heavy street fighting he survives, as always.

The afternoon after the shooting, Yvonne Fletcher's mother Queenie and her father Tim were fetched to West End Central police station. Some of the officers present in the square took Yvonne's mother to one side and told her that nothing was as it seemed that morning, something was not quite right though none could put their finger on it. Their suspicions were well founded. The afternoon after the shooting, Dr Iain West, a Home Office pathologist, carried out a post-mortem. Her body was photographed and the line of the bullet analysed. The pictures showed that she was shot with a single bullet, which entered her right shoulder blade, passed through her liver, bounced off her lower spine below her pelvis, emerged on the left side of her stomach and then passed through her uniform, ending its journey in her tunic by the left elbow. West wrote that the fatal bullet was fired at 'an angle of sixty to seventy degrees, from the upper floors of an adjacent building'. Eleven days later, the police took possession of the embassy building and carried out a meticulous search. No murder weapon was found, but there on the window sill and curtains of the first floor were the unmistakable traces of gunpowder from a recently discharged weapon.

But there was a big problem. From this window, there was only a fifteen-degree angle to the street. This angle matched the bullet wounds in the demonstrators but did not match her wound. It was simply not steep enough. The police experts searched the rest of the building but no gun had been fired from anywhere else in number five.

At the inquest, the coroner Paul Knapman was suspicious

and questioned West on this point. West said that Yvonne Fletcher must have been turning when she was shot and this somehow reduced the angle of the wound from sixty plus degrees to fifteen. One expert who was not called but who drew a very different conclusion was Hugh Thomas, who worked for years as chief surgeon for the British army in Northern Ireland, a man who has operated on and seen hundreds of bullet wounds. He described West's conclusions as 'a nonsense' adding 'the fact is that if you turn, the lumbar spine still remains in roughly the same area.' After visiting the square, he added, 'It's almost impossible that she was shot from number five, because there's no floor in the building which would give an angle of sixty to seventy degrees.' Ten years later, when West wrote his autobiography, he had a different story. He no longer claimed that she was twisting and bending but instead argued that 'the film showed she had her arms folded across her chest at the moment she was shot.' In fact, there was no camera pointing towards her at the moment she was shot.

After two days, the inquest jury had no alternative but to return a verdict of murder by persons unknown, firing from the Libyan People's Bureau.

The police had one other crucial piece of evidence, the third video tape shot by one of the demonstrators, which had the words 'of no evidential value' written on it – but which actually contained the key to what happened. According to the police expert, two sub-machine guns were used, one firing nine bullets, the other firing three. The missing evidence shows this to be incorrect: two guns were used, but one was not a sub-machine gun. Matching the video tapes from this camera with the others shows there was a single continuous burst of eleven bullets, after which there was a two-and-a-half second gap, when a twelfth bullet was fired. But the audio signature of this bullet was totally different. The sub-machine bullets were light and comparatively soft. This final bullet was much louder. A bang not a tap. According to an audio expert, Simon Heyworth, this was 'a separate shot entirely, which suggests there's another weapon, another gun firing a single shot'.[4]

This was the bullet that killed Yvonne Fletcher. There were two further clues. When the bullet entered her shoulder, it left a small hole, 'almost round, measuring 7 mm × 7 mm' with 'an elliptical rim of abrasion set obliquely up and to the right,' further confirmation that she had been shot from someone looking down on her from a steep angle. The bullet then travelled down through her body into her liver, where it left a hole '3 inches in diameter', ten times the size of the original entry point. After it bounced off her spine it came out of her lower chest, leaving behind an odd shape, 12 mm × 8 mm. As West observed, this was 'a tumbling bullet,' but not only did it sound different to the sub-machine gun bullets, it was travelling much more slowly. The bullets from the submachine gun flew one hundred and sixty five metres across the square and through a plate-glass window. The bullet that killed Yvonne Fletcher was travelling so slowly it did not even have enough energy to pass through the sleeve of her uniform, after it came out of her body. She was standing ten yards from the pavement and her killer had a clear line of sight from his gun to her left shoulder blade.

This issue was not raised at the inquest, a surprising omission as Iain West was a gun fanatic and should have spotted this contradiction. Had she been shot at thirty yards by the sub-machine gun the bullet would have passed cleanly through her and it would not have tumbled.[5] It could not have been a ricochet bullet either as it was less than thirty metres from the first-floor window to her right shoulder and there was nothing in between for a bullet to bounce off.

There is only one building in the square which gives a steep enough angle for this twelfth and fatal bullet: number three, a building with an excellent view of the People's Bureau. The occupants of every floor can be accounted for, except one. In the weeks before the shooting an upper floor was taken over by MI5.[6] They had their own key and came and went via a back entrance so they would not have to be seen by the embassy staff.

Mrs Thatcher was horrified. She was very close to the Americans and, in particular the CIA Chief William Casey, so she knew about the intercept. When she challenged MI5 on it, they lied and told her that the police had been tipped off, a claim which the Metropolitan Police Commissioner Sir Kenneth Newman was able to prove was untrue. Thatcher was all for closing down MI5 and handing over their work to the police special branch who she respected far more. She ordered an inquiry report from the Home Secretary Leon Brittan, into the workings of the security services. As he concluded his report, which was very critical of the security services, MI5 began to spread a vile – and completely untrue – rumour throughout Fleet Street about his sexuality, character assassination of the worst sort. Eventually it was exposed in *Private Eye* by Richard Ingrams who spotted the smear, after which the large number of journalists who had been taken for a ride moved on to the next rumour.[7]

While Leon Brittan was compiling his report, there was a second murder in London, which went largely unreported, but which carried the clues to unlock the mystery of who really shot Yvonne Fletcher. Ali al-Gihour was a small-time Lebanese businessman with a confused and troubled past. He was arrested the summer after Yvonne Fletcher's death for his alleged involvement in a series of small bombs which went off in west London, apparently against anti-Qaddafi dissidents. The bombings were strange: they were small, did relatively little damage, apart from generating some anti-Qaddafi headlines, and were very much out of character for the Libyans, who preferred to target the opposition and then assassinate them. Even though al-Gihour was the driver for the group, he was also a member of a shadowy but very well-financed group called Al Burkan (the volcano) which had suddenly appeared as the main opposition group against Qaddafi. But this was not all. He told his solicitor, Anthony Elletson, that he was also working for someone else as well – British intelligence – a claim the lawyer regarded as 'quite plausible'.

Given the serious nature of his crimes, al-Gihour was initially denied bail and was happy to spend the summer in prison, where he felt safe. But then inexplicably he was given bail, a decision he considered with horror, telling his solicitor that he was now a dead man. According to Elletson, 'He felt that he was really no longer of any use to any of the people for whom he'd previously been working. His useful life had come to a grinding halt, effectively.'

A few days later, on 20 August 1984, a woman living in a mansion block in Marylebone, west London, complained of a strange smell coming from one of the flats. It was the rapidly decomposing body of Ali al-Gihour, forced to kneel, hit across the face and then shot, just once, in the back of the head. Though this was a classic execution, all similarity to a professional hit ends there: the assassin left the gun, a Walther PPK, behind, with a big clue. The gun had a serial number, 176979, which took police straight back to its owner in Germany. From there the trail led straight to a major criminal gang who were involved in drugs, murder, terrorism and a US-financed plot to overthrow Colonel Qaddafi.

The gang was headed up by a wealthy German businessman, Hilmar Hein. In public he ran a prominent construction company in Berlin. In private he headed up a huge criminal organization, whose biggest client was Al Burkan. According to one gang member, Helmut Nagler, 'Al Burkan commissions Hein to organize weapons, even groups and an organization to kill Qaddafi.'

As the Hein gang quickly discovered, running a terrorist organization for a financier with an apparently limitless budget is a great business to be in. In early 1984, the Hein gang started supplying Al Burkan with handguns and silencers, home-made in his workshops, some of which were delivered to Britain.[8] But this was a business which was not without risk. Nagler was given the task of delivering three Walther PPK handguns to

London. As he drove off the ferry, he ran into trouble with British Customs, who searched his car. They removed the panels from the doors, even looked in the engine, but they did not remove the sump where the guns were hidden, heavily wrapped in plastic. A relieved Nagler drove on to London to the Royal Lancaster Hotel where he met the head of Al Burkan, Ragev Zatoot. Back in Germany, Hein's organization was involved in a firebomb attack on the Libyan People's Bureau in Bonn as well as assassinating Qaddafi supporters throughout Europe. But these acts of terrorism were just the taster before the main course. The Hein team started to train anti-Qaddafi Libyan students in the basement of a large build-ing on a Berlin industrial estate. The course was a standard assassination primer, reminiscent of the one which the CIA had used thirty years before in Guatemala, though much less sophisticated.

Hein had already been well paid for his work but the future rewards were far greater. The next stage was a planned *coup d'état* against Qaddafi – and once a new regime had been installed, he was promised lucrative building contracts as well as profitable dealerships and concessions.

In early 1984, some of the Hein gang met in a Berlin brothel. According to Hein's right-hand man Manfred Meyer, they decided that they needed an inflammatory incident to galvanize world opinion against Qaddafi. Various options were discussed and according to another gang member, the idea emerged that they should kill a British police officer in a way that the blame would be pinned on Libya.

On the day Yvonne Fletcher was shot, Manfred Meyer went to Hilmar Hein's Berlin flat where he found his boss in a dressing gown, drinking champagne and dancing round. He shared his good news with Meyer, telling him 'a police woman's been shot!' According to Meyer, 'Hein was euphoric as he said "Pack your bags, we're off to Libya!" Meyer was in no doubt that the assassination of Yvonne Fletcher was down to the Hein gang, 'It was talked about as "our weapon" quite openly. It was "our piece". That was how we used to talk. We weren't beating about the bush. It was our weapon. It worked out fine.'

For the next three weeks it all looked fine for Hein and Al Burkan. The diplomats were not wiped out by the SAS but instead returned to Tripoli. Among their number were several members of Al Burkan, who confidently expected to be part of a new pro-Western government, once the proposed coup was successful. But once again Qaddafi survived, crushing the plotters. The students trained in the basement of a Berlin building were no match for the Libyan National Guard.

A full-time criminal, Meyer had become increasingly worried about the activities they were sliding into. Dealing cocaine in small amounts, stealing large-scale plant machinery from building sites was one thing but this was big international politics, a different league entirely. He sought reassurance from Hein, asking him who would stand behind them. Hein told him, 'Don't worry, Reagan's people have said nothing can happen to us.' Hein then gave him two names: John Poindexter and Oliver North. At the time, these two names meant nothing to him, but Meyer wrote them in his diary. Both men were key members of the Reagan White House and the architects of many of the dirty tricks which the CIA refused to touch, including Iran Contra, when the American government ran drugs and guns to pay for a closet, dirty and illegal war to destroy the Sandinista regime in Nicaragua.

The role of the Americans was curious. Al Burkan was clearly the creation of the Reagan White House, who had grown frustrated with the lack of progress in removing Qaddafi. The CIA had traditionally supported the National Front for the Salvation of Libya (NFSL) but by 1983 it was an ineffective talking shop of intellectuals and émigrés, long past their effective sell-by date. Reagan's men bypassed the CIA and set up their own organization. Al Burkan appeared from nowhere, a complete surprise to most in the anti-Qaddafi opposition who were shocked to suddenly discover this overgrown and heavily financed cuckoo in what was, by now, an old and battered nest. It had no grass roots, no foundations. Unlike any other revolutionary organization, it was top down and run by a man with a bottomless cheque book. There was no central group of revolutionaries and no ideology, simply a desire to remove Qaddafi. In the absence of any base, they created their own using a gang of German criminals to inject the backbone which was missing in the NFSL.

After the coup failed, everything went quiet until the assassination of Ali al-Gihour. As soon as the gun was traced back to Berlin, the Hein gang were picked up by the German police and once inside a cell, they soon discovered the harsh realities of life for those who are suckered into working for the intelligence services. They were now expendable. Meyer began to talk and once he started he didn't stop, telling them about everything from al-Gihour to Yvonne Fletcher. According to Berlin's senior state prosecutor, Clemens-Maria Boehm, Meyer was a good witness in the box, a career criminal but a reliable witness of events. The court believed him and Hein, Nagler and Meyer all went to prison for terrorism.

Meyer was visited in prison by a man from British intelligence. He told him his story but never heard from him again. He was also visited by the Metropolitan Police, but again no action was taken. Meanwhile, Al Burkan's leader Ragev Zatoot fled to the USA, where the Germans tracked him to an address in Virginia Beech. Boehm had a cast-iron case against Zatoot as a major terrorist: there was a long paper trail, including regular bank transfers of over two million Deutschmarks at a time from Zatoot to Hein. He tried to bring him back to Germany for trial but he met with heavy resistance from the US State Department, who made it very clear that they were not going to allow Zatoot into a German court, where his testimony could be a massive embarrassment to the Reagan White House.

Zatoot stayed in the USA until the mid-1990s but then his various business ventures failed. He turned to his former US paymasters but like the Hein gang he discovered that he too was now expendable.

And so he did what many other Libyan dissidents have done before and since. He made his peace with the colonel and returned to Libya, taking the final secrets of the Fletcher assassination with him.

Meanwhile, the plotters had learned well from history. The case of Julius Caesar had cast a long shadow. Mindful of what had happened to his killers, they did what smart assassins have always done: they got someone else to do their dirty work for them – and they had successfully stigmatized their enemy, Colonel Qaddafi, with the crime.

This pattern of using someone else has been the dominant one since the end of the Second World War, since which time the majority of governments worldwide have used assassination teams at one time or another. Paramilitary death squads are widespread throughout South America, Africa and South East Asia. Wherever there is a military dictatorship or a coup backed by the military, assassination follows as a means of securing power and eradicating the opposition. In all these countries, the military ensure the absence of any effective judiciary or respect for the rule of law and so state-sponsored assassination and repression flourishes, often with the support of the first world nations who are their sponsors.

In October 1976, Henry Kissinger, the US Secretary of State under Richard Nixon, gave the green light to the military junta in Argentina, allowing them to pursue their policy of assassin-ation, repression and torture with the covert blessing of the US government. In a meeting with their Foreign Minister, Admiral Cesar Augusto Guzzetti, Kissinger told him that the US government would support its friends. A week before the meeting, Kissinger was given a US State Department report which noted that 'extra-legal right-wing goon squads' were operating with impunity abducting and murdering hundreds, including 'foreign nationals, politicians, students, journalists and priests'. Among the foreign nationals were several American citizens who were brutally tortured.

Kissinger knew his way round the assassination business. He kept it simple and got someone else to do the dirty work for the US government, telling his Argentinian visitor, 'Our basic attitude is that we would like you to succeed. The quicker you succeed the better. We want a stable situation. We won't cause you any unnecessary difficulties. If you can finish before Congress gets back the better.' But the goon squads continued their grisly work for years to come and in all an estimated thirty thousand Argentinian civilians would be identified by the state intelligence service and then assassinated.

At the time all this was fervently denied, but as always with an operation this size there was a huge paper trail and the minutes of Kissinger's meeting have been declassified,[9] revealing the hidden hand of the US government in one of the most outrageous modern incidents of state terrorism. Here was a world superpower, the United States, encouraging and promoting a violent campaign of terror by a state against its own people. What compounds Kissinger's crime is that he then subsequently berated his aides when he discovered they had supported reports condemning both the Argentinian and Chilean governments for practising repression and state-sponsored assassination.

Argentina and Chile were not alone. As the carpet of colonial and imperial power has been rolled back since the 1950s, death squads have now frequently become the invisible branch of government throughout the developing world, especially in South America, where trade unionists, civil rights lawyers and journalists are 'disappeared' in their thousands. Though criminal charges are rare no one is ever in any doubt who is responsible.

Kissinger was not alone. First world governments always try and use this option and get someone else to do their dirty work. After three hundred years of empire and commonwealth, the British are better at it than most. During the Troubles in Northern Ireland, British intelligence recognized the corrosive

140   HITMEN AND ASSASSINATIONS

nature of assassination within terrorist organizations and leveraged this against the paramilitaries on both sides.

The key figure here was Howard Smith, the civil servant who called for the 'killing' of Patrice Lumumba in 1960. By 1971, he was the UK representative in Northern Ireland, responsible for intelligence coordination, before returning to London a year later to take responsibility within Whitehall for British policy in the province. This was the hottest period of the civil war. The internment of three hundred and forty-two Catholics in the early hours of 9 August 1971 was a disaster. The intelligence was weak and many innocent people were wrongly jailed and then released. It was also out of date, as fathers were detained where it should have been sons. Many internees were tortured and beaten. Increasingly, the Provisional IRA took the war to the UK mainland and the early 1970s became a peak time for assassination on all sides as they settled in for a long civil war.

The British policy was one of containment. For the most part, the war was confined within the paramilitaries on both sides who were regularly culled through assassination, much of which was organized and manipulated by MI5, the army and the Royal Ulster Constabulary (RUC) Special Branch (though they did not work together and ran their own internecine wars against each other). The vast majority killed were Catholics, but Protestants were killed as well. In 1975, Smith became Head of MI5, which by then had won the turf war with MI6 and was running the intelligence war against the IRA.

Unlike all the other civil wars fought elsewhere in the world since 1945, the sectarian violence did not spill out and pollute the general community. There was no wave of refugees fleeing the country and, though tragic, the total number of dead – three thousand six hundred in just over thirty years – is small compared with the other long-running civil wars.

The British were effective because they kept it simple. Throughout the conflict there was continual dialogue with paramilitaries on both sides, both through back channels and face-to-face meetings. One aspect of containment was an early agreement with the leaders of the IRA. In a round-table meeting, British Army commanders warned their IRA counterparts that the royal family was off limits. The British admitted that ultimately it would not be possible for them to totally protect the royals against attack so they told the men sitting across the table that if anything should happen to any member of the royal family and the IRA was responsible then they would kill them all before midnight. It is a tactic straight out of the Hashshashin handbook and it worked. Hasan ibn el-Sabah would have been proud of them.

The assassination of Lord Mountbatten appeared to contravene this agreement, but the British army's own internal investigation concluded that the bomb (a mercury tilt switch activated by a slow fuse) was identical in its key elements to those used by INLA, the Irish National Liberation Army. However, at the time, it suited their propaganda purposes to blame the IRA.[10]

The Mountbatten assassination is much murkier than it seems. It is a classic case for investigation. At the time, there was no shortage of powerful forces with a strong motive to kill him, even though he was seventy-nine years old. But having very good reason for wanting him dead is long short of proof that they were actually responsible. But just to further complicate matters, the absence of that final convincing piece of evidence is not proof of innocence either. There are three schools of thought, which attribute the killing to the Americans, the British and the Russians, all of whom had both motive and opportunity.

The renegade Conservative Unionist MP Enoch Powell claimed that it was the work of the CIA though he failed to provide any concrete evidence and Maurice Oldfield, the coordinator for security and intelligence in Northern Ireland, declined to meet him. Powell's claim is not so bizarre. For years, many in US and British intelligence circles had believed that Mountbatten was a long-term Soviet asset and with good reason. Throughout his life Mountbatten made pro-Bolshevik

and pro-Russian noises and shortly before his death he attacked
the US for not being more enthusiastic about nuclear disarma-
ment. Even more worrying for the professional paranoids in
Western counter-intelligence, Mountbatten had frequently used
back channels to communicate secretly with the Russians. As
First Sea Lord in the mid 1950s, one of the frostiest periods in
the Cold War, he had clandestine talks with the Kremlin and
his life-long companion (and probable lover) Peter Murphy,
was a Soviet agent. Had Mountbatten been a man of obvious
integrity this would not have mattered, but he was narcissistic,
rampantly dishonest and obsessed with intrigue. Field Marshal
Templer once shouted at him across a table, 'Dickie, you're so
crooked if you swallowed a nail you'd shit a corkscrew!'[11]

Though many of these events were long in the past, Ireland
was a key Cold War issue and Mountbatten's crooked behaviour with his friends in the Kremlin was a major security
issue. Eire was not a member of NATO and therefore was a
hole in the European defence umbrella. Northern Ireland was
even more important as the deep water ports were crucial for
monitoring the Russian submarines coming out of the Baltic.
But what made Mountbatten's perceived treachery such a
pertinent issue was the rumour which flashed round some
circles of Western intelligence in the late 1970s that he had
betrayed some crucial Office of Strategic Services (OSS)
operations to the Russians shortly after the end of the war.
Whether he did or not is largely immaterial. A generation of
American intelligence officers had seen their friends and allies
killed by the Russians who had defeated them across the
frontlines of Eastern Europe and many knew this was because
they had been betrayed right at the heart. Many suspected
Philby but if Mountbatten was complicit as well then this
would have been enough to sign his death warrant, even though
he was seventy-nine years old.

There were many in British intelligence and army circles who
had good reason to hate Mountbatten. His vainglorious
behaviour and poor judgement had caused the deaths of

thousands of soldiers. But though this was in the past there was something much more current in the 1970s. Many within British Intelligence circles in Northern Ireland knew him as a visitor to Kincora, a boy's home used by the paedophile and gay members of the Protestant Order, civil servants and intelligence officers. There was a visceral resentment against Mountbatten and many were furious that he was protected. As one British Intelligence insider subsequently remarked, 'We were all over INLA. We must have known about the Mountbatten hit beforehand. I guess we looked the other way. Put it this way, no one was upset.'[12]

Having ensured the security of the royal family, the British then manipulated both sides, constantly disrupting their activities through a classic counter-terrorist operation, underpinned by assassination, either carried out vicariously or directly.

One key tactic used by the British both here and in other colonial wars was to lift a 'terrorist' and hold him or her for several days before releasing him a few days later. This would then be followed by the rumour that he or she had talked. This was often a death sentence and many were then tortured and assassinated by their own side. The beauty of this strategy was that anyone who was released without a rumour attached became equally suspicious, as the paramilitaries then worried that one of their number had been turned. Both sides had active units enforcing internal discipline, with assassination being their ultimate sanction. But assassination has its own imperatives and the British were not the only ones who practised vicarious murder. In this fetid world, paranoia is ever-present and, periodically, paramilitary leaders on both sides ring their counterparts on the other side of the struggle to arrange the removal of one of their own, usually as a way to resolve one of the endless series of internal power struggles.

Though both sides of the sectarian divide committed atrocities, the British saw the Catholics and the paramilitary Provisional IRA as the enemy and so worked closely with the various Protestant terrorist organizations, particularly the

Ulster Volunteer Force (UVF), providing them with intelligence, information, explosives and weapons to use in their war against the IRA and the Catholic community.

One of the key Protestant assassins was called Robin Jackson, nicknamed 'The Jackal', who carried out at least twenty assassinations of Catholics, many with the collusion of both the British and the RUC. Much of the detail of Jackson's activities is contained in the affidavit of John 'Jock' Weir, a Sergeant in the RUC between 1970 and 1980 before he was convicted of the murder of a Catholic, William Strathearn; a killing which Weir believed was carried out with the approval of senior officers at the highest level in the RUC, who at the time were running an assassination programme against Catholics. From the start, his police unit was what he describes as 'basically an Orange Lodge', a Protestant organization which even plotted to assassinate a fellow RUC officer as they believed he had Catholic sympathies. Weapons handed in under a gun amnesty in 1971 were then redistributed from the police station straight to Protestant paramilitary groups. Weir and his colleagues moved round south Armagh with impunity, driving through RUC roadblocks with the most notorious Loyalist paramilitary in the car without anything other than an exchange of pleasantries. On the occasion that Strathearn was assassinated, Weir went to meet another RUC officer who had a gun from Lurgan police station which had not been used. Together they collected Jackson and drove him to the village where Strathearn lived. Jackson then went and shot him twice before returning to the police car. The two police officers then dropped Jackson back at the lorry of his helper. Weir then drove his colleague to his father's house where they left the gun and he then took him back to the police station. Jackson and his helper then continued on their journey delivering chickens.[13]

But being an assassin's accomplice is a dangerous occupation, especially when there is another war on your own side, in this case between British Intelligence and the RUC Special Branch, both of which warned him against the other. Weir knew too much and he became suspicious that he too was being set up to be assassinated by his colleagues when they suggested he plant illegal weapons on an IRA suspect. He believed that as soon as he set off they would tip off the army and he would be shot as a suspected terrorist. He wisely declined the request.

In the world of assassination, fear is rampant but it often keeps people alive.

Part 3
COVER-UP

Since 1945, assassins have had to become more sophisticated. The growth of the mass media and the ever-increasing uptake of democracy have forced assassins and their paymasters to become ever more scientific in their approach. As well as the assassination of Julius Caesar, one other stands out – the slaughter of Thomas Becket in Canterbury Cathedral. This too backfired spectacularly on the assassins and it has been one of the key defining precedents for everything that has happened since.

The lessons from Thomas Becket are ever clear: assume your appointed assassins will get caught and build plausible deniability and plenty of top cover into every plan. These lessons then underpin the work of every major intelligence service and they are the key to understanding the complex relationship between the CIA and President John Kennedy, the most assassin-obsessed of modern US presidents.

High-profile assassinations have therefore become more complex and this has demanded ever-increasing levels of skill. Quite simply, the assassins have got better: there are remarkable similarities between the choreography of the assassinations of Robert Kennedy and Yitzhak Rabin, as if the Israelis had used the earlier assassination as the template and then improved on it. In both cases, the killers got away with it.

Though assassins have improved so have the investigators. There has been a problem with virtually every modern high-profile assassination: cover-ups have unravelled and official inquiries have been exposed as whitewash, often contradicted by the ballistics and other forensic evidence. Official reports have a common thread: all the evidence points to one inescapable conclusion, yet the judges conclude the opposite, which is one not supported by the evidence. As each successive official version has crumbled the public has become increasingly cynical and many opinion polls in different countries show that the conspiracy theory of assassinations is now generally accepted, but this does not necessarily mean that where there is a mysterious death there is necessarily an assassination.

It's all, ultimately, a matter of evidence . . .

6

GET YOUR COVER STORY STRAIGHT

'Will no one rid the kingdom of this turbulent priest?'
Henry II of England 1170 *CE*

'I found in my experience that presidents used the entire range of
the English language from euphemisms on the one extreme to
very explicit talk on the other.'
Richard Helms, Director CIA 1966–73

**Westminster Abbey, London, 19 December 1154 CE,
the coronation of Henry II, King of England ...**
By any measure Henry II of England is smart, becoming King
of England in 1154 CE. Aged just twenty-one, he inherits a vast
and unruly area stretching from Scotland to the Pyrenees,
including half of France. On day one, his big problem is that he
is taking power after decades of anarchy. His lands are not
really under his control, but ruled by barons, protected by
mercenary armies in fortified castles. Bursting with the sort of
energy which would have made Alexander the Great proud, he
puts together a strike force and smashes them one by one,

unifying the kingdom and installing order, peace and security. At his side is an equally smart young chancellor, Thomas Becket, a brilliant middle-class lawyer whose precocious talents have been spotted by Theobald, the Archbishop of Canterbury, who sends him to Europe to fine tune his legal skills. When the young Becket returns, he goes into the church, becoming Archdeacon at Canterbury. The king is similarly impressed by the remarkable administrative skills of this man and makes him Secretary of State, shortly after taking the crown.

At thirty-six, Becket is a worldly man, a pre-Renaissance figure and fifteen years older than his king. He is equally devoted to his friends, hosting the best banquets in England, while never forgetting his Christian duty of helping the poor. In war, he is a clever commander, strategically acute in the campaigns he plans. On the battlefield, he earns the respect of his knights, leading seven hundred of them into combat. No back-seat general, he fights hand to hand in close-quarter single combat. In peace, he is a clever bureaucrat and quickly organizes the machinery of government to run smoothly for his king. All the nobles are obliged to pay monthly taxes, proper records are kept and he fires the incompetent and stupid from local government, replacing them with a new class of civil servants. The partnership of king and chancellor is devastatingly effective. Though everyone is taxed more heavily than before they get a lot in return: stability, the introduction of jury trials and the establishment of the rule of common law to replace the previous capricious feudal lottery of the courts. On the diplomatic front Becket is superb. When Henry sends him to Paris to negotiate with the French he astounds his hosts with an opulent display of power and wealth: eight chariots, forty horses and two hundred servants, prompting the gossips to ask, if the chancellor is that rich, how wealthy is his boss, the king?

Back home, the major domestic issue is the administration of justice. While they are reforming the courts, Henry and Thomas Becket are confronted with a major problem: one in six work for the church and are therefore covered by their own courts, which puts them outside the criminal law and beyond the reach of the state. Henry wants the 'criminous clerks' brought under the royal courts in a system of equal justice for all. As it stands, even if they are found guilty, the usual punishment is demotion to the status of layman, so Henry's legal system can then only pick them up if they re-offend.

Everything is going well for the young king and his chancellor until 1161, when the Archbishop of Canterbury dies. Though the Church is not under his strict control Henry manipulates the appointment to ensure that his closest ally gets the job, after all this is the man who once ordered a lord to 'hold free and fair elections and elect my man Robert into the post'. Thomas Becket tells the King that this is not going to be a wise choice because if he heads up the Church he will inevitably have to defend its interests against the crown. Hot-blooded and sure of his own judgement, Henry overrules his friend, assuming that once Thomas is the leading Churchman in England then reform of the antiquated and deeply divisive system of church courts will go ahead. It is his single biggest mistake.

As soon as he becomes Archbishop, Thomas Becket changes, turning his back on his old life, giving up his palace, the robes celebrating his sumptuous earthly magnificence as well as his posh friends. He wears a hair shirt next to his skin, gives up the extravagant feasting of the Plantagenet court for a frugal vegetarian diet of vegetables and grains and – as part of his routine of penance – washes the feet of thirteen beggars every night.[1] The man who is now the closest to God (outside Rome) is obdurate: he refuses to even negotiate with the king and demands to keep the restrictive practices, protecting criminals on the Church payroll.

As often is the case, it is a single incident which inflames all sides. A Canon at Bedford, Philip de Brois, is charged with murdering a knight but acquitted by the judge, who (conveniently for him) is the Bishop of Lincoln. Henry, a man with a choleric temper, is incensed and tries – without success – to have him re-tried in a civil court. Becket tries to appease the king and banishes Philip de Brois, but this only angers Henry even more. Sending Philip de Brois out of the country carries a strong presumption of guilt, but once out he is even further from the justice he deserves. Henry is trying to repair the civil order after the corrosive destruction of a bitter civil war. What greater affront can there be to his authority than to watch a murderer walk free? Henry suggests a compromise: that the civil courts only deal with serious offenders but this too is rejected by the fundamentalist archbishop. All sides meet and try to resolve the dispute through a sixteen-clause contract.[2] Becket prevails on the bishops to sign it, but then repudiate it immediately afterwards, which is exactly what happens, enraging the king even more.

The dispute escalates. Henry has Becket convicted on trumped up charges and forces him into exile, where he stays for the next six years, only returning in 1170 CE, when the king's son, Henry the Younger, is crowned by the Archbishop of York at Becket's old church, the cathedral at Canterbury. Snubbed and with his mortal pride wounded, Becket decides to return and crown the King's son himself for a second time. Everything is agreed with Henry and reconciliation even looks possible, but as soon as Becket returns to England he immediately excommunicates the bishops who have collaborated with Henry in his absence, including the Archbishop of York. Henry is at his Christmas court in Normandy when he hears the news. This is the point at which he explodes, famously shouting, 'Will no one rid the kingdom of this turbulent priest?'

Four knights – Reginald Fitz Urse, Hugh de Merville, Richard le Breton and William de Tracy – mount up their horses and set off across the Channel to Canterbury, where they try to persuade Becket to return with them to explain himself to the King. Becket refuses. They return the next day to the cathedral to arrest him and take him back to France. According to the main eyewitness of the assassination, Edward Grim, the knights enter the cathedral 'in a spirit of mad fury' shouting, 'where is Thomas Becket, traitor to the king and the realm?' Becket makes no attempt to flee, making the argument of martyrs everywhere (and more recently suicide bombers), telling them, 'I am ready to die for my Lord, that in my blood the Church may obtain peace and liberty.' The knights try to drag him outside but when this fails they each strike him on the head with their swords. As Becket lies dying on the floor, a clerk who comes in with them puts his foot on the Archbishop's neck, scattering his blood and brains about the stone floor of the cathedral. Becket is dead before they mount their horses to flee. And before they reach the coast, the locals swarm on the church, collecting souvenirs of his blood and torn-off fragments of his blood-soaked clothes. His pallium (outer cloak) is given to the poor to pray for his soul, but they promptly sell it 'for a paltry sum of money'. The local monks are so worried that his corpse will be stripped and 'so precious a treasure taken from them' that they bury him without washing or embalming the body[3] . . .

This is one of the classic assassinations, one which has greatly influenced what has happened subsequently. Henry II (even though his hand was not on the sword) had his immediate wish satisfied, which was the removal of the turbulent priest who was thwarting him at every stage. But the savage murder – on consecrated ground in a deeply religious time – backfired, as Becket first became an instant martyr and then a saint two years later. Henry was forced to do public penance, walking the last three miles to Canterbury barefoot. At the cathedral, he prostrated himself at the tomb of the man who had once been his closest ally and begged the monks to flog him, which they duly did. Thousands of pilgrims flocked to the cathedral and, predictably, miracles were reported. Canterbury became one of the great holy sites of Christendom where the judicious installation of a souvenir shop at the shrine also helped make it one of the wealthiest. Though the archbishop was out of the way, the problem of the 'criminous clerks' remained unsolved and the uneasy peace between church and state continued to dominate British politics for centuries to come.

Historians and commentators have been uniformly harsh towards Henry, condemning him as a vile murderer of a decent and saintly man, but a re-examination of the original documents suggests a very different interpretation. Henry was a great reforming king opposed by an unyielding religious fundamentalist, who simply refused to negotiate and took every opportunity to use his power base in the church to snub his king. Furthermore Becket was the one man protecting a system which allowed murderers and major criminals to walk free simply because they were loosely attached to the church. Henry's frustration was clear, particularly when Becket arbitrarily excommunicated those senior clerics who were prepared to work with the Crown. The king did not call for Becket's assassination, only for him to be removed from the kingdom. The eyewitness statement of Edward Grim, who was there in the cathedral at the time, makes this clear: 'then they made a rush at him and laid sacrilegious hands upon him, pulling and dragging him roughly and violently, endeavouring to get him outside the walls of the church and there slay him or bind him and carry him off prisoner.' Far from being a passive martyr, Becket fought them off, after all this was a man who not so long before had been a brilliant soldier, fighting in hand-to-hand combat on the frontline. Grim continues, 'but as he could not easily be moved from the pillar, one of them seized hold of him and clung to him more closely. The archbishop shook him off vigorously, saying, 'Touch me not Reginald. You owe me fealty and obedience. You are acting like a madman, you and your accomplices.' At this point, things got out of hand. 'All aflame with a terrible fury at this rebuff, the knight brandished his sword against that consecrated head,' telling Becket that he owed him neither obedience nor faith, his loyalty was to his king. What had started out as an arrest turned into murder when the knights lost sight of their mission and lost control of themselves as the first knight struck Becket with his sword and the others then joined in.

From a narrow legalistic point it is difficult to sustain the charge of murder against Henry as he did not order his knights to assassinate Becket. His crime was a loose use of language. He only called for Becket's removal, not his assassination, and it is clear that the knights' original intention was to arrest Becket and take him back with them. The eyewitness Edward Grim makes it clear that they were trying to drag him out of the church, he believed either to take Becket back to France or kill him outside, though this is unlikely as the knights would be circumspect about murdering him in front of the inevitable crowd which was gathering in the cathedral grounds.

This is not to condone the assassination of Becket but Henry's frustration is understandable. The archbishop had simply refused to negotiate in any meaningful way. He had rejected the excellent compromise offered by the king (that only serious criminals were tried in the state courts and the rest were dealt with by the church) and he stubbornly insisted on offering the Church's protection to murderers and major criminals. At its heart this was a row about power between a nationalist sovereign who believed that he should govern his country in the best way he could and an overbearing, arrogant and inflexible church in Rome, which believed in its own absolute power and the complete obedience of all monarchs to it. For Henry, this was an intolerable straitjacket, made worse by the fact that his closest ally had changed sides, effectively moving to head office, from where he could torment his former boss with impunity, tightening the straps at will.

This single assassination and the gap between command and deed is crucial to understanding the use of assassination by modern democratic states, particularly by the British and Americans. The significance of this single killing was far greater than an early skirmish between the modern state and the medieval church. It created the notion of plausible deniability, which was then automatically built into all subsequent British and American assassination plans. Modern assassins study their precedents and though Americans are often accused of knowing little history (even their own) this particular assassination and the valuable lessons that came from it are seared into the CIA consciousness. According to their longest-ever serving head, Richard Helms, the example of Henry and Becket 'spans the generations and the centuries'.[4] The context for this remark was the US Senate Committee, which convened in 1975 to investigate the assassination of foreign leaders. The two key points they wanted to establish were: did the various American presidents know of the assassination attempts against foreign leaders and more importantly, did they authorize them? Discovering what had happened was relatively easy. Finding out where the orders came from and exactly who authorized the assassinations was a very different matter and the inquiry spent a great deal of time camped in the linguistic territory first mapped out by Henry II and Thomas Becket in twelfth-century England. Despite many skirmishes with the English language, they still emerged confused.

As they tried to unravel the numerous CIA plots to assassinate Fidel Castro, the intractable issues were euphemism and meaning but the context they used to understand what had happened was England in 1170. Helms outlined to the senators how he used euphemisms to skirt round the problem and was asked whether he was alone in this or whether presidents used euphemisms as well. Helms, who was CIA director under Presidents Lyndon Johnson and Richard Nixon, replied, 'I found in my experience that presidents used the entire range of the English language from euphemisms on the one extreme to very explicit talk on the other.' Senator Mathias then brought up Henry II, asking 'when Thomas Beckett was proving to be an annoyance, as Castro, the king said who will rid me of this man? He didn't say to someone go out and murder him. He said who will rid me of this man and let it go at that.' Helms replied enigmatically, 'that is a warming reference to the problem'. Having agreed this example spanned the generations and centuries, Mathias then asked whether this was 'typical of the kind of thing which might be taken by the director or by anybody else as presidential authorization to go forward?' Helms replied, 'That is right' adding 'one sort of grows up in the tradition of the time and I think that any of us would have found it very difficult to discuss assassinations with a president of the United States. I just think we all had the feeling that we were hired out to keep those things out of the Oval Office.' Mathias was still not happy because there clearly had been assassination plots, yet no one seemed to have given any orders for them. He and the other committee members clearly suspected that the assassination orders came directly from the president, the question was exactly how. He pursued Helms, asking 'and yet at the same time you felt that some spark had been transmitted that that was within the permissible limits?' Helms replied 'Yes.'

The 'spark' was transmitted with great clarity. The Kennedy White House ordered the CIA to 'get rid' of Castro and there were no limitations on just how they did it, short of military invasion. After the fiasco of the Bay of Pigs, no one had any stomach for that, but there was no shortage of support for assassination. Everyone was frustrated and there was no shortage of 'nutty schemes' suggested as the White House turned up the pressure on the CIA, 'white heat' as Helms called it. One senior CIA officer, Richard Bissell (who was at the heart of the assassination programme) described meeting the Kennedys and being 'chewed out in the cabinet room of the White House by both the president and the attorney general for sitting on my ass and not getting rid of Castro and the Castro regime'.[5] This pressure was then amplified as it got passed down the line, with the US Secretary of Defense, Robert McNamara remarking that 'We were hysterical about Castro . . . and there was pressure from JFK [President Kennedy] and RFK [his brother Robert] to do something about Castro.'[6] The minutes of one meeting were clear, 'No time, money, effort or manpower is to be spared.'[7] The note continued, 'Yesterday the president had indicated . . . that the final chapter had not been written – it's got to be done and will be done.' For Helms, the meaning was clear. Writing Castro's final chapter meant assassinating him. The problem for the Committee investigating the assassination plans was that the Kennedys knew their history and the story of Henry II. Plausible deniability was built into their every move.

Echoing the CIA assassination manual written over twenty years before, Helms told the Committee, 'Assassination plots would not be authorized in any formal way'.[8] Specifically, he argued, 'These schemes would have taken place in the context of doing what you could to get rid of Castro and the difficulty with this kind of thing, as you gentlemen are all painfully aware, is that nobody wants to embarrass a president of the United States discussing the assassination of foreign leaders in his presence.' In a telling remark, Helms went on, 'This is something which has got to be dealt with in some other fashion' adding that 'even though you use euphemisms you've still got a problem.' As another CIA officer, Bill Harvey, remarked, 'No one wanted to charge the president personally with the complete, dirty-handed details of the assassination plans.'[9]

To get round the formal reporting structure, Kennedy did what subsequent presidents have also done: he set up a special group outside the normal CIA/White House nexus.[10] The operation was called MONGOOSE and Edward Lansdale was put in charge. McNamara's Deputy, Roswell Gilpatric, was asked whether the killing of Castro by a paramilitary group was within bounds. A career diplomat who lived his political life in the space between words, he replied, 'I know of no restriction that would have barred it.'[11] Lansdale had no doubts either and put together plans for biological and chemical warfare against Cuban sugar workers as well as dropping leaflets on Cuba offering rewards, ranging from $5,000 for anyone who assassinated an 'informer' to $100,000 for anyone killing a 'government official,'[12] a scheme devised to set neighbour against neighbour. One utterly bizarre nutty scheme of Lansdale's was to spread the rumour that the Second Coming of Christ was due and on that date an American submarine would fire star shells over Cuba, a scheme dubbed sarcastically 'elimination by illumination'.[13] More seriously, the Caribbean Survey Group (which was one of its other cover names) then contacted the mafia to enlist their help in assassinating Castro.

This operation is one of the most embarrassing in CIA history. Lyndon Johnson asked for a report from the Agency's Inspector General but the contents were so damaging that neither he nor his successor Richard Nixon were allowed to see it. No secretaries were used and the Inspector General typed his own report. Only one copy was kept and then burnt along with all the source materials. It was, however, reconstructed from the ribbon.[14]

The CIA's technical staff were at their most ingenious. They built a special assassination weapon as ingenious as anything the Soviets had ever produced: a Paper Mate pen with a syringe full of a poison called Black Leaf 40. The needle was so fine the victim would not feel it as it punctured their skin. Its creator boasted that it would be like a scratch from a shirt containing too much starch. Poison pills based on a shellfish toxin were also made and passed to the mafia but these plans also failed. The CIA got ever more imaginative. There was a contaminated skin diving suit to be given to Castro as a present and a booby-trapped sea shell to be put in an area where he was known to dive. This scheme was abandoned after the CIA bought a couple of books on molluscs and found that the shells they were planning to use did not come from the Caribbean and there were no local ones either big enough to hold the explosive or attractive enough to catch Castro's eye. There was one other problem: the mini submarine which was to detonate the explosive did not have a long enough range to get sufficiently close.

Other schemes included one to spray LSD into the radio station while Castro was on air, as well as cigars full of mind-altering drugs that would cause him to behave weirdly

and a depilatory drug to make his beard fall out. As always with
the 'nutty schemes' of any intelligence service, farce was built
in. One of the CIA officers was unconvinced that the poison
pills would work so he gave Dr Gunn, the scientist from the
Agency's technical services department, some money to go and
buy guinea pigs for testing. The guinea pigs then dutifully
chomped their way through the most deadly poisons the CIA
could produce and carried on snuffling their way round their
cages. Further research demonstrated that they were immune to
this poison. Monkeys were drafted in and they obediently died
when given the toxin. Though they could kill monkeys in cages,
it was a different matter trying to assassinate a smart and
resolute foreign leader. When all else failed, the CIA went back
to simpler technology: explosives, detonators, twenty .30
calibre rifles, .45 calibre hand guns, high-powered rifles, night
sights and silencers.

On May 7 1962, Helms and other CIA officers briefed
Robert Kennedy, the Attorney General and the president's
brother, telling him that they were working with the mafia to
assassinate Castro and had agreed to pay $150,000 to Sam
Giancana, the Cosa Nostra boss of Chicago, to find a gunman
to go down to Cuba and kill Castro. Kennedy then briefed the
FBI boss Edgar Hoover about his meeting. Hoover's detailed
note read, 'Robert A. Maheu, a private detective in Washington
DC, to approach Giancana with a proposition of paying
$150,000 to hire some gunmen to go into Cuba to kill Castro'.
A week later the CIA official note of the meeting was circulated
but it contained no mention of the assassination plot. But there
can be little doubt that Robert Kennedy was briefed and that
he in turn told his brother, a briefing which must have been
excruciating for Jack Kennedy who was sharing a mistress,
Judith Exner, with Giancana.[15]

Exner was not called as a witness and Giancana never got to
testify. In the middle of the Church Committee hearings he was
assassinated with a bullet in the back of the head. Six further
bullets were fired into his face, making a neat circle round his

mouth, the symbolism of which was not lost on anyone.[16] His assassin has never been found. The day after, the CIA Director William Colby made a bizarre announcement, saying 'We had nothing to do with it.'

In another exchange, the committee explored the verbal chasm between orders and actions, pursuing this with an executive assistant who had passed on the orders though he had not been present when they were agreed. First of all he told the committee that he 'wouldn't expect any president to sign a piece of paper directing an assassination for any reason. I don't think that is done in any government,' adding that they would not find 'a piece of paper for everything that this Agency or any other Agency has done . . . There are lots of things that get done by word of mouth.' It soon became clear that once the orders were handed down no subordinate would ever go above his boss's head to check or confirm their veracity. When he was challenged that the orders to assassinate Castro were based on assumption or speculation, he made an extraordinary claim saying, 'I think it is based upon the integrity [sic] of the people who passed on the orders. And it is all oral.' So that was it. Though they were involved in a whole series of conspiracies to commit assassination, the men at the top were men of integrity who could be trusted to honestly carry out the wishes of their president. And as a further mark of their integrity some of these CIA officers then bragged to the senators that they would then lie to protect their president.'[17]

In the end it all came down to language, which was both clear in its meaning and opaque in its accountability. As one CIA officer said, 'if he [Castro] had disappeared from the scene they [the Kennedys] would not have been unhappy.' Henry was also probably not unhappy that Becket had disappeared from the scene, though upset that, unlike any president of the United States, he had to do public penance. Worse still, he was indelibly linked to Becket's murder, which made the reform of the courts he so desperately wanted, virtually impossible. The CIA had learned from Henry and, like the presidents they served, they understood the potential backlash from assassination and had devised a system that allowed them to carry out the president's wishes (which included the assassination of foreign leaders) with the orders (such as they were) emanating from a crack in the system, or which no one could ultimately be held responsible. They had learned from Henry's example and inserted layers of deniability into the system so that no American president would ever have to do public penance.

The superbly articulate Helms summed it all up neatly, a masterpiece of prose defining the relationship between any spy master and his political masters: 'In my twenty-five years in the Central Intelligence Agency I always thought I was working within authorization, that I was doing what I had been asked to do by proper authority and when I was operating on my own I was doing what I believed to be the appropriate business of the Agency as it would have been expected of me.' In a proactive world this meant assassination. 'No member of the Kennedy administration ever told me that assassination was proscribed or ever referred to it in that fashion. Nobody ever said that assassination was ruled out.' As far as Helms was concerned, delivering poison pills to Cuba 'seemed to be within the permissible part of this effort,'[18] even though he told the committee that he personally did not like assassination and banned its use when he became Director of the CIA, though others in the Agency at the time are highly sceptical that Helms imposed any such ban.

The Secretary of Defense Robert McNamara was also asked to explain what went on in this strange political hinterland where the relationship between command and action, word and meaning was entirely fluid. Before he attempted clarification, he warned the committee that his answer would only further their uneasiness. His answers were sublimely contradictory. On the one hand, he did not accept that the CIA was a rogue elephant rampaging out of control, instead arguing that it was a highly disciplined organization under the control of senior officials (of which he was the most senior) and everything they had done had been authorized. He did not believe that there had been any misunderstanding and he accepted that there had been assassination plans. He then claimed not to know of them, even though he would have been the person to authorize them, something he found 'impossible to reconcile'. He concluded, 'I just don't understand how it could have happened.' Had Senator Church and his colleagues decided at this point to retreat to a darkened room with a set of cold towels to put on their heads no one would have blamed them.

After months of investigation, dozens of witnesses and millions of words the committee was, ultimately, not much wiser. All the assassinations (both actual and attempted) were exactly what the president and his closest adviser (the attorney general, Bobby Kennedy) wanted. These operations took place over months, some over years. Dozens of CIA officers and others were involved and millions of tax dollars were spent, but no one ever appeared to have actually given any clear orders. The line of command was fractured and full of black holes where the audit trail simply disappeared. No one was responsible as ultimately everyone was a man of integrity who had behaved honestly and properly even though they were all involved in the greatest crime of all, cold-blooded premeditated murder of other human beings.

The committee would have been better off taking their cue from Alice in Lewis Carroll's,[19] *Through the Looking Glass*, written just over a hundred years before. She challenges Humpty Dumpty over his use of the word 'glory' which he claims means 'there's a nice knock down argument for you!' When she objects, he tells her, 'When I use a word it means what I choose it to mean – neither more nor less.' Alice retorts, 'The question is whether you can make words mean so many different things?' but he has the final word, telling her, 'The question is which is to be master, that's all.'

There is one incident which would have helped the committee to understand exactly what was going on here and who was master, but at the time the key witness kept silent. Edward

Lansdale was the American general who had run Operation MONGOOSE, the White House's secret war against Cuba.

Lansdale was also a Vietnam veteran and in autumn 1963 he was summoned to the White House for a clandestine meeting. Present were two others: President Kennedy and his Secretary of Defense Robert McNamara. Kennedy asked Lansdale if he would go back to Vietnam to try and persuade President Diem to separate himself from his brother Nhu, whom he described as 'an evil genius'. A career soldier and enthusiast for anything clandestine, Lansdale indicated that he was willing to take on the mission, but then Kennedy put the bite on him, asking him what would happen if he failed and he could not persuade Nhu to leave. 'If that didn't work out – or if I change my mind – and decide that we have to get rid of Diem himself, could you go along with that?' Though Kennedy did not use the words 'kill' or 'assassinate' Lansdale was in no doubt that this was what he was being asked to do. Lansdale was anything but morally squeamish, having been quite happy to assassinate Castro, his brother and any number of anonymous Cubans, but he shook his head slowly and told Kennedy, 'No, Mr President. I couldn't do that. Diem is a friend of mine and I couldn't do that.' Kennedy had chosen the one man in the intelligence apparatus who would not take part in his murderous plans. For Lansdale, assassinating a close friend and a long-term ally of the United States was a kill too far. Besides, Lansdale, like others in the American intelligence services, believed that Diem was their best choice of defeating North Vietnam. The meeting ended and McNamara was furious. As they drove back to the Pentagon, McNamara told him, 'You can't talk to a president that way. When the president wants you to do something, you don't just say to him, no you won't do it.' McNamara never spoke to Lansdale again, whose career ended at that moment. He did not receive the promotion he was expecting and a month later – as he was clearing his desk at the Pentagon – he heard that Diem had been assassinated.[20] Others had done the president's bidding.

But assassination as a clandestine tool of foreign policy is an addictive drug. Gerald Ford, who was the White House incumbent during the Church Committee hearings, recognized this and signed the presidential ban on the assassination of world leaders,[21] which was further endorsed by his successors, Jimmy Carter and Ronald Reagan. But while Carter believed he should obey his own orders, Reagan did not. The ban remained – in public at least – but deniability was all and by the time he was installed in the White House in 1980, assassination was once again high on the clandestine foreign policy agenda. His new CIA Chief Bill Casey was his victorious campaign manager and a fundamentalist Cold War warrior who knew best. Casey had little recent intelligence experience and no time for anyone in the CIA who did not tell him exactly what he wanted to hear. Like the Kennedy brothers before him, he wanted a general assassination capability, which could be accessed by the White House to remove the troublesome, wherever they were on the globe. However, there were many in the CIA who were still smarting from the embarrassments of the 1970s and were opposed to the use of assassination, but they would be outmanoeuvred by an aggressive White House, which – as ever – held all the high cards.

There was tension from the start when the CIA analysts told the White House that the Soviets were now pretty much out of the business of sponsoring international terrorism, but this was not intelligence which either Reagan or Casey would tolerate. As far as they were concerned Russia was the evil empire and the Kremlin was the puppet master pulling the strings of their surrogates throughout the world. Unfortunately for the White House, the Kremlin was inconveniently silent and refused to match the Reagan stereotype, but there was one man who was wonderfully noisy, Colonel Muammar Qaddafi of Libya, who had long been regarded by many American politicians, particularly the neo-conservatives, as the world's most evil man and the source of most global terrorism.[22]

Shortly after Reagan came to office there was little intelligence that suggested that Qaddafi was going to assassinate the

American president, and many senior CIA analysts were highly doubtful that he had either the desire or the capability. Regardless of their scepticism, a major news story broke – on cue – about Libyan assassination hit teams in the United States whose target was Ronald Reagan. The story played very big in the American media and the nation stepped up a gear into near panic mode. Qaddafi was interviewed on American television and though he passionately denied he was trying to assassinate Ronald Reagan it was round one to the White House. His denials were discounted and the story was later shown to be a fabrication, the source being an Iranian arms dealer, Manuchar Ghorbanifar, who wanted to stir up trouble for the Libyans.[23] But none of that mattered. The public agenda was set: Qaddafi was an assassin and something must be done about him. Having been burned by what was little more than single source intelligence, the CIA analysts then took a more considered position and throughout the early 1980s briefed the White House that though Qaddafi was in the assassination business, his hit teams only killed other Libyans, the 'stray dogs' as he called them. But this intelligence was ignored by the Reagan White House which preferred to believe its own propaganda, particularly the work of Claire Sterling, who was busy extruding a steady diet of Cold War nonsense of plots and conspiracies, all leading back to the Soviet bloc.

Her two main books: *The Terror Network*, which was the public expression of every neo-conservative prejudice about the Soviet Union; and *Time of the Assassins*, a preposterous 'investigation' which attempted to prove that the Bulgarians were behind an all-reaching conspiracy surrounding the attempt to assassinate Pope John Paul II in 1981. When challenged in 1985 to produce a single shred of hard evidence to support her book, she conceded that 'it was a hypothesis'. A brilliant propagandist, her work had been done by this time and many (including the BBC) had bought into it, but her greatest fan was President Reagan, who read her stuff in the *Reader's Digest* and believed it, even though it was the CIA's own 'cooking'.

The more worldly view among the CIA's expert analysts was that the really dangerous countries in the Middle East, like Syria, were too big for the US to tackle so whenever anything went wrong it was much easier to attack Libya, 'kicking the cat' in the words of Vincent Canistraro, the highly articulate former head of the CIA's Counter Terrorism Centre. Qaddafi was the perfect target for the Reaganites: he liked being attacked by the Americans as it enhanced his credibility in the Arab world and he could easily be provoked into making inflammatory statements, pretty much on cue. It was a balanced symbiotic relationship where everyone benefited even though it had little reference to anything that was actually happening in the real world.

Throughout Reagan's first term, the White House kept up the pressure both on Qaddafi and their allies. The State Department lobbied anyone who would listen but even the British were not buying, despite the incredibly close relation-ship between the British Prime Minister Margaret Thatcher and Ronald Reagan. The British Foreign Office rejected the American calls for invasion for three very good reasons: Qaddafi was an essential bulwark against Islamic fundamental-ism in north Africa; there was a substantial amount of trade between the two countries; and there were 6,500 British expatriates living happily in Libya, who would become potential hostages in the event of any precipitate action.

The Americans, with French help, fostered an attempted *coup d'état* following on from the assassination of WPC Yvonne Fletcher outside the Libyan People's Bureau in St James's Square in April 1984, but this was suppressed after several days of heavy street fighting. Qaddafi narrowly escaped assassination though he was shot in the buttock, a wound he proudly showed to visitors as his badge of courage in the great anti-imperialist struggle. This was not the first attempt to assassinate Qaddafi. It would not be the last.

At the end of January 1981, three days after being installed as CIA Chief, William Casey had received a twelve-page assessment of Qaddafi and Libya. Throughout his tenure, there were endless discussions in the CIA, the State Department and the White House about how to assassinate him. Getting an assassin inside his inner circle was impossible and the memories of trying and failing to do exactly this against Castro were still fresh. They financed exile groups like the National Front for the Salvation of Libya in the hope that they could assassinate Qaddafi during a coup. When this group (which consisted largely of intellectuals and students) failed they created their own. Millions of dollars were poured into a White House-created anti-Qaddafi group called Al Burkan, whose members then received military training in Berlin, but they were no match for Qaddafi's troops. Legal opinion to justify an assassination was sought and in case anyone had doubts about the quality of the advice, Reagan settled the issue. He told a meeting in 1985 that he would ignore his own ban on assassination and take the heat.

Finally, in 1986, after six years of relentless pressure, Reagan and Casey got their best chance to assassinate Qaddafi. The affair was carefully coordinated but, like previous assassination operations, the CIA and the White House left their fingerprints everywhere.

The battleground chosen for the US assassination operation was the long-standing issue of Libyan territorial waters, which had been a sore point since Carter's presidency. Five years earlier, in August 1981, the US had shot down two Libyan fighter jets there and the Reagan White House knew they could always provoke a Libyan response by challenging them over it, which they did at the beginning of 1986. Qaddafi immediately reasserted his claim to the Gulf of Sidra, poetically proclaiming a 'wall of death' which no one should cross. Two months later the Americans, with 45 ships and 200 planes from the Sixth Fleet, were anchored off the Libyan coast trying to provoke Qaddafi into a conflict, which he was guaranteed to lose. On 24 March, there was a series of minor skirmishes, during which the Libyans claimed to shoot down five American planes.

President Reagan dismissed this, saying there were no American casualties but a confidential Russian report by Air Force Marshal Koldunov was probably the closest, noting that Soviet specialists put the figure at three American losses.[24]

The Americans lobbied furiously throughout Europe to get support for an attack on Libya but there were no takers. Every European intelligence service could see what this was leading to and no one wanted a part of it.

Then on 5 April 1986 there was the single incident, the *casus belli* which the Americans needed for war, a terrorist bomb which exploded in the La Belle discothèque in Berlin. The nightclub was a well-known haunt for US forces stationed in Germany and this was a direct attack on the USA. A twenty-one-year-old US sergeant, Kenneth T. Ford, and a twenty-nine-year-old Turkish woman, Nermin Hannay, both died at the scene. Another sergeant, James E. Goins subsequently died of his injuries. Dozens of others were permanently disabled. Shortly afterwards, journalists were briefed that US Intelligence had intercepted cable traffic from the Libyan People's Bureau, implicating Tripoli and, by inference, Colonel Qaddafi. President Reagan was unequivocal, saying the US had 'direct, precise and irrefutable' proof that this was a Libyan-sponsored attack. However, West German intelligence officers who had seen the same intercepts were much more sceptical, arguing they were nothing more than unanalysed raw intelligence and therefore should be handled carefully. But imposing regime change in Libya was top of the Reagan agenda and such niceties were irrelevant. Then as now, politicians playing at being intelligence analysts and cherry-picking bits of intelligence to justify something they are going to do anyway is highly dangerous. The Reagan White House had just enough of a pretext to launch a military strike against Libya – and that strike was the cover for what was in reality an assassination attempt on Colonel Qaddafi.

The bomb which exploded in the La Belle discotheque looked remarkably like Libyan retaliation for the American

sinking of a couple of their patrol boats. Three months before
this President Reagan had warned that if Libya used terrorists
against American citizens, the US government would treat it as
if it was an attack by Libyan frontline troops and this would
justify a military response. It was a bizarre warning as the CIA's
own assessment was that Libya scrupulously avoided killing
American citizens, let alone servicemen on a night out. The
bomb gave the White House everything they needed to justify
their military attack. As far as they were concerned, they had
given a clear warning to the Libyans which was then ignored.
The Libyans had therefore invited the inevitable fatal consequences upon themselves.

The La Belle bomb was enough to change the attitude of the
British government. Three days after the explosion, President
Reagan sent a personal note to Margaret Thatcher asking for
permission to fly US planes from Britain. Late that night, Sir
Percy Craddock, the Chairman of the Joint Intelligence
Committee, was summoned to Downing Street. Though Mrs
Thatcher was keen to help the Americans, she was concerned
that the request was vague and she was also worried about both
the response in the Arab world and the risk to British hostages
in Lebanon. She also knew that just three months before she
had publicly condemned retaliatory strikes, which was exactly
what Reagan was now proposing, but she expressed general
support and fired back a list of questions. The US response was
immediate and tough. They told the British that they were
going ahead anyway, but Thatcher's questions had at least
focused US thinking. The US targets were now defined as
Qaddafi's headquarters, the offices of Libyan security and other
intelligence centres. Mrs Thatcher was also reminded of the
shooting of WPC Yvonne Fletcher outside the Libyan People's
Bureau two years before. It was enough to sway her though
there was the question of legality. The Attorney General Sir
Michael Havers suggested that the actions could be justified
under Article 51 of the United Nations Charter, which permits
military action in self-defence.[25] Though no Britons were killed

in the La Belle disco, the little coterie round Mrs Thatcher decided that they could get away with this assassination as it was part of 'a continuum of terrorist activity and we had the right to defend ourselves against coming dangers'.[26]

Had the little informal group in Downing Street known just how shaky the US intelligence on Libya was, it is doubtful they would have sanctioned the attack – for there was very little here which was as it seemed.

The La Belle bombers were a mixed bunch. Their leader, Musbah Eter, was a Libyan who worked at their embassy in Berlin and was very close to the CIA, a fact well known to the KGB and the Stasi, the East German secret police, who followed him to his regular meetings with his American paymasters. Another of the bombers, Mohammed Amairi, was an alleged Mossad agent. The rest of the gang were mercenary terrorists who would work for anyone who would pay them. The KGB and the Stasi decided that the whole gang were working for Western intelligence[27] and subsequently concluded that the sole purpose of the bombing was to implicate Libya. But none of this would be revealed until over a decade later. For the moment, the US occupied the moral high ground and had a pretext for attacking Libya.

Just over a week after the La Belle bomb, on 13 April 1986, Soviet Intelligence warned Qaddafi that an American raid was imminent,[28] but the Libyan leader ignored them. The Russians were right on the money. The day after, twenty-four F-111 jet fighters took off from Lakenheath air base in England, along with other US planes from RAF bases at Upper Heyford, Fairford and Mildenhall. By the time the fighters reached north Africa, the Americans had enough hardware for a full-scale modern war – in fact, they had more aircraft and combat ships than Britain used during the entire Falklands War. The Americans also flew three SR-71 Blackbird spy planes which had just entered the US Air Force, though this was never announced publicly. This was their first major combat mission but it was one dogged with technical problems. The first plane had engine trouble and the second suddenly veered to one side causing the pilot to smash his helmet as he tried to regain control. The third eventually got over the target and watched the damage unfold. All told, five targets were chosen, including one, the Murrat Side Bilal base, which the Pentagon said was being used to train terrorist frogmen for the PLO and other organizations, a slightly bizarre claim as combat swimming and naval commando operations have never been high on the weapons list of an organization better known for suicide bombers. While the planes were still in the air, President Reagan publicly described the operation as a matter of self-defence against Libya's state-sponsored terrorism. It was a bold claim but untrue. Operation El Dorado Canyon had one sole purpose: to assassinate Colonel Qaddafi.

The statistics and structure of the operation gave the game away. Shortly after 3 a.m., the US Navy began firing unmanned drones from the sea. At 3.35 a.m., the planes which had set off from Britain the day before flew in from the desert at fifty metres, under the Russian radar and took out the Libyan air-defence system. Twenty-five minutes later, they homed in on the only target that mattered: the barracks where the Americans believed Qaddafi was based. In all, five F-111s fired sixteen 2,000lb laser-guided Paveway II bombs (designed to take out major structures like bridges, command bunkers and SCUD launchers) at his tent, over a quarter of all the bombs dropped on the operation. This was the first time they were used and though they were advertised as delivering 'accuracy, reliability and cost-effectiveness previously unattainable with conventional weapons', they were useless as an assassination weapon if the target was not at home. Qaddafi was elsewhere that night and instead the US pilots killed an innocent non-combatant, his four-year-old adopted daughter.

The confidential Soviet report into the attack revealed that the Libyan defences were a shambles. On Qaddafi's orders, the Libyan air force of three hundred jet fighters, including eighty Mig-25 jet fighters, stayed on the ground. There was no command and control, the training had been abysmal and few knew how to operate the expensive Russian radar defences they had bought. Worse still, cowardice was rife and some crews fled as soon as the attacks started. The final upset for the Russians was that though they had advised the Libyans to upgrade their radar to pick up planes coming in below fifty metres, this was a recommendation which the Libyan military – 'due to its own arrogance' – had rejected. In a final affront, the Russians noted that their planes were not properly maintained, unlike the French aircraft which were, though none of this made any difference as all the Libyan planes stayed on the ground.

In the event, though Qaddafi ignored the Russian warnings about an imminent US attack he was also tipped off by the French who picked up the huge amount of aerial activity round their coasts. The Americans knew that the French had warned Qaddafi and were furious. On the way out of Libya one of their planes bombed the French embassy in Tripoli as well as causing huge casualties in the hospital next door, a publicity disaster for the Americans as these were the pictures which set the international news agenda. One of those involved afterwards said that they regretted bombing the hospital. When asked about the French embassy, he repeated, 'We very much regretted the bombing of the hospital.'[29] When asked again about the French embassy, he repeated himself, saying 'We very much regretted the bombing of the hospital' making it very clear that the attack on the French embassy was deliberate, revenge for what the Americans saw as Gallic treachery. Publicly, the Americans dismissed it as 'an accident'.

Though Mrs Thatcher was fêted in Washington, the consequences for the British hostages were fatal. Before they had agreed to give help, Mrs Thatcher and the little coterie round her had feared there would be reprisals in the Middle East. Their fears were spot on: three British hostages held in Beirut were shot. An English journalist, Alec Collett, who had been in Beirut working for the United Nations reporting on the plight of Palestinian refugees was assassinated, after being kidnapped the year before. His murderers, from a pro-Qaddafi group, released a shaky video of a black-hooded man being hanged in front of a cheering crowd. John McCarthy, a television reporter, and a group of other westerners were also kidnapped and would not be released for another five years. In all, it was far too high a price to pay for loyalty to an ally. It has been justified since by arguing that it calmed Qaddafi down and that he then abandoned his role as international terrorist in chief. However, there are many in both the British and American intelligence services who believed at the time that he was inactive on the terrorist front, solely concentrating on killing his Libyan opponents.

At no time did the Reagan administration ever admit publicly that this was an assassination attempt on Qaddafi. Neither did they own up to the fact that his assassination had been swirling round the top of the White House agenda for the previous five years. Mindful of the lessons of Henry II and Thomas Becket, as well as the presidential ban on the assassination of foreign leaders, it was dressed up as self-defence, though few, least of all those inside the White House or Downing Street, actually believed it.

The legal foundation for this attack was shaky at best. The US and the British both claimed it was allowed under the self-defence provisions of Article 51 of the United Nations Charter, but this was fatuous. This section of the charter says that countries have 'the inherent right of individual or collective self-defence if an armed attack occurs against a Member of the United Nations, *until* the Security Council has taken measures necessary to maintain international peace and security.'

Powerful Western governments have continually hidden behind this tiny legal fig leaf, but Article 51 does not sanction assassination. It deals specifically with an armed attack on a member state, not the murder of a soldier on a night out and a long way from home. There has to be a real, present and imminent danger to the nation as a whole and action can only be taken to protect the sovereign state until the UN can intervene.

But none of this mattered to the Reaganites. The La Belle discothèque gave them the excuse they wanted to attack Libya. Trying to assassinate Qaddafi was something they were going to do anyway and now they had a pretext. There was no major debate. In the words of Vincent Canistraro, the Reagan White House 'was looking for a *casus belli*, who is sponsoring it, let's punish them, let's retaliate'.[30]

The problem was that Britain had not been under attack so the close coterie round Mrs Thatcher came up with a second argument, which was no firmer than the first but at least it provided some small level of comfort. They argued that there was a continuum of Libyan terrorist activity against the West and therefore both Britain and the US had the right to protect themselves against unspecified but future dangers. The shooting of WPC Yvonne Fletcher two years before outside the Libyan People's Bureau in London helped Mrs Thatcher firm her position, though she knew nothing of the US involvement with Yvonne Fletcher's killers.

The British pledged their support to Reagan but emphasized that he needed to put this in the context of self-defence rather than retaliation. When Reagan went public with his response he took his cue from his closest international ally, arguing that the strike on Libya was not just a right but a duty under Article 51, a claim which stretched this clause way beyond its meaning.

But in reality this was little more than a legal fan dance. Though Mrs Thatcher and her close advisers publicly supported the Reagan White House, her Intelligence Chief Sir Percy Craddock (who also supported the raid) gave the game away in his memoirs, noting that the Americans were 'not too concerned with the niceties of international law'.[31]

The true nature of this charade would have become immediately apparent if two facts had been revealed at the time. The first is the true nature of the La Belle disco bomb. Had Mrs

Thatcher and her advisers known that it had been planted by someone close to the CIA, they would never have countenanced supporting the strike. The US Secretary of State could not have argued this case in front of the United Nations General Assembly. Justifying an assassination attempt against the head of a sovereign state on the basis that a small bomb in a disco on another continent constitutes an armed attack, especially when the device was planted by a terrorist who was subsequently on the American payroll, would have taken chutzpah of the very highest order. The second unpleasant fact was that the Reagan White House was intimately involved with the killers of WPC Yvonne Fletcher.

There was a second 'continuum' of state-sponsored terrorist activity here but it originated in Washington not Tripoli.

The simple legal fact is that in peacetime, the assassination of another is premeditated murder. Nothing more, nothing less. In wartime, it is different and the killing of another is sanctioned by law. But war has to be formally declared and a loose argument that this is part of the 'war on terror' does not apply any more than arguing that it is justified as part of the 'war on poverty' or 'the war on drugs'.

Though the US government did not sign the Kyoto Agreement, there is one area of recycling on which they are very keen: pretexts for assassination. Seven years later, the missiles flew again. Different president, different type of missile, different Arab despot but same old dodgy intelligence underlining a paper-thin pretext for assassination.

Fast forward to 16 June 1993. Twenty-three Tomahawk Cruise missiles were fired from US Navy warships in the Gulf and the Red Sea. Their target was the headquarters of the Mukhabarat, the Iraqi Intelligence Service. Once the missiles left the sea, they hugged the land through TERCOM (terrain counter matching) and were then guided to the target through a series of advanced electronics called DSMAC (digital scene matching area correlation). This abundance of acronyms (so loved by the military everywhere) is supposed to guarantee an accuracy of ten metres. In the event three missiles completely missed their targets, hitting nearby houses, killing eight, including one of Iraq's leading artists, Layla al-Attar. Clinton's popularity ratings jumped eleven points the next day, which at a million dollars a missile is PR money well spent.

The hope was to assassinate Saddam but as usual he was elsewhere. The specific justification for the attack was that the Iraqi leader had attempted to assassinate George Bush on a visit to Kuwait, but the evidence was even thinner and more questionable than it had been for the assassination attempt on Qaddafi. The prime source was the Kuwaitis, who already had a distinguished record for manufacturing untrue stories (Iraqi soldiers throwing babies out of incubators, post-war attempts to invade Kuwait) and then being caught out. The source for the assassination attempt story was a bunch of cigarette smugglers who had been captured, brutally tortured and confessed. Hardly reliable witnesses but their testimony was supported by the claim that the car bomb found matched similar car bombs used by the Iraqis in the Gulf War, but this turned out to be untrue. The parts used were standard issue and could be bought in any toy shop. There was one further very big clue that this was not an assassination attempt: the assassins were captured in the desert one day before George Bush was about to leave. They had been in Kuwait City, drinking illegally for three days and were on their way home.

But even if this had been an assassination attempt against the former president it still fell short of an armed attack against a country. Furthermore, in this case, the alleged plot had taken place two months before. Had Clinton believed that the USA was under armed attack, the response should have been immediate. Instead it was dictated by his fear that the FBI report into the affair would be leaked and he would look weak.

But the key problem with the liberal interpretation of this clause is that it cuts both ways. If powerful Western states assume to themselves the right of what is little more than a pre-emptive strike, is it surprising that the fundamentalists on the other side also believe that they too have the same right?

In August 1998, US missiles flew again. At least seventy-five Tomahawk cruise missiles were fired against Al Qaeda camps in eastern Afghanistan which US Intelligence believed were being used for training guerrillas. But the specific target was the Al-Badr base east of Kabul where NSA intercepts had led them to believe Osama Bin Laden was meeting with the Al Qaeda high command. This camp, ironically built by the CIA in the early 1980s, was virtually invisible from above and had a network of rooms underground with hydroelectric power from water running off the mountains. The Clinton administration had a legal ruling which said that the presidential ban on assassination did not apply to military targets. Bin Laden's farm was categorized as a military camp and so that legitimized the operation. But for the third time in twelve years, the missiles missed their target. It was not just the operational performance which was poor. The intelligence was dreadful and on the same day cruise missiles were also used to destroy the El Shifa factory in the Sudan. The CIA believed and Clinton then claimed that the factory was being used to make chemical weapons. In fact, it was a completely innocent installation, making medical drugs for commercial use, pharmaceuticals which were desperately needed in one of the world's poorest countries. While the attacks on the Al Qaeda camps were at least the right target, cynics were quick to point out that this action had conveniently taken the Lewinski sex scandal off the front pages, though the respite was only a brief one.

Clinton then turned to the CIA and their Afghan agents and authorized them to assassinate Bin Laden and his lieutenants. After the embarrassments of the Church Committee, the CIA insisted that President Clinton personally sign off on any assassination. The White House lawyers agonized over the wording and eventually it was agreed that lethal force could be used but there should be a good faith effort to arrest Bin Laden and the other Al Qaeda leaders. This was little more than legal casuistry as no one expected that anyone would be taken alive. Indeed, Bin Laden had stated that – if cornered – he would die fighting. The case history of Henry II and Thomas Becket continued to cast a long shadow. Verbal ambiguity was the trick here, the problem was that the CIA were reluctant to play the game so over the months the memos became stronger, ever greater levels of certainty being added. But regardless of what form of words was used, no one was in any doubt as to just what was being demanded. As Clinton's security adviser told Congress in 2002, 'It was no question, the cruise missiles were not trying to capture him. They were not law enforcement techniques.' As each was carrying 1,000lb of high explosives and not an arrest warrant, this was the ultimate statement of the obvious.

Each of these missile raids cost the US taxpayer millions of dollars but the final score was three assassination attempts (Qaddafi, Saddam, Bin Laden) and three expensive failures. The retaliation, when it came in the late 1990s, was lethal and devastating: attacks on the USS *Cole*, two US embassies in east Africa and then 9/11. Clinton characterized the struggle as one between freedom and fanaticism. The problem was that the fanatics had also assumed that they too had the right to launch retaliatory strikes, in what they also saw as the right to self-defence against the enemy.

In their determination to 'kick ass' and exploit the PR advantage of being seen to be tough, both Reagan and Clinton had forgotten the very first rule of assassination: cover your tracks.

7

WHENEVER YOU CAN, SET UP
A PATSY

'Did you shoot the president?'
'No, they've taken me in because of the fact that I lived in the
Soviet Union ... I'm just a patsy!'

Lee Harvey Oswald

King's Square, Tel Aviv, Israel, 4 November 1995 ...
The Israeli Prime Minister, Yitzhak Rabin, addresses a peace
rally. Though he is much admired by other world leaders for
his attempts to bring peace to the Middle East, he is loathed at
home. As he addresses the faithful, he knows that fewer than
one in five Israelis support the peace process with the
Palestinians, the rest want a national referendum, a vote he is
guaranteed to lose. Even more worrying for Rabin, he knows
that his imminent assassination is being widely discussed in
cafés and synagogues everywhere from Los Angeles to Tel
Aviv. Several months earlier, two words – *rodef and moser* –
had suddenly been injected into the conversation of daily life

for Jews everywhere. Until then, both had only ever been known to obscurantist Talmudic scholars. Under ancient Talmudic law, *din rodef* is a sacred duty laid on all Jews to kill another Jew who imperils the life or property of a Jew and *din moser* is the duty to eliminate a Jew who intends to turn another Jew over to non-Jewish authorities.[1] Though these two laws are many centuries old and apply to a completely different time in Jewish history, the rabbis on the far right argue that Rabin is both a *rodef* and a *moser* for giving away Jewish land to the Palestinians.

The country's intelligence services and the opposition Likud party, who oppose the peace process, stir up the right-wing religious fanatics. Rabin is smeared as a Nazi and a poster appears of him in a full German Nazi uniform. It is hard to think of a greater insult for a Jewish leader. It is now open season on Rabin and he is especially vulnerable as the fractured nature of Israeli politics is reflected in the security services, where there are many who also believe he is a *rodef*. By late 1995, Rabin is both powerful but vulnerable, the two key characteristics of the likely assassination victim.[2] As with other assassinations, the subject of his impending murder is in the air, just part of the daily gossip round. There are only two serious questions: where and when. The who is largely irrelevant. There are major political forces at work now and if one assassin does not get him, another one will.

Inside the stadium, Rabin clutches a song sheet and pleads the case for peace but outside a young law student, Yigal Amir, his head full of dodgy theology, nurses a Beretta semi-automatic handgun.[3] The *din rodef* argument is crucial: for Amir, it makes the issue simple. Rabin wants to give Israeli land to the Arabs. He is therefore a *rodef*. It is the binding duty of every good Jew to assassinate him and as he is a good Jew he has no choice. Amir subsequently tells his interrogators, 'without the halakhic ruling or the *din rodef* which were issued against Rabin by a number of rabbis that I know of, I would have had difficulty murdering him. Such a murder must have backing. If I had no backing . . . I would not have acted.'[4]

Though Rabin's bodyguards should be on heightened alert, they are not. Amir is a well-known fundamentalist, part of a group which is noisy about their desire to assassinate Rabin, yet he is left unchallenged in what should be a sanitized area. On the roof above, as Rabin walks out, is an accountant, thirty-seven-year-old Ronni Kempler from the State Comptroller's Office, who films the whole event. He is not searched or questioned beforehand, a strange omission, as he could just as easily have been a sniper, with a very easy shot.

The Deputy Prime Minister Shimon Peres comes out first and hangs around, followed a couple of minutes later by Rabin, flanked by bodyguards. As Rabin walks towards his car the bodyguard on his left shoulder stops walking, leaving Rabin unprotected. Amir steps forward, draws his pistol and fires. Some of the security pounce on him, hurling him to the ground. According to Yoram Rubin, Rabin's head of personal security, 'We jumped, really jumped. I'm surprised that a man his age could jump like that.' They bundle him into his limousine and drive to the nearby Ichilov hospital.

Rabin is pronounced dead at 11.15 p.m. that evening, another statistic in a long tradition of Jews assassinating other Jews. According to one estimate he is the ninety-second political assassination in the previous one hundred years.[5] Dr Gabi Barabash, the hospital director, is asked by a television reporter about the wounds and he replies, 'There was a wound to the spleen and a gaping hole in the chest leading to the backbone. The first bullet was not necessarily fatal. The other bullet tore apart vessels leading to the heart and shattered his spine . . . The prime minister died of spinal shock.' An hour later, the Health Minister, Ephraim Sneh appears on television to tell a shocked Israeli nation that Rabin had taken three bullets, 'one in the chest, one in the stomach and one in the spine'.[6] This line is picked up by the world's media (including the BBC) and faithfully repeated . . .

* * *

So there it is: an open and shut assassination of a major world statesman cut down as he tried to drag a recalcitrant Israeli nation down the road to peace with its neighbours.

Yigal Amir was immediately identified as a 'lone nut' by the Israeli security services, another one in the great tradition of crazed assassins, both well known like John Wilkes Booth (Abraham Lincoln), Lee Harvey Oswald (Jack Kennedy), Sirhan Sirhan (Robert Kennedy) and James Earl Ray (Martin Luther King) as well as the not so well known, including Leon Csolgosz (President William McKinley), Al-Sayyed Nussair (Rabbi Meir Kahane) and Romeo Vasquez Sanchez (Castillo Armas). Amir confirms his lone-nut status, telling the judge that 'my whole life, I learned Halacha [the Jewish legal code]. When you kill in war it is an act that is allowed' When asked whether he acted alone, he replied 'It was God.'

Famously, Lee Harvey Oswald shouted out that he was just 'a patsy', an innocent who was set up to take the rap. The problem with patsies is that some refuse to go quietly and continue to protest their innocence but Yigal Amir was the perfect choice. He was so convinced he had assassinated Rabin that he refused to believe the ballistics, video and other forensic evidence that proved that he could not possibly have killed his prime minister.[7]

The big problem for the Israelis behind the assassination was that the official version of events was carefully laid out for the public but then a couple of months after the assassination, Kempler popped up with his video, which undermined all the official announcements. His video showed that Amir approached to about five feet *behind* Rabin's left shoulder before firing. He was never *in front* of Rabin and could not therefore have fired the fatal shot into his chest ('a gaping hole in the chest leading to the backbone'). Neither does he fire three times. Not for the first time is there a complete mismatch between the number of bullets claimed and the actual number fired.

Ever since then, the official version of events has slowly unravelled as more of the forensic and other evidence has been revealed.[8] The Shamgar Commission, which investigated the assassination, concluded that Amir shot Rabin twice in the back, once from about fifty centimetres and then in the lower back while standing thirty centimetres above him. The commission then said that he also shot Rabin's bodyguard, again from about thirty centimetres above. However, there are serious problems with this: it does not match the footage, which does not show Amir firing from above. This could be explained away by editing or camera fault. But much more importantly, it does not match the forensic analysis of Rabin's jacket. This evidence was given at Amir's trial in January 1996 by Chief Lieutenant Baruch Gladstein from the Israeli Police laboratories.

His analysis showed that Rabin was shot from much closer by one bullet (measured by the amount of gunpowder) and at point blank range by the other (which left a distinctive tear), almost certainly while kneeling. This was not speculation but exact science as the distance at which a gun is fired is measured by the amount of gunpowder deposited. Furthermore, bullets fired at point-black range leave a distinctive tear, which was evident in this case.

Not only was Rabin shot from far closer than the footage shows but there was one other clinching piece of evidence which literally blew a hole in the official version of events. Dr Mordecai Gutman, a highly experienced surgeon, kept a handwritten note, which reads 'Bullet wound in upper lung lobe of 2.5–3 cm. Exit wound in the direction of D5–6 with a shattering of the vertebrae,' in other words, he was shot in the chest, the bullet then shattering his spine. This is not a mistake any surgeon could make. It is the definitive proof that Amir could not have killed him but it also calls into question the evidence of his bodyguard who claims that Rabin dived into the car. Had his spine been shattered as the surgeon noted then he would have collapsed to the ground, not 'jumped' anywhere.

It is only a short distance to the hospital but it took between eight and twelve minutes to get there, as the road was packed and the driver tried to find a back route. By the time Rabin arrived there was no doubt he had been shot and was bleeding profusely.

As the official version of events slowly began to collapse, fingers inevitably began to point at the Shabak, or Shin Bet, the Israeli counter-intelligence and internal security service, who had Rabin under their control at all crucial times. This is not that surprising as the history of modern Israel is one of conspiracy interrupted by assassination, a volatile and feverish democracy underpinned by the world's most ruthless intelligence services, for whom there is no moral debate about ends and means. All that matters to them is the defence of the state, a duty that transcends all other considerations, legal, spiritual and temporal.

The evidence of their complicity is substantial.

Many believe that this was a staged event. At the time, several eyewitnesses said the bodyguards shouted '*Srak, srak*' meaning blanks. The Shabak agents who took Rabin's wife, Leah, to the hospital assured her that her husband was fine and that the assassin had used a toy gun. By this time, he was already dead.

Given the ballistics and other evidence, it is clear that he was not shot outside the stadium but had been by the time he arrived at the hospital. There is one further and highly suspicious moment on the Kempler tape. As the bodyguards move towards the limousine both back doors are open, with the chauffeur sitting in the front seat. Just before they reach the car, the door furthest from them shuts, yet according to the bodyguards there was no one in the car.

Rabin was clearly shot while under the control and protection of the Shabak, but their complicity does not end here. Yigal Amir did not act alone but was a prominent member of Eyal, a far-right militant Zionist organization, run by a long-term Shabak agent and *agent provocateur*,[9] Avishai Raviv, operating under the code name 'Champagne'. But Raviv was not just a religious zealot who hated Palestinians. He was photographed with a T-shirt carrying a picture of Rabin and the slogan 'No

Rest For Traitors' and was the distributor of the placards featuring Rabin in full Nazi uniform. He ran paramilitary terrorist training camps, staged a secret late-night signing in ceremony for the TV cameras and continued to agitate, often with violence. In a country where domestic security is the first and main issue, all these actions would have brought him constantly to the attention of the intelligence services. But though the incidents were many, the prosecutions were few. Clearly, he was being protected by the invisible but warm embrace of the security services. Shin Bet created and ran Eyal, with some prominent Jews like Rabbi Benny Elon alleging that they financed the whole group as well.

In a closed session of the Shamgar Commission, some young women described how Raviv was the constant companion of Yigal Amir throughout the summer, continually goading him to assassinate Rabin ('You keep talking about killing Rabin. Why don't you do it? Are you frightened? You say you want to do it. Show us that you're a man! Show us what you are made of). Other witnesses told the Shamgar Commission that Raviv described Rabin as a *rodef*, a man to be killed. The section of their report dealing with Raviv remains classified, none of which is surprising as the Shamgar Commission was anything but impartial. Apart from the judge, the other commission members included a former head of Mossad.

In the summer of 2004, Raviv was finally put on trial for failing to prevent the assassination of Rabin. Not surprisingly, his lawyer complained that crucial documents from Shin Bet were being withheld from his client.

The Rabin assassination is typical of many modern political killings as the official version of events is founded on the physically impossible. It is absurd to believe that an assassin, no matter how creative, can shoot someone in the chest while standing behind him. But official inquiries and investigations, whose conclusions defy all known science, are surprisingly common. It is a generally accepted principle of ballistics that bullets travel in straight lines, particularly over very short distances. The only time they do not is in assassination world, when the science of ballistics crosses over into a matrix universe where – if the official reports are to be believed – bullets can change direction as effortlessly as space vehicles in a graphic cartoon.

The patsy is crucial. Their role is that of a magnet to attract the media attention away from the ballistics and other forensic evidence.

Amir was a brilliant choice because he desperately wanted to believe he shot Rabin and no amount of forensic science was going to convince him otherwise. The architecture and ingredients of this assassination are remarkably similar to that of Robert Kennedy. If Robert Kennedy was the prototype, then Rabin was the advanced model. The basic template of ingredients is the same. There is a high-profile and much-hated politician in a crowded area after a public meeting. He is apparently under the protection of a security service, many of whom loathe him and wish to see him dead. They have some control of the evidence and there is enough confusion to believe they can get away with it. The key element in both assassinations is the patsy. In the case of Robert Kennedy it was a confused Palestinian, Sirhan Bishara Sirhan.

The 4 June 1968 was a crucial day for Bobby Kennedy as he attempted to secure election to the White House. America was torn apart by the war abroad in Vietnam and by the battle for civil rights at home. Martin Luther King was not long in his grave, having been shot just two months before. Kennedy promised to end the war, heal the divisions between rich and poor and step up the war against organized crime, none of which made him popular with US vested interests. He won the crucial California primary and after a night of celebration left the Ambassador Hotel in Los Angeles shortly after midnight. In a suit from the Georgetown University shop, a navy blue silk tie with grey stripe and plain oval gold cufflinks, he was every inch the man of the people. Only the shirt, custom-made from Wragge's of New York, gave away his affluent roots.

But as he worked his way through the food service pantry, a short, slightly built former jockey, Sirhan Sirhan, stepped in front of him and fired at the senator with a .22 handgun. Kennedy fell to the floor as the guards pounced on the man with the gun, who was immediately subdued, arrested, tried and convicted and has been in prison ever since.

Like Yigal Amir, it looked like an open and shut assassination. But just like Amir, Sirhan was convicted of a murder he could not possibly have committed.

Kennedy's body was taken to the morgue, where the pathologists discovered that the fatal bullet was a shot to the head, 0.5cm in diameter, 'right to left, slightly back to front, upward'.[10] Using infra-red photography, the pathologists immediately discovered large deposits of soot in his hair. They then carried out a series of 'pig ears' ballistics tests in which they fired a gun at a pig's ear, each time moving it back one quarter of an inch. They got an exact match, one and a half inches from the back of Kennedy's head. As Sirhan Sirhan was standing five feet in front of him he could not have fired this fatal bullet. There are two other wounds, both near his armpit. One entered at the back of his right shoulder and left by the front right shoulder. The other was about an inch away and lodged in his neck. Both bullets were fired upwards from someone standing behind him. It was physically impossible for Sirhan Sirhan to have fired any of these three bullets.

What makes these two assassinations so fascinating is they are mirror images of each other. Rabin's assassin was behind him and he was shot in the chest, Kennedy's assassin was in front of him and he was shot in the back.

The prosecution then withheld the post-mortem information until after Sirhan Sirhan's lawyer had pleaded guilty. He never raised the post-mortem evidence at trial and his client was duly convicted of a crime he could not have committed. There was no proper investigation, but the most extraordinary aspect of the case was the behaviour of the LAPD, the Los Angeles Police Department. They may not have been complicit in the original crime, but they were certainly guilty of both fitting up Sirhan Sirhan and protecting whoever did kill the senator. They ignored the evidence which showed Sirhan did not commit the crime, they did not investigate the most likely suspect and then routinely destroyed the evidence. Those witnesses who described a second gunman were hectored and bullied. The photographer who chronicled the whole event was arrested, his pictures taken from him never to be seen again. Over two thousand four hundred other photographs relating to the event found their way into a local hospital incinerator. The door frame which carried the evidence that ten bullets were fired in all, two more than existed in Sirhan's gun, was removed and destroyed. There was clearly more than one shooter but the Los Angeles police did not impound all the guns at the scene for testing. They got the post-mortem report within forty-eight hours, which showed that they needed to be looking elsewhere for the assassin, but suppressed and ignored it.

He has always denied it, but there was one other possibility for the actual assassin: Thane Eugene Cesar, the uniformed security guard standing directly behind Senator Kennedy. A man of pronounced right-wing views ('His brother John sold us down the river. He literally gave the country to Commies, the minorities, the blacks'), Cesar supported the vituperative racist governor of Alabama, George Wallace, and loathed the Kennedy brothers. He was interviewed on 24 June, by which time the LAPD had had the post-mortem for nearly three weeks. They knew that Bobby Kennedy was shot in the back of the head at point-blank range and that the other two bullets were from a gun fired by someone kneeling down and pointing his weapon upwards. They also knew from all the witnesses and the photographs that Cesar was the man standing in the spot the assassin must have occupied, yet the interview was light and cursory even though Cesar admitted to kneeling down and drawing his gun. Though he denied firing it, several witnesses contradict this claim. He even showed the officer a .22 calibre gun, the same size as Sirhan Sirhan's, but this roused no suspicions. The police then re-interviewed him several months later, but only after several witnesses refused to withdraw their testimony and insisted that they saw him fire his weapon. By then it was all too late as he told the police that he had sold the gun.[11] He then changed his story yet again, claiming that he had never shown the gun to the police at his interview and could not have done so as he had sold it before the shooting. This is untrue as the police have his handwritten receipt showing he only sold it three months *after* the shooting. Any competent detective confronted by all this evidence would then regard Cesar as their prime suspect, but LA's finest regarded none of this as suspicious.

But just to really spice up the rich fabric of this tale, the two key police investigators, who did such a brilliant job at not doing their job, both had intelligence backgrounds with connections to the CIA. But this was Los Angeles and it was inevitable that this killing should have had all the elements of a conventional Hollywood assassination thriller, though there was an extra twist. There was evidence suggesting both that Sirhan was highly susceptible and that – according to psychiatrists who examined him – he was certainly under some sort of hypnotic influence at the time. This is not as bizarre as it might first appear. Throughout the 1950s and 1960s, the CIA spent millions of US tax dollars on a whole series of mind-control experiments[12] part of which was the elusive quest for the programmed assassin. Many believe that Sirhan was the result of those experiments as he clearly had no idea where he was and what he had done.

However, there is a problem with this in that there is no other case history of hypnotically induced assassination and few psychologists believe it is possible to brainwash someone in this way. However, there is a much more simple explanation for Sirhan's behaviour. MK-ULTRA was a huge programme, with hundreds working on it. There is a vast literature showing this programme was responsible for the arrival of LSD (one of the main drugs they were experimenting on) and its subsequent leaking on to the street. One of the other drugs they worked on was scopolamine, which derives from a Colombian tree called *burundanga*. Initially it was used for interrogation (both by the Nazis and the CIA in the early stages of the Cold War) but abandoned as anyone who took it was totally compliant. They would tell their interrogators whatever they wanted to hear and would admit to whatever they were accused of. As a drug it is very close to Rohypnol, the date rape drug, though scopolamine is more powerful: the effects are immediate, the subject is completely unaware of what they are doing, they have absolutely no memory of what has happened to them and they are completely under the control and influence of whoever is with them. It is widely used by criminal gangs in Colombia, who slip the drug into their target's drink. The hapless victim then wakes up the following morning to discover that they have made numerous visits to a cashpoint machine, persistently withdrawing money, but have no recollection of what they have done. If this was the particular drug used (and clearly Sirhan was under the influence of some sort of hypnotic) then it would clear up one unresolved aspect of the case. For those who believe that Sirhan Sirhan was a brainwashed, hypnotized assassin this is further evidence, though circumstantial.

The use of the patsy is common throughout assassination history. One of the earliest examples is Pausanias, who assassinated Philip of Macedon, the father of Alexander the Great. Pausanias was a former gay lover of Philip, a rampant bisexual who had cast him aside for a younger and prettier man. Pausanias then stabbed Philip to death at a major gathering in front of all his closest allies. Pausanias was portrayed as a lone-nut assassin, bitter because he had been gang raped by one of Philip's favourite generals, his dinner guests and then his servants. Pausanias had demanded justice against the rapists but Philip had rejected his pleas. The public motive was therefore revenge. But Pausanias had been set up and manipulated by Olympias, Philip's fourth wife and the mother of Alexander the Great. Philip had married for a seventh time and had just produced a completely Macedonian heir, meaning that Alexander would no longer inherit the empire. Olympias provided Pausanias with getaway horses but he was conveniently captured and killed by the palace guards. She then assassinated Philip's young children and anyone else who threatened to prevent Alexander inheriting his father's empire.

The 1960s is the decade of the patsy in the USA, and Robert Kennedy's was the third major assassination (after his brother Jack and Martin Luther King) where the convenient patsy featured prominently.

Lee Harvey Oswald was the prototype and even identified himself as such. In the training manual chapter on how to set up a patsy he would have been the case study. By the time President Kennedy was shot he had a back story which made him perfect. He had a questionable past, which linked him to both Cuba and Moscow, there were multiple sightings of him (though he seemed to be able to continually change height), he had the requisite skills (just about) and he was a drifter on the edges of society, classic fodder for any disinformation specialist. A famous photograph appeared of him in his backyard, holding a copy of a communist newspaper and a rifle, which was enough to convict him in the eyes of the American public, even though this photograph was almost certainly a fake.[13] Though there was a mountain of evidence suggesting that the CIA had got their fingerprints all over him, there was still much evidence which put him in the frame, though it is highly doubtful that he was the sole shooter. But that was never his role. He was there to be the focus of media attention, the man forever thought of as the shooter, the lone assassin who shot the glamorous young president.

The next big assassination in 1960s America was Martin Luther King, shot dead in Memphis, Tennessee, 4 April 1968, the day after making a famous speech predicting his own death. To begin with the investigation went badly and after two months, the FBI had still not made an arrest. Then on June 5

1968, the Los Angeles Police arrested Sirhan Sirhan for the assassination of Robert Kennedy and three days later, the FBI got their man. James Earl Ray was arrested at Heathrow Airport, England on his way to Belgium[14] and extradited back to the USA to face charges for the murder of Martin Luther King.

James Earl Ray was an alcoholic, drug user, hypochondriac, frequenter of prostitutes, fantasist and virulent racist, a perfect match to fit the profile of lone gunman. In the shadows was another fantasist and virulent racist, Edgar Hoover, the Head of the FBI, who for years before had been running a vicious campaign of character assassination against King. The FBI bugged King for years, distributing the tapes round Washington, to both Kennedy[15] and Johnson. Hoover hated King, describing him as 'a tomcat with obsessive degenerate urges' and even had him smeared as a bisexual, a bizarre claim as King was a devout and overactive heterosexual and Hoover was a closet transvestite, who lived with his long-term boyfriend. Famously Hoover called for the 'removal' of King from the political scene and told his aides to achieve the 'desired result' of 'neutralizing King as an effective Negro leader'. In the climate of the 1960s, 'removal' only really had one meaning, but Hoover was an adept politician. The language was elliptical enough but the meaning clear.

Though James Earl Ray initially confessed he then withdrew this, saying he was forced into it by the FBI, who had threatened to jail his brother and his father if he did not. He then continued to deny his guilt for the next thirty years, until his death, claiming he was framed to cover up an FBI plot to assassinate King. In 1978, the US House Select Committee on Assassinations concluded that Ray was probably the shooter but that he was part of a wider conspiracy. This was never properly investigated and the documents are sealed until 2029.

As with many other modern assassinations, this one is very murky. There are major problems linking James Earl Ray to the crime, as the forensics and ballistics are weak. Many promising

leads pointing to other potential assassins were ignored by the
FBI, an organization which had both the motive and the
opportunity, and whose boss was playing the Henry II role
('Who will rid the kingdom of this turbulent priest?'). Motive
and opportunity are not evidence but several things are beyond
doubt. The US government waged a semi-public and illegal war
against King.[16] They were very close to and supportive of many
of the virulent segregationist groups circling round King and
the FBI, in particular, sent a very clear message to these people
that the government wanted him dead and that it was therefore
safe to assassinate him. Once he was dead, many in Washington
(and particularly the higher echelons of the FBI) celebrated his
passing. They had done what Henry II had failed to do and
created the conditions under which the assassination took place
but without any clear ties between them and the murder. The
key difference was James Earl Ray as the patsy. He took the
focus away from the FBI and Edgar Hoover, who reinforced
the message by denigrating King and trying to plant stories that
he had been murdered by a jealous husband. The only people
who cried different were the black leaders in his circle, like
Ralph Abernathy, and they were discounted by the FBI smear
machine, which by this time was a major operation.[17]

Once the patsy has had his brief moment in the publicity
spotlight, he has served his purpose and is generally silenced,
either by death or prison.

Lee Harvey Oswald was an unwilling patsy and was not
going to go quietly. If he had been able to have his time in court
with a smart team of US lawyers, then there were enough
conspiracies going on around him to keep grand juries busy for
years. Their investigations would have inevitably wandered –
uncontrolled – round the murky hinterlands occupied by the
CIA, the mafia, international crime, the White House and
inevitably the entire security and intelligence structure of the
US. The risk was simply far too great for far too many powerful
interests. Oswald was led out of the police station with no
protection and summarily executed by Jack Ruby.

At the time, the murder of Oswald was a great shock but assassinating the assassin (alleged or not) has a long and effective tradition, dating back two thousand three hundred years to ancient Macedonia, and Pausanius, one of the earliest known patsies.

Operationally, it is a very smart thing to do as it drops a bar over any future investigation.

In 1948, as he was about to make an announcement at a public meeting Liaquat Ali, the first prime minister of Pakistan, was assassinated by Saad Akbar, who was then immediately killed by the security forces. With no one to interrogate, the inevitable Commission of Inquiry never resolved the issue of whether he was a lone nut or the instrument of the security forces who had so spectacularly failed to protect the prime minister.

The clever variant on this strategy is to then smear the dead assassin and use his corpse for propaganda purposes. The CIA installed Castillo Armas as their chosen leader in Guatemala in 1954 after removing the democratically elected government of Arbenz. But Armas was too brutal and stupid even for his Cold War paymasters in Washington and he was assassinated three years later. His killer, a palace guard called Romeo Vasquez Sanchez, was found dead immediately afterwards, having committed suicide, though no one believed this to be the case. But some sharp operator did not miss the PR opportunity here. In the three years that Castillo Armas was in power, his secret police picked up and imprisoned tens of thousands of the opposition, but somehow missed the most dangerous one of them all, one of the president's own bodyguards. The police immediately portrayed him as a lone communist fanatic, embittered by the Liberator's 'patriotic policies'. They even produced some leftist propaganda which they claimed to have found in his pockets and a 'diary', which surprised those who knew him, as none of them ever described him as a man with left-wing views. However, it fitted the Washington-spun image of Armas as a heroic martyr cruelly chopped down on the frontline of the Cold War, even though privately they viewed him as an incompetent disaster.

The golden age for the patsy ended in the late 1960s. By then the public had become suspicious of the regularity with which the lone crazed assassin conveniently appeared every time there was a high-profile assassination. But, at the same time, the press began to come of age, the counter-culture spawning a new generation of journalists. Magazines and newspapers began to print long investigative pieces, in which the intricacies of complex assassination conspiracies were unravelled. The various congressional inquiries and court cases tore the veil of secrecy from the CIA and the American public was shocked to discover that many of their tax dollars had gone on bizarre plots to assassinate foreign leaders they had never heard of from countries about which they cared even less. The Warren Commission report into the assassination of President Kennedy was picked apart and ever since there has been a constant drip-feed of books parading different theories as to who was behind the killing. All start from the same premise that Oswald was a concoction created by the US intelligence services and was not what he appeared to be. James Earl Ray appeared on TV and gave a very good impression of an innocent man. Even Sirhan Sirhan has attracted media attention pointing out that it was impossible for him to have committed the murder for which he is still incarcerated.

In a climate where the press is naturally highly suspicious of anything which might link back to the intelligence services, it would be a very foolish assassin planner who now tried to insert a patsy into the equation. As with Oswald, virtually every day of their lives would be picked clean. Even in a country like Israel, where the intelligence services can hide behind national security, Avishai Raviv's links into the secret state have been painfully exposed, even though it took nearly a decade to bring him to trial.

Though few in a functioning democracy would now build a patsy into their plans, if one comes along then they can expect to be fully exploited by everyone with an interest. One of the best modern examples, because it is still an enduring media fantasy, is 'the Bulgarian plot to kill the Pope'.

In May 1981, a young Turkish fascist and a member of a terrorist group called the Grey Wolves, Mehmet Ali Agca tried to kill the Pope in St Peter's Square, Rome. The Pope survived and a passing nun, full of the strength and vigour that flows from Jesus, knocked the slightly built assassin to the ground, from where he was taken into custody. Once in prison he became yet another item of propaganda in the Cold War. The media specialists from the CIA and Italian intelligence popped him into the propaganda washing machine and in no time the grey stains were washed away and he came out looking like a terrorist controlled by the Bulgarian secret services. Much of the Western media fell for this and he was portrayed everywhere (including major reports on ITV and the BBC's *Newsnight*) as being their puppet.

Where the victim is a prominent figure, the assassins have taken the subsequent media coverage into account. But it is the very existence of spin doctors, often closely allied to a nation's intelligence services, which gives the game away – and any serious analysis of an assassination needs therefore to look at their role. Nowhere demonstrates this more powerfully than the case of Mehmet Ali Agca, the man who shot Pope John Paul II. Agca was a member of the Grey Wolves, a right-wing Turkish terrorist group, but much of the impetus for the 'Bulgarian Plot' came from Claire Sterling, a long-term CIA propagandist, and Michael Ledeen, another CIA asset working closely with the Italian intelligence services. Ledeen was the *spinmeister* who subsequently manufactured the Billygate scandal against President Carter and is now a key advocate of Bush foreign policy, spinning across the American media as a 'foreign policy expert'.

The case against the Bulgarians collapsed when it was revealed that Agca had been heavily coached in prison by the Italian secret services (working closely with the CIA) who got many details wrong. In court, Agca described the crucial planning meeting with his Bulgarian secret service masters in a hotel in Sofia. Sadly for the Italian and American intelligence services, this was not true – the hotel was not even built when the meeting was supposed to have taken place.

The author was in court when the Bulgarians were on trial in the early 1980s. Agca was caught in yet another preposterous series of claims in which he contradicted himself minute by minute. Eventually the prosecuting counsel lost all patience and denounced his star witness as 'a liar!'. And this being Italy, the judge flounced out and the chief prosecutor then held an impromptu press conference in the court to further denounce Agca.

Agca finally blew what little credibility he had when he told the court that he was Jesus Christ. The Bulgarians, against whom the evidence had once seemed unassailable, walked free. But the damage had been done. Most believed that the attempted assassination of the Pope had been masterminded and carried out by the Bulgarian secret service, acting on behalf of the KGB.

But media fantasies like this are hard to shift. The story is front page, the correction (if it appears at all) is buried away and the myth remains etched in the vague public consciousness. The Paris crash, in which Princess Diana and her lover Dodi Fayed were killed, was blamed entirely on the driver Henri Paul, who was treated as the patsy from the start. From the start, it was in the interests of the newspapers and the French government to blame him. But like the great patsies of the past, he was not to blame for the deaths attached to his name.

8

BEWARE THE POWERS AT WORK

'For secret assassination, either simple or chase, the contrived accident is the most effective technique. When successfully executed, it . . . is only casually investigated.'

CIA Assassination Manual, Guatemala, 1954

'But I don't want to go among mad people,' Alice remarked.
'Oh, you can't help that,' said the Cat: 'we're all mad here. I'm mad. You're mad.'
'How do you know I'm mad?' said Alice.
'You must be,' said the Cat, 'or you wouldn't have come here.'

Alice in Wonderland

Serpentine Gallery, London, 30 June 1994 . . .
She is the most photographed woman on the planet, able to command the global media at will. When her estranged husband uses a fawning TV documentary to try and rehabilitate himself with a sceptical British public, she turns up to a local art gallery event, wearing a tiny black off-the-shoulder chiffon dress.[1] She takes the headlines, he gets the inside pages. She

looks fabulous, a million dollars, all translucent skin and glistening teeth – and there is just enough hint of cleavage to guarantee her front page on the world's media. In contrast, he looks old, grey and pallid, a squalid throwback from a previous age, now long gone and best forgotten. Once again Princess Diana, a former kindergarten teacher with few academic qualifications, completely outwits and humiliates the Buckingham Palace PR machine.

In public she looks strong, a modern woman in control of her life and her emotions. In private, her life is a debilitating cocktail of self-doubt, tantrums and paranoia – none of which is surprising. After her wedding she discovers that her husband is having an affair with the woman next door and has no intention of giving her up as he thinks this is his god-given right. Worse still, though she has escaped from one of Britain's most dysfunctional families she has only married into another. Her new in-laws are a bizarre bunch of the emotionally defective and the physically challenged, warped by generations of inbreeding and wrapped in a surreal cotton wool world of fawning courtiers and sycophantic servants. Desperately lonely, she soon discovers that seeking the intimate friendship of men from outside this ankle-deep gene puddle is dangerous, both for them and for her.

Early on in her loveless marriage, she becomes close to her personal detective, Barry Mannakee,[2] but the palace has him transferred to other duties and he dies in a suspicious motorbike crash in July 1987. Deeply suspicious, she believes that this is the work of MI5. She begins an affair with a young army major, James Hewitt, after meeting him at a party. He is everything her husband is not: charming, kind and attentive to both her and her children. Given her desperate loneliness and the fact that she is trapped in a madhouse, it is hardly surprising that she falls in love with him.

Buckingham Palace condones the affair as it gets her out of the way and allows her husband to be with his mistress.[3] But then in 1990, when Hewitt is due to be moved to Germany with his regiment, the palace becomes worried that she will become unstable again and cause trouble. A beauty parade of young army officers is shuffled in front of her but none appeals. The palace wants to break up the relationship and get her settled with someone new. The phone calls start to Hewitt's unlisted number, telling him that 'they', whoever 'they' are, can no longer guarantee his safety or his security, the traditional death threat used by the British security and intelligence services.[4] At first Hewitt does not take them seriously, dismissing them as crank calls, but then he receives similar warnings from Patrick Jephson, the princess' private secretary, as well as other courtiers. Hewitt does not possess the sharpest brain so just to make sure he gets the point, one of the anonymous calls tells him that he will be murdered, 'just like Barry Mannakee'.[5] When he asks Diana about this, she tells him her belief about Mannakee's death.

After this, Hewitt is genuinely nervous and fully expects to die in an 'accidental' incident of friendly fire during the first Gulf War. He survives but is lucky. Shortly before he goes to the Gulf, a member of the royal family is at a British army regimental dinner. When everyone is drunk, the royal starts railing against James Hewitt, describing him as 'a fucking traitor' and starts prodding the officers asking them 'when are you lot going to do something about it – he's fucking the future King of England's wife ... your commander in chief!'[6] The soldiers present are in no doubt that Hewitt's assassination is being called for but none decides to follow it up.

With talk like this in royal circles – and there is more than one person involved – it is hardly surprising that the princess is nervous. After an incident when her brakes fail, she confides in a very close friend her belief that her car has been tampered with. She tells others that she is frightened she will die in a helicopter crash. After she separates from Charles, she is often harassed but is never sure whether it is always the paparazzi who are buzzing her car.[7] She divorces Charles on 28 August 1996 and shortly after this, in October, she writes an extraordinary letter to her butler, Paul Burrell, telling him, 'This particular phase of my life is the most dangerous – Prince Charles is planning "an accident" in my car, brake failure and serious head injury in order to make the path clear for him to marry.' When she gives him the letter, she tells him to keep it safe . . . 'just in case'. Subsequent to this, the Queen also confides in Burrell, warning him, 'there are powers at work in this country about which we have no knowledge'.

By the mid 1990s she is a transnational brand, the People's Princess by popular vote – but increasingly hated by political establishments everywhere who are worried by her unpredictability and her awesome media pulling power. In January 1997, she visits Angola with a small army of the international media and pushes landmines to the top of the international agenda, wrong-footing those British and American diplomats who had managed to stall progress towards a well overdue international ban. Later that year, in June, she visits Bosnia-Herzegovina to keep up the pressure. According to a witness at her inquest, Princess Diana was passionate about exposing everyone involved in this trade. She was planning to publish a report, *Profiting out of Misery*, in which she would name many high-ranking public figures, as well as the Secret Intelligence Service, who she believed were behind the sale of British-made landmines. There was panic in Whitehall. Publicly, Conservative politicians describe her as 'a loose cannon', who is not being 'helpful or realistic' and warn her to keep her nose out of politics.

But her campaign works. A TOP SECRET memo written after her death in December 1997 by a US intelligence officer based at the American embassy in London notes that landmines have become 'a very emotional issue because of the late Princess Diana's involvement'. The memo goes to the National Security Council in Washington and the writer warns them that 'the pressure that the Labour government will be subjected to should not be underestimated,' and this issue 'could have negative effects upon the NATO alliance and become a divisive issue between the US and UK' because 'NATO countries could get rid of a defensive weapon that in a few years' time they might need in an unforeseen region of Europe or the world.'[8] The 'powers at work of which we have no knowledge' hated Princess Diana. Her 'crimes' were upfront and visible. There was the landmine campaign, she had been publicly unfaithful to the future king of England and she was dating a Muslim Arab, the son of the man who they believed had stolen their corner shop, Harrods. All that was irritating enough, but there was something else, something far worse.

Their view of the world is locked in Tudor mythology, straight out of Shakespeare and the court of Elizabeth I. They see their role as the defence of the realm and the realm is represented by the crown and the court – there can only be one of each. Quite simply, her court was now more powerful than his. She was threatening to splinter the crown and fracture the realm. In their eyes, she had to go.

And then in the summer of 1997 she begins a very public affair with Dodi, the son of Mohammed Al Fayed, the man the British establishment hates more than any other and the owner of their corner shop, Harrods. They dislike him partly because he is Egyptian (and no one should ever underestimate the closet but virulent current of racism running through British public life) but loathe him because he helped bring down the Tory government of John Major after it was revealed that he had a couple of dozen Conservative MPs on his payroll, his parliamentary foot soldiers in his long-running feud with his former friend, Tiny Rowland, the buccaneer founder of Lonrho, an international trading conglomerate. Bizarrely, newspaper commentators largely direct much of their venom at him, for whom it is not an offence to pay the bribes rather than the politicians for whom it is to receive. He is portrayed as the great corruptor when all he has done is book a seat on a gravy train that has been running quietly through British politics for decades.

Post-divorce, the world's tabloid industry is obsessed with Diana's sex life. Her affair, largely conducted in front of the world's paparazzi in the Mediterranean off the south coast of France, is the big story of the summer of 1997, the first 'kiss' picture fetching a rumoured $2 million in international sales. But with an ever-increasing number of powerful forces ranging against her she begins to look increasingly like a candidate for assassination, meeting the two critical tests identified by one of the mafia's major victims: she is both too powerful and she is unprotected and unloved by the state.[9]

When the world wakes up on 31 August 1997 to pictures of a mangled Mercedes in a Paris tunnel and the news that Princess Diana has died at 4 a.m. on an operating table in a French hospital, it does not seem that much of a surprise, as if there is a collective but unstated public feeling that she has been living on borrowed time . . .

Her last twenty-four hours alive started on Mohammed Al Fayed's yacht the *Jonikal*, moored in the Mediterranean. It was the end of the holiday for Diana and Dodi and they decided to return to London via Paris, taking Al Fayed's private jet to Le Bourget airport. Inevitably there was a security leak, the paparazzi were tipped off and by the time the couple arrived there was a small posse waiting for them, which then followed them into Paris.[10] They were collected in a Mercedes by Philippe Dourneau, a regular chauffeur for the Ritz, who often drove Hollywood stars visiting Paris. It was low-intensity conflict from the start. According to their statements the paparazzi said they simply followed Dourneau and the back-up car to see where they were going. Their targets told a very different story. As well as being a supremely competent driver, one of Philippe Dourneau's great skills was to be able to drive through Paris at great speed, while paparazzi fired their camera flashes in his eyes. It was a skill he needed that afternoon. Dourneau told the police that although it was a very bright and sunny day, as the paparazzi buzzed alongside the car on their motorbikes, they partially blinded him by firing their camera flashes in his face.[11]

Welcome to Paris, Princess Diana.

The two bodyguards, Trevor Rees-Jones and Kez Wingfield, followed in a Range Rover, driven by Henri Paul, the Deputy Head of Security at the Ritz. On the high-speed road into Paris, Wingfield told the police that one of the paparazzi, driving a black Peugeot (whom Kez Wingfield identified as Christian Martinez)[12] twice swerved in front of Henri Paul, braking sharply to try and break up the convoy. Both times, Henri Paul, who had been on several defensive-driving courses, swerved and avoided them. It was a good piece of driving. Martinez denied this but it was not the first occasion when the paparazzi version of events was the opposite of everyone else's. It would not be the last.

Meanwhile, Dourneau, a much more experienced Paris driver,[13] managed to shake off the pack of cars and motorbikes. Diana and Dodi then visited the former home of the Duke of Windsor and Wallis Simpson, a magnificent detached house in its own grounds near the Bois de Boulogne, which Mohammed Al Fayed had acquired. It had much that she was looking for: it is secluded, discreet and well protected.

As soon as they headed back into the centre of Paris, they were surrounded again. There was to be no privacy for the young lovers and throughout the rest of the day they constantly had to change their plans as they were harassed by the pursuing pack. Diana was used to the antics of the paparazzi but she had never seen anything as bad as this, telling her bodyguards that she was worried that one of them was going to get killed through their reckless driving. Kez Wingfield remarked subsequently that the paparazzi were so close he could have wound the window down and touched them.

After having to cancel their dinner reservation at a local restaurant they ended up at the Ritz Hotel shortly before 10 p.m. Henri Paul arrived shortly afterwards at 10.08 p.m., having finished work earlier that day at 7 p.m. Outside, a crowd of two dozen paparazzi patrolled the front and back entrances of the hotel, working in pairs connected by mobile phones.

Some time before midnight, Dodi came up with a plan, which was without a single redeeming feature: the couple would leave from the back door, in just one car, Diana and Dodi in the back, their bodyguard Trevor Rees-Jones in the front and Henri Paul at the wheel. The best chauffeur would drive the diversion car and the least-qualified driver (and a man who disliked driving cars) would take them. Though three cars were involved in the plan, there was to be no back-ups and the diversion from the front would never work as the hotel was surrounded. Before they set off, their plans were leaked: at midnight, a Ritz employee tipped off one of the paparazzi, Christian Martinez, that the couple were about to leave.

The paparazzi outside were seething. Many had been on call since lunchtime.[14] They knew that Dodi had bought a ring and they expected an announcement but there had been none. They also knew that whoever got the first photograph of Diana's left hand, with the ring on that crucial wedding finger, would make a lot of money – but after a day running round a hot and sticky Paris they had got nothing. No picture, no reward.

The Mercedes left the back door at 12.18 a.m. It was an ordinary Mercedes, one of a fleet and not the bullet-proof limousine of journalists' imagination. Though it had been in an accident some time before it had been thoroughly overhauled and was in excellent condition. A small detachment of paparazzi was already waiting for them on the pavement. The young man who delivered the car from a local hire company, Frederic Lucard, had a creative imagination[15] and enjoyed his brief moment of fame by persuading the gullible that Henri Paul shouted out to the photographers and journalists, 'Don't try to follow us, you'll never catch us.' Sadly for him (and the many journalists who were happy to go with this single source) it was a figment of his imagination. The four journalists/paparazzi who were all within a few feet told the police that Henri Paul simply smiled at them, got in the car and drove away, without speaking.[16] At 12.18 a.m. at the back of the hotel, Alain Guizard, a journalist working for the Angeli Agency, called his photographer, Christian Martinez, who was patrolling the front, to tell him that the couple were on the move. Guizard jumped in his Peugeot 205 and followed the Mercedes. It took a couple of minutes for the Mercedes to reach the traffic lights at the nearby Place de la Concorde, but in that time the posse caught up with them and they were surrounded by cars, motorbikes and scooters.

The official crash report estimated that the car was travelling at around 80 mph on the straight and around 60 mph when it hit the pillar, a figure confirmed by independent experts.[17] Nowhere near the exaggerated speeds reported at the time, which suggested that the car was travelling at over 130 mph when it hit the pillar, which would give it a speed of over 150 mph on the straight, before he slammed on the brakes.

The paparazzi deny taking any pictures here but the nearest eyewitness tells a very different story. Jean Louis Bonnin, a financier, was in a green Fiat Punto at the lights when the Mercedes drew up on his left. He watched the Mercedes, drenched in white light, as the flashes popped and fizzled at the couple in the back, who looked trapped, dejected and miserable. Dodi was holding the security grip with his left hand and covering his face with the other. Diana was trying to hide. The photographer subjecting them to this miserable experience was on a scooter/motorbike,[18] with two men on it, the pillion passenger taking the pictures. These pictures (along with hundreds more taken that night) have never turned up. When the lights changed, the Mercedes was hemmed in and the car in front refused to move. Henri Paul had to reverse and then drive round it as once again they desperately tried to make their escape from the pack, which had now been pursuing them for nine hours solid.

The Mercedes set off, a posse of cars behind, motorcyclists and scooter riders alongside. A motorbike with two men on board then overtook Bonnin along with a light-coloured Peugeot 205,[19] whose driver blasted his horn at him to get him to move out of the way so it too could join the chase.[20]

As the Mercedes left the Place de la Concorde the pack was in hot pursuit. A consultant engineer, Thierry Hackett, was overtaken by the Mercedes travelling at 120–30 km/h, being chased by four to six motorbikes, some with two on board. The route taken was a quite common one for chauffeurs and cab drivers as it avoids the Champs Elysée, which is slow moving and crowded, especially at midnight, the perfect place for the paparazzi to ambush the Mercedes. The normal route taken by all the chauffeurs is to travel along the Cours la Refine on to the Cours Albert 1er and then turn right and make the short cut towards the Arc de Triomphe and Dodi's apartment, but Henri Paul could not do that as there was a motorbike on his right blocking the exit.[21] The whole journey was only a matter of minutes. Unable to turn right, Henri Paul had no choice but to go via the Alma tunnel. Ahead of him an off-duty police officer, David Laurent, spotted a white Fiat Uno driving very slowly near the entrance, 'As if the driver was waiting for someone,' he noted at the time, but this was Paris, late at night, the roads were full of crazy people and so he drove on. By the time Henri Paul reached the tunnel entrance, the Fiat Uno was straddling the white line in the centre of the road and the Mercedes just clipped it.

Benoit Boura, a photographer's assistant, described a motorbike following the Mercedes at speed. Marine Boghen, a student, was in a Lancia with her boyfriend which was overtaken by a motorbike in hot pursuit travelling at 110–20 km/h. Annick Catheline and her husband Jean Claude, who were on foot, both saw the Mercedes speed by, with another big car in the next lane about a metre away. Their daughter Marie-Agnes also saw a motorbike close up with two people on it. A motorbike flashed through the tunnel at high speed immediately afterwards, swerving round the crashed car. In a car coming the other way, a financial analyst, Christophe Lascaux, saw two motorbikes just behind the Mercedes as it went into the tunnel.

Thierry Hackett, who was overtaken at speed near the Place de la Concorde, followed the convoy until his exit one hundred and fifty metres short of the tunnel. His evidence was crucial because he told the judge that the driver of the Mercedes was having problems holding his trajectory and that a lighter-coloured motorbike was alongside throughout. As he turned right, the Mercedes was still being hindered. Crucially this witness put the white motorbike next to the Mercedes as it entered the tunnel. At this time, the convoy was travelling at about 120 km/h. Less than five seconds later two of the occupants would be dead and one would be fatally injured.

As the Mercedes entered the tunnel, three witnesses described seeing flashes of light surrounding the vehicle. Benoit Boura, who worked as an assistant in a photographic laboratory, was in a white Renault with his girlfriend coming the other way, while two others, Clifford Gooroovadoo and Olivier Partouche, were both standing near the tunnel entrance. Partouche also told the police something very significant. It looked to him as if the car in front of the Mercedes was braking to allow the bike to get alongside, a common manoeuvre for the paparazzi and one tried the afternoon before.

A witness, François Levistre, driving in the tunnel ahead of the Mercedes also saw the same motorbike. In his account, the bike had two people on it, swerved in front of the Mercedes, there was a huge flash of light and the Mercedes lost control, zig-zagging first to the left, then to the right and then to the left. The French police and the judge took an instant dislike to him and dismissed him as unreliable for completely irrational reasons. He worked in the black economy and did not have a formal job. He had a long-lapsed minor conviction for fraud and he talked to the newspapers. But according to a hand-written note on the file, the detectives had one major reason for not believing him – Levistre was a bald man in his fifties who could not be trusted because he had a much younger and very attractive wife.[22] Levistre says the police put a huge amount of pressure on him to change his story (and he was not the only witness to make this claim) and when he refused, they rubbished him to any journalist who would listen.

However, there were several things in his favour. He accurately described the skid pattern of the Mercedes (left, right, left) long before this information became public, he described the presence in the tunnel of a small white car (two weeks before the French police even knew of the white Fiat Uno) and he was clearly describing the same motorbike seen by other witnesses going into the tunnel with the Mercedes. He was also scrupulously honest about the fact that he was speeding. Many other witnesses confused matters and threw out all the timings by saying they were driving within the speed limit but he was quite open about the fact that he was driving at over 80 km/h when he entered the tunnel.

There was further confirmation of this same motorbike from two other witnesses. Severine Banjout described a motorbike fleeing the scene at high speed, while Grigori Rassinger, a photographer, also described a high-powered bike, with a touch of white, which drove off immediately afterwards.

Other witnesses who supported this version of events were simply ignored by the police. Brian Anderson, an American marketing consultant, was in a taxi coming the other way and saw three motorbikes pursuing the Mercedes in an aggressive manner. As they approached the tunnel, one of the motorbikes overtook the Mercedes after which there was the crash. In a TV interview he said that the motorbikes contributed to the Mercedes' driver losing control. The French police did not interview him but instead wrote derogatory remarks about American tourists on the file.[23] Brenda Wells, an English secretary, who also saw a motorbike carrying two men following the Mercedes, was not interviewed by the French police and has since disappeared.

According to the two police officers who were first on the scene, Sebastien Dorzee and Lino Gagliardonne, none of the photographers did anything to help the victims. The witnesses said much the same, describing a scrum of paparazzi, taking a huge number of pictures and fighting among themselves. According to the police Romuald Rat shouted at Martinez,

'This is all your fault!' which Martinez denied, though others also witnessed it. The witnesses described him as volatile and aggressive towards the police, telling them that if this was Bosnia he would be allowed to get on with his job, a claim he subsequently admitted.

Diana did not reach hospital until 2.05 a.m., an hour and forty minutes after the crash. The journey itself taking forty minutes, even though it should have taken five, the ambulance driving slowly to avoid bumps. The French practice is called 'stay and play', where the medics do whatever they can at the scene and in the ambulance. The American and British practice is called 'scoop and go', get the victim to the hospital as soon as possible. Her post-mortem shows she had massive injuries. The experts are divided, some arguing she was unlikely to survive, whatever happened, others saying she might have had a chance, though a very slim one, if she had got to an operating table earlier.

Despite all this evidence, the French judge drew two conclusions, neither of which has any basis in evidence.[24] One, that the presence of the paparazzi did not cause the Mercedes to speed, a ridiculous conclusion because it is a matter of common sense that had the paparazzi not been harassing them they would have just got in the car and driven quietly to Dodi's flat. Given that it was not a huge distance and it was a warm night, they might even have walked it. His second conclusion was that there was no clear underlying link between the speed of the Mercedes and the presence of the photographers following the vehicle. Again, it is a fatuous conclusion. Diana was not only an icon, she was also a target and Henri Paul had no idea whether the pursuing pack, which by now was extremely aggressive, were photographers or terrorists. Any other professional driver would have taken off in exactly the same way to escape.

The judge hid behind the fact that none of the witnesses was able to describe the make and model of the motorbike, though several described its colour (white), and that the witness statements did not match in all their detail. But this is common in any event like this. The psychology of memory is that people take away different snatches of the same event. In this case, all the witnesses described a car chase with the Mercedes as the quarry. No one describes the Mercedes alone, apart from the paparazzi, who made a series of preposterous claims in their numerous interviews with the police and judge, saying that they only followed at a distance, obeyed the speed limit (which, if true, would be a first for a French paparazzo) and were therefore unable to keep up with the Mercedes.

Stephane Darmon, on a 650 cc Honda motorbike, with Romuald Rat on the back (the most aggressive photographer pursuing the couple for the last month) told the police he was only travelling at 60 km/h. Alain Guizard said he followed the Mercedes at a sensible distance, decided to call it a night and then – by an extraordinary coincidence – arrived in the tunnel. However, at 00:23:34 he rang his boss and then at 00:24:18 he rang the ambulance. A minute later at 00:25:32 he rang his boss again. All the calls were made in the Alma tunnel area,[25] an area he would not have reached this quickly if he was travelling as slowly as he claims. Jacques Langevin, one of the paparazzi at the back of the Ritz, told the police he was on his way to a friend's house when he noticed something odd in the tunnel and walked in, taking four or five pictures from a distance of about fifteen metres. Yet the police recovered eleven of his pictures taken at less than a third of that distance, only four to five metres away. Christian Martinez, who arrived with Arnal, said he took a few pictures from five to ten metres away. Yet in his case, the police recovered thirty-one, many taken from close up at a distance of about a metre and a half. He was right on the ambulance man's shoulder when he was trying to treat Diana. David Oderkerken is another one who told police that he had decided to call it a day, arriving in the tunnel just by coincidence, even though (according to four other paparazzi) he had moved quickly enough to be in pole position next to the Mercedes at the Place de la Concorde, a fact he only reluctantly admitted after two police interviews and two interviews with the judge.

Faced with a catalogue of lies, falsehoods and dodgy claims (all made under oath) the judge's only criticism was to express a mild disbelief about their claims. Of those who said they were on their way home, his criticism was less than mild, remarking that 'it is difficult to understand why professionals, reputed to be "persistent" and who had already waited for hours would have given up in this manner.' He also argued that there was no 'hounding of the couple by the photographers', a bizarre claim to make as there was not a single independent witness statement in his investigation which supported this claim. In fact, the photographs and video footage show the exact opposite.

This is typical of Judge Hervé Stephan, who many thought did everything possible to exculpate the paparazzi. As far as the public and the press were concerned, the judge's investigation has always been portrayed as thorough and complete. In fact, the very opposite was the case.

A movement to acquit the paparazzi regardless of the evidence seems clear, starting from the moment the pack first ambushed the couple at Le Bourget. In the judge's report, he says that only Kez Wingfield recalled the dangerous behaviour of some of the paparazzi on the road from the airport. The report states, 'Both Trevor Rees-Jones and Philippe Dourneau, on the other hand, testified that the photographers had always remained behind the Range Rover.' This is a very partial account. Rees-Jones described a scene 'which made the London car chases seem tame'. According to him, they were 'surrounded by screaming motorcycles, darting round the target vehicles so that the photographer could wield his camera and focus the powerful zoom lens'.[26/27] Crucially, the judge fails to mention the other key piece of Philippe Dourneau's testimony, when he tells the police that he was dazzled by the flashing in his face,[28] ('*Lorsqu'ils ont pris leurs photos, les flashes, m'ont ebloui*'). Both British bodyguards also told the French police about Diana's remarks that she was worried that one of the paparazzi might go under the wheels and be killed, so aggressive was their behaviour.

Seven of the paparazzi were arrested that night and inter-viewed by the police. The other three, who fled the scene, only turned themselves in four days later. From the start they were unreliable, contradicting each other, changing their stories, lying and providing implausible and unconvincing explana-tions. Of this, there is no mention in the judge's report.

In his first interview with the police, Serge Arnal told the police that he rang the emergency services number 112, and despite it being a bad connection he was able to provide them with the first pieces of information. He claimed that he then started taking pictures twelve minutes after the police arrived. In his second interview he shortened this time period to five minutes. In all he was interviewed three times by the police and twice by the judge. In his second interview with the judge, he repeated his claim that he saw the crashed car in the tunnel, rang 112, returned to his car, before going back down into the tunnel, where he saw three, possibly four other paparazzi.[29] He then took some more pictures, before returning to his car, parking it in a nearby road and then ringing his editor. In fact, he lied throughout. He was the very first journalist there, taking the very first photograph,[30] which showed smoke coming from the car, the lights on and the air bag still inflated. He then took another seven pictures, going round the car before any other paparazzo was there and at no time was he more than five feet away from his victims. When the police seized his mobile they discovered that at 12.23 a.m. he rang 12, not 112, information not emergency services. He then rang his editor, a minute before a passerby, Paul Carril, called the fire brigade at 12.24 a.m. The judge excused him by saying he acted to call the emergency services, though he clearly did not speak to them and lied about the content of the call. He was not criticized for lying consistently to the police and the judge in his various interviews. Given that he was the first on the scene, there was an even more serious question to be asked of him: one of the witnesses described a small dark car in front of the Mercedes trying to slow it down. Was it him?

Arnal was not the only paparazzo with a flexible attitude to the truth. Nikola Arsov told the police and the judge that he only arrived at the tunnel late after following the back-up car. The judge asked him to describe the route, but even though this interview took place months after the event, Arsov still got the details wrong. The judge did not recall him or challenge him on this point and in his report he just remarked that because Arsov's alibi had collapsed it did not mean he was at the scene of the crime. However, there were two witnesses who placed him at the Place de la Concorde. Fabrice Chassery, one of the paparazzi who knew him well and Jean Louis Bonnin, the financier who was stopped at the lights, who recognized Arsov's distinctive bike, a white 1000 cc BMW. When Bonnin arrived at the tunnel he noticed the bike there.

The quality of the French police work was very low grade. The statement-taking was minimalist and lazy. Obvious follow-up questions were simply not asked. Many witnesses described a distinctive-looking bike but the police did not pursue this with any vigour. But despite this, there was only one possible conclusion on the evidence gathered: the paparazzi *en masse* caused the accident by harassing and pursuing the couple relentlessly all day. The key figure was the bike alongside the Mercedes in the tunnel.

The view of Anthony Scrivener QC, one of Britain's most experienced barristers, who has reviewed much of the same evidence as the judge, was that the driver of the motorbike caused the accident and was guilty (at the very least) of manslaughter, which was the only reasonable conclusion that anyone would draw after reading the evidence.

Short of a confession, the issue is unlikely ever to be resolved. The police made little attempt to identify the motorcyclist and the judge never made it a priority. However, in the summer of 1998, they were approached by a former British intelligence officer, Richard Tomlinson, who told them that when he was

working for MI6 in Bosnia (under UN cover) there had been a
plan to assassinate President Milosevic of Yugoslavia using two
men on a motorbike, armed with a high-powered flash gun.[31]
The thinking was that the flash would disable the driver causing
the car to crash in a suitable place where there was enough
concrete to guarantee the deaths of the occupants. Such guns
are commercially available and use a single high-powered flash
of light to stun their victim. The military version of this weapon
is exceptionally powerful, rendering the victim immobile for a
good five minutes and still in shock half an hour later.

Though this method of assassination may seem far-fetched,
it is not. The West German authorities have been investigating
whether it was used by assassins from the Soviet bloc and
specifically by a highly trained and well-financed East German
assassination team, which operated between 1976 and 1987.
One specific assassination under investigation was that of Lutz
Eigendorf, an East German footballer who defected to the West
in 1979 and died in 1983 in a car crash on a straight road. The
suspected method was the flash gun to cause the crash, the Stasi
assassins then pouring alcohol down his throat to make it look
like an accident. Two former Russian Spetsnatz (Special Forces)
have also boasted that they 'killed a man without firing a shot.
He was belting along in a Mercedes . . . It was dark and he was
doing 130 km/h. We blasted him with an electric light-gun,
through the windscreen and, bang, that was the end of him.
When the car was opened, all those inside were pulp.'

But the French inquiry had already steered well away from
anything which might link the motorbike to the crash and did
not investigate this. Instead Tomlinson was arrested at gun-
point, beaten up by the French police, and had a rib broken just
before he was due to see Judge Stephan. His laptop and
organizer were taken away and given to MI6. As he remarked
in his affidavit, 'The lengths which MI6, the CIA and DST have
taken to deter me giving this evidence and subsequently
to stop me talking about it, suggest they have something to
hide.'

Instead of pursuing the obvious cause of the crash, the judge pinned his verdict on the blood test carried out on the driver Henri Paul, but this was a very shaky foundation. The first samples were simply scooped out of his chest (which was badly smashed in the accident), improperly labelled and then analysed. This method of analysis is very prone to contamination and is so inaccurate that no pathologist in Britain would rely on it. The results were then given to the press. Proper tests were only carried out five days later, this time taking blood from the femoral artery, which is generally regarded as more reliable. In what many pathologists regard as a happy coincidence this second test confirmed the results of the first, to an accuracy of two decimal places. As one pathologist remarked, 'The odds on this happening are not high – you're lucky to get the same result five minutes apart!' It is even more remarkable as there is no record of the original samples being stored correctly.

Both blood tests also showed that Henri Paul had an unusually high level of carbon monoxide poisoning, just over 20 per cent. When this was raised in a television programme,[32] the judge commissioned a report to explain it. In the spirit of impartial enquiry that characterized his investigation, the doctor given the job of providing an explanation was the same man who had carried out the original flawed blood test. Dr Pepin told the judge that the carbon monoxide had come from the air bag and that Henri Paul must have breathed it in. This line has been endlessly repeated by journalists ever since – but it is nonsense. According to Mercedes the gas they use in their air bags is nitrogen not carbon monoxide, a fact that could have easily been checked by the French investigators (and the journalists who have so eagerly endorsed it). Just as important, Henri Paul's post-mortem shows he died instantly, his neck snapped and his aorta ripped away from his heart. He breathed in nothing and no blood was pumped round his body.

If Henri Paul did not get the carbon monoxide in the crash, then he must have been carrying it when he arrived at the Ritz just after 10 p.m. But here, the mystery deepens. Carbon monoxide has a half-life of four hours which means that when he arrived (just over two hours before the crash) the carbon monoxide level in his blood would have been just over 30 per cent. If the blood test was correct he had also had the equivalent of seven single whiskies – all on an empty stomach. But if he had had this amount of alcohol and the carbon monoxide on top, he would have been disoriented and slurring his speech. Yet the Ritz Hotel security footage shows that he is in total command of his situation. He moves fluently, stopping to tie his shoe laces, has a lengthy conversation in English with Dodi's two bodyguards, both of whom have since said that he was not drunk and showed no signs of drinking. In the words of Professor Alistair Hay of Leeds University, it's 'an enigma'. The judge failed to resolve the problem and did not mention it in his final report, a disgraceful omission.

Henri Paul's family do not believe the blood sample can be from their son. Since May 1999, they have been trying to recover it so they can submit it for independent DNA analysis, but have been resisted at every turn by the French courts and the state,[33] which prompts the question: if the French government is confident in their pathologists why are they so reluctant to have their results independently confirmed?

The problem with the French legal system is that it is, to all intents, a subsidiary of the state machine. Unlike Britain or America there is no right to independent pathology reports, and Henri Paul's parents have now taken their case to the European Court of Human Rights. This lack of impartiality is further compounded by French judges who traditionally have a strong sense of the national interest. After the crash, the Hollywood A list came out fighting. Elizabeth Taylor spoke for many when she said, 'the paparazzi murdered her'. Tom Cruise told CNN of his frightening experiences at the hands of the Paris paparazzi in the same tunnel. He talked of 'being chased by paparazzi, they run lights and they chase you and harass you the whole time.' George Clooney attacked the editor of the *National Enquirer* asking him how he slept at night. Right from the start it was very clear that French national interests would not be served by an inquiry that confirmed the fears of the Hollywood elite and found the paparazzi guilty.[34]

The only explanation that makes any sense is that the sample is not Henri Paul's – and this is not as far-fetched as it sounds. The administration of the Institut Medico-legal morgue in Paris was a shambles. In a properly run unit, both paperwork and samples are meticulously kept. This did not happen here. The basic paperwork was not done. There is no mention of the time, the origin, the quantities or the volumes taken. No proper histological investigation was carried out and so there is no guarantee that the samples were authentic. They also should have been deep-frozen but there is no record of this happening either. In the case of Henri Paul, the documents attached to the experts' reports refer to different samples. One just has the word 'Andrieux' followed by a reference 'X masculine', which is then replaced by the word 'Pau'. These are not fresh labels clearly marked as are required under French law or European law. In the words of one British coroner's officer, 'I would not dare go into court with paperwork as bad as that. My coroner would simply throw me out!'

Henri Paul's samples are not the only ones with inaccurate paperwork. The handling of Dodi's samples was even worse. His official post-mortem report was drawn up at 6.45 a.m. on the morning after the crash by Commander Mules, who had assisted Professor Lecomte in her work. It referred to 'blood, urine and other habitual samples' being taken from his body, which then prompted the rumour that he had tested positive for cocaine. Five days later, there was a new official report which said that 'no sample under any form whatsoever was taken,'[35] which prompts the question as to how much anyone could trust a laboratory which does not even know if samples have been taken or not. Mules explained this by saying that these words were automatically inserted, but they do not appear in the post-mortem reports for Princess Diana or Henri Paul. But even more worrying is why such routine samples were not taken, yet more evidence of the unprofessional management of this morgue. In Princess Diana's post-mortem report, there is no pregnancy test, even though this would be standard procedure for any sudden death in a woman of child-bearing age. Despite acres of wild speculation in the newspapers, there is no evidence that such a test was carried out.[36]

In all, there were twenty-three autopsies carried out that steamy weekend in Paris. Given the appalling lack of basic housekeeping of paperwork in just two of them, it would be surprising if unlabelled samples did not get mixed up. In fact, it would be a surprise if they were not.

Once the world's press had the drunk-driver story they were off the hook. In the days immediately after the accident, the papers took a lot of criticism for their use of paparazzi photographs and Diana's death was beginning to look like a commercial disaster for them. The 'drunk-driver' story was perfect but there is a problem: there is an acute shortage of evidence anywhere else in his life that he was an alcoholic. For a start he played tennis before breakfast that morning, not normal behaviour for a binge drinker. He had dinner once a week with a group of friends but drank sparsely. France is a country where people socialize in brasseries, but the barmen are not helpful. Bernard Lefort, the *maitre d'hotel* at Le Bourgogne, told the police he had served him three times the previous year but never with an alcoholic drink. He also told the Paris police that visiting British journalists had offered him money to say that Henri Paul was a drunk, an offer tabloid journalists were making all over Paris in the days after the crash. Lefort's sister (who knew Henri Paul better) told the police he would drop in once a week and just have a single drink. David Evanno, a former barman at a bowling alley said the same, as did his former girlfriend, Laurence Pujol, and a writer friend called Sylvie Lambert. Many journalists and others then argued that he must have been a closet drinker, but his cleaner (who would know better than anyone if he was a closet alcoholic) assured the police that he did not drink at all, as did a student,

Badaia Mouhib, who stayed with him. A local policeman, Pierre Houssais, who saw and talked to him every day also confirmed what everyone else was saying: he was not a drinker.

A week before the crash, he renewed his pilot's examination, which involved a detailed physical examination and rigorous medical. He passed and according to his instructor, 'He was a good private pilot, looking to progress all the time.'

The only evidence of him drinking came from a doctor, Dominique Melo, who gave him Prozac and Noctamide to help treat the depression he felt after the break up of his relationship with his girlfriend, Laurence Pujol. She also told police that as Henri Paul was worried he might become alcohol-dependent, she had prescribed him Aotal, a drug which diminishes the desire to drink. However, despite his fears, she also confirmed to the police he was not an alcoholic. Even if he had had that tendency, he clearly had it under control, as there is no evidence of him drinking either in public or in private. This was further confirmed by his post-mortem, which revealed that his liver was in excellent condition and carried none of the tell-tale scars of heavy drinking. The French government doctors argue that the blood test was accurate and that he could carry such a huge volume of alcohol without showing it because he was such a heavy drinker. The only questions are, where and when did he drink?

Henri Paul was secretive about his private life and for a very good reason. According to former MI6 officer Richard Tomlinson, he was a spy working for the British, bugging guests who stayed at the Ritz. Tomlinson came across him in 1992 when he was working in the Soviet Operations Department. Henri Paul was regularly supplying the British with bugging tapes and intelligence on guests, like Yasser Arafat and Jonathan Aitken.[37] Aitken visited the Ritz in September 1993, which resulted in a story in the *Guardian* newspaper. He famously sued for libel, lost his case and went to prison for perjury. In the early 1990s, MI6 was involved in a large and complex operation to smuggle advanced weapons systems out of the

Soviet Union and many of the Russian arms dealers they were dealing with were regular guests at the Ritz. It is standard practice for the world's intelligence services to recruit security managers in five-star hotels and Henri Paul was well paid for his work.

At the time of his death, he had fourteen bank accounts at four different banks. In the first nine months of 1997, he paid large cash sums into his account, generally FF40,000 (£4,000) on eight separate occasions. The size of the amounts is crucial, as anything over £5,000 would trigger a money-laundering investigation. By the time of his death, he had FF729,716 on deposit and FF490,803 in cheque accounts, a total of FF1,220,519, which at the exchange rates at the time was around £122,000. The French judge discovered all this but dealt with it the same way he dealt with every other difficult area of the investigation: he simply ignored it, a pattern seen elsewhere.

Instead of pursuing the motorcyclist and the other vehicles that caused the crash, the police spent a huge amount of time trying to find a white Fiat Uno, which the Mercedes grazed on its way into the tunnel. They never found the car or the owner.

Under French law the examining magistrate issued *lettres rogatoires* which gave the police specific instructions as to the areas of investigation they were to undertake. In this case the judge issued them but then in the latter stages of the investigation he verbally countermanded them, telling the police that he had nothing left for them to investigate. When he did this, the police had not found the white Fiat Uno, identified the two motorbikes involved in the crash, secured all the paparazzi mobile phone records, located all the witnesses, identified the other vehicles which were there that night or interviewed their owners. As for the driver, they had not explained the carbon monoxide in his blood sample, solved the mystery of the non-drinking alcoholic or discovered where his money came from. They had not even managed to find out where Henri Paul was that evening between 7 p.m. when he left work and 10 p.m. when he returned, the final piece of evidence that France's finest were more Clouseau than Maigret.

The morning after the crash, the royal family (who were on holiday in Scotland) went to church as usual, with Diana's sons. During the sermon, no mention was made of the crash or Diana's death. In London, a massive crowd grew outside her house. Though Charles went to fetch his ex-wife's body, the rest of the royal family refused to leave their holiday home. There was a huge row when the courtiers refused to drape the coffin with the royal ensign, Charles losing his famously short temper.

At Buckingham Palace there was no flag at half-mast and by the middle of the week, the mood in the crowd was very angry. The television and newspapers were badly out of synch with the public mood and did not realize just how short tempers were becoming. By midweek, they suddenly caught on and every British newspaper launched a series of furious attacks on the royal family.

A meeting was called in Whitehall. Present were civil servants from the Cabinet Office as well as officers from the police special branch and the security service MI5. Both the police and MI5 who had spent the previous thirty-six hours working the crowd reported that it was a million strong. It was leaderless but growing increasingly militant with only one demand: they wanted the union jack at half-mast. The police told the Cabinet Office that there was no way they could control a crowd that size, now parked inconveniently a short walk from the essential organs of state. Should they choose to march in any direction, the only way they could be stopped would be to bring the army out of its barracks, an unthinkable act in peacetime, which would also result in heavy loss of life. An anxious civil servant asked if there was a precedent and was told 'Yes, Paris 1789, Russia 1917. Neither of which had a favourable outcome for the incumbents!' The Whitehall machine moved quickly. The prime minister was briefed and so was Prince Charles. That night he rang his mother and father to explain the final reality to them. If the flag did not go up, the crowd could well march on Buckingham Palace to put it up themselves. Once inside the palace, they would be unlikely to leave and that would be the end of monarchical rule in Britain.

The flag went up and an unrepentant monarch bowed to the inevitable. She gave up her holiday and came to London to read a speech to the nation, a speech written for her not by her courtiers but by Downing Street. But by then, the damage had been done. Diana got a huge funeral and royal popularity ratings slumped, particularly among the under-forties.

Sir John Stephens, the former Commissioner of the Metropolitan Police, was asked to produce a report for the coroner. He dutifully portrayed the deaths of Princess Diana, Dodi Fayed and Henri Paul as a tragic accident. The coroner, Lord Justice Scott Baker, then limited the range of verdicts, only allowing the jury to say it was either unlawful killing, accidental death, or leave it open. He did not allow them a verdict of murder. The jury did not buy the conclusion of Lord Stephens' report and returned the strongest verdict they could – unlawful killing – blaming the paparazzi, the pack of cars and motorbikes following her Mercedes, and the driver, Henri Paul.

The coroner's decision to deny them a verdict of murder was crucial. Had they returned this, the British police would have had to extradite the obvious suspects and put them on trial. As it stands, the authorities walked away and the paparazzi who harassed her to her death went free, unnamed and unidentified, thanks largely to the Inspector Clouseau-like incompetence of the original French investigation.

Two years before her death, on 30 October 1995, Princess Diana talked privately with her solicitor, Lord Mishcon, at Kensington Palace. There were three others at the meeting, including her private secretary, Patrick Jephson. She told Mishcon she was afraid that efforts would be made to either get rid of her or silence her. She suspected this would be achieved by an accident in her car, such as a pre-prepared brake failure or something similar. At the very least, the purpose was to see that she was so injured or damaged that she could be declared unbalanced.

Three weeks after her death, Mishcon gave his note of the meeting to the Metropolitan Police Commissioner Paul Condon and a senior officer, David Veness. They put it in a safe and did not disclose it either to the French judge or the original English coroner, Dr John Burton. Instead, this important piece of evidence, which would have been routinely divulged in any other similar police investigation, remained locked in a safe at New Scotland Yard. Lord Stephens finally revealed its existence, but only after Paul Burrell had gone public with a letter from Princess Diana in which she claimed her husband was planning to kill her.

After the inquest, Mike Mansfield, QC, who represented Mohammed Al Fayed, wrote a lengthy piece for *The Times* newspaper, arguing cogently that her death was not an accident. 'Diana's fears for her safety and her preoccupation with surveillance were thoroughly canvassed, and in my view were found to be entirely justified. Unfortunately her predictions came to pass.'

Part 4
AFTERMATH

Benjamin Disraeli famously argued that assassinations never change the course of history. He was wrong. Some assassinations have profound effects. The killings of Archduke Ferdinand, Judge Giovanni Falcone and President Diem changed the course of the twentieth century and still profoundly affect the daily lives of billions of people. Some failed assassinations have been equally as important. Had the assassins been successful against Hitler, Stalin, Hirohito and Churchill, the Second World War would have been profoundly different.

Mathematicians have applied complex formulae to try and reveal the hidden patterns of assassination, to discover if there is any underlying relationship between assassination and other types of historical events, but such linkages are elusive. Though assassination is often an essential element in any coup d'état it is not inevitable. There is no clear relationship between political murder and different types of regime. Well protected despots can still be taken out while vulnerable leaders can walk the streets without protection.

The law of unintended consequences applies here but – just to confuse matters further – it only works randomly. Few assassins achieve their aim and often watch – horrified – as their predictions unravel and the outcome is exactly the opposite of what they had predicted or hoped for.

Some assassinations of major public figures, like JFK, have little impact on the body politic even though they traumatize the public soul, while others carry a long delayed time fuse. In 1981, the assassination of Anwar Sadat was dismissed as a minor hiccup in Middle Eastern politics, the work of a small band of largely unimportant religious zealots.

Few heard the time bomb ticking away in the basement of Egyptian politics, which would then erupt in the greatest ever terrorist atrocity in New York on 11 September 2001 ...

9

DECIDE WHAT YOU WANT TO ACHIEVE

Rue des Cordeliers, Paris, 1793 . . .
Charlotte Corday, an attractive convent-educated young woman takes the coach from Caen to Paris, stopping off to buy a kitchen knife with a six-inch blade and a black ebony handle. A devout nationalist and democrat, her intention is to kill Jean-Paul Marat, a member of the Jacobins who she correctly identifies as the architect of the worst excesses of the Reign of Terror during the French Revolution. Unlike many other assassinations, all the evidence suggests that there is no conspiracy and she acts alone. It is premeditated and her plan is to assassinate him in the most public way possible, at the National Convention in front of the massed ranks of his fellow revolutionaries. She is fortified by her belief that this will shock the French out of their lethargy and they will rise up to stop the endless slaughter of her fellow citizens as the country lurches from being a monarchy to a republic.

It is high summer and when she gets to Paris she discovers that Marat has not been seen for a month and she will therefore have to rethink her plan. She decides to kill him at home, knowing that because he is such a high-profile figure, the shock value will be just as great. The night before the assassination, she checks into a cheap hotel and writes her speech to the French, *L'Adresse aux Français*, in which she explains her desire to destroy 'the savage beast fattened on the blood of Frenchmen' and her belief that his assassination will bring peace and restore the rule of law in a country where public executions, often on the flimsiest evidence, are the currency of everyday life. The following day she goes round to his house, her knife concealed in her dress, but the *concierge* refuses to let her in. A smart and resourceful woman, she leaves an enticing bait, which she knows that Marat, a man now consumed with bloodlust, cannot resist: the promise of juicy details of anti-revolutionary activity in her hometown. When she returns again that evening the *concierge* once again refuses her entry but Marat hears her voice and invites her in. A journalist, Marat loves writing lists of his enemies to be slaughtered in the name of the people and, given the increasingly short supply of locally based victims, he is delighted to be able to mine a new and rich seam of counter-revolutionaries who can be rounded up and brought to Paris for the mob and their heroine, Madame Guillotine.

In public, Marat swaggers around, dressed as a *sans-culottes*, a man of the people, pistols stuck in his belt. In private, he conducts much of his business sitting in a hip bath to treat his skin complaint (almost certainly psoriasis) with a vinegar-soaked turban round his head. Across the bath is a plank of wood which functions as a desktop, on which he rests his pen and paper as he scratches the names with his quill pen. His pistols lie, loaded but impotent, on the shelf behind him as he assures her that – on the basis of her testimony alone – all those she has named will be arrested and guillotined within days. If she ever had any doubts about his infamy and contempt for the rule of law these assurances dispel them. Enraged, she stands up and stabs him to death with a single blow, the knife going through his ribs, slicing his aorta as it slides into his heart. Death is virtually instant and, like the religious assassins who preceded her, she is secure in the utter righteousness of what she has done. She makes little attempt to escape and is captured immediately.

Both victim and assassin acquire instant celebrity status. Marat is painted by one of his supporters, a fellow revolutionary, Jacques-Louis David,[1] a brilliant and visceral portrait of a once powerful man on the very cusp between life and death. At her request, she is painted by a National Guard officer, Jean Jacques Hauer, who she thanks with a lock of her hair, 'a souvenir of a poor dying woman'. Her portrait shows a handsome young woman, clear-eyed and defiant. While in prison she writes, 'I am at peace and delightfully content, for the last two days my country has been happy and so have I.' She waits expectant in the firm belief that her actions will inspire the real citizens of France to seize control, trusting that her example will 'inspire the people with that energy which had been at all times the characteristic of republicans'.

Like many other politically motivated assassins she is convinced that the single high-profile assassination of a key individual will dramatically change the course of history, in this case stopping the relentless tide of state-sponsored assassination and violence, delivering peace and re-installing the rule of law back into the heart of the state. But there is no popular uprising. Confronted by a spineless and indifferent populace, she complains, 'There are so few patriots who know how to die for their country. Everything is egoism. What a sorry people to found a Republic.' Despite her gut-wrenching disappointment, she goes to her death with great dignity, 'with Roman firmness' according to one contemporary account[2] . . .

The sad irony of her death is that Marat was seriously ill and unlikely to live much longer. But even if she had known that, it is doubtful if this would have made her change her plans. This was never about his death but the shock value of his assassination, which makes this killing the ideal starting point for the question: *do assassins ever achieve their aims?*

First of all, they have to actually kill their victim. This is an obvious point but one often overlooked by the assassins themselves. When the CIA was running an assassination course in the early 1950s, the trainer reminded his apprentices: 'The essential point of assassination is the death of the subject. A human being may be killed in many ways but sureness is often overlooked by those who may be emotionally unstrung by the seriousness of this act they intend to commit. The specific technique employed will depend upon a large number of variables, but should be constant in one point: death must be absolutely certain.' To enforce his point he reminded them that 'the attempt on Hitler's life failed because the conspiracy did not give this matter proper attention'.

Actually, there was not a single conspiracy to assassinate Hitler but several dozen, some of which got remarkably close. But in every case, the assassins had very specific goals, which they failed to achieve.

By June 1944, the war was effectively lost, but those around Hitler still believed it was worth risking everything to assassinate him. In the most famous attempt on his life, Colonel Claus von Stauffenburg, a Bavarian Catholic from a noble family, planted a time bomb under the table, where the Führer was chairing a meeting. Stauffenburg made his excuses and left for Berlin, believing that Hitler would be dead by the time he arrived. But Hitler was protected by the table leg and survived. Stauffenburg and his fellow plotters were shot. A devoutly religious man, Stauffenburg was horrified by the treatment of the Jews and prisoners of war and regarded Hitler as the epitome of evil. His motive was simply to make Germany a better place by ridding the Third Reich of its leader, in the belief that once he had gone some sense of normality and civilized behaviour would return.

There was another even closer and much more significant near miss. But despite eight months' planning, the assassin failed to make Hitler's death 'absolutely certain'. In November 1938, a carpenter, George Elser, visited the Burgerbraukeller Hall in Munich on a reconnaissance mission. He got a job as a renovator and over the next year – only ever working at nights – he meticulously built an intricate bomb, concealing 50 kg of high explosive, six clock movements and a small battery, which allowed him to set the detonator up to six days ahead. He tested it and it worked perfectly so he set it for 9.20 p.m. on 9 November 1939 when, he believed, Hitler would be in mid-rant. He then set off for the Swiss border. As expected, Hitler began on time but then fifty-seven minutes into his speech, just at the point when he would normally be stepping up a gear into full eyeball-bursting froth, he suddenly finished, gave a Nazi salute and left. As his heavily armoured motorcade reached the station just a few minutes later, the bomb exploded, killing eight and injuring dozens of others. Had Hitler still been present in the hall he would have been assassinated and the course of the rest of the twentieth century would have been very different.

Elser is often portrayed as the ultimate lone assassin, an obsessive who planned this killing over an eight-month period. Others think he received help from highly placed Nazis, who provided him with the sophisticated tools and equipment he needed. There is further suggestive evidence that someone was looking after him. Though he was captured immediately afterwards he was not executed, and only died at the end of the war in Dachau.

Hitler was not alone. History is littered with the survivors of assassinations, especially that unique breed who are impregnable and repeatedly survive the assassins' best efforts. All are lucky but there are often other factors at work.

Queen Victoria survived at least seven attempts, her image of a remote and unassailable figure being reflected by the reality, though she was helped by the amateurishness of the assassins. Fidel Castro is the easy winner of the assassination survivors' sweepstake, having emerged unscathed from dozens of attempts on his life. The Church Committee, which investigated US assassinations of foreign leaders, found concrete evidence of eight CIA plots to kill him between 1960 and 1965,[3] including one on 22 November 1963, the day President Kennedy himself was assassinated in Dallas. On that day, a US government emissary met Castro to discuss the possibility of better relations between the USA and Cuba, while a CIA case officer was hooking up with a would-be Cuban killer to give him a poison pen with which to assassinate the Cuban leader. This was the Kennedy White House at its duplicitous best. Castro's survival is due primarily to two factors: the operational brilliance of the Cuban intelligence service which consistently outwitted the CIA, and the often farcical incompetence of the Agency.[4] Colonel Qaddafi of Libya has also survived numerous attempts by the CIA and MI6; the closest they ever got was a bullet in his buttocks.

Again, Qaddafi has been kept alive by his cunning, but principally by the astute skills of his intelligence chief, Moosa Coosa, who has been with him since he first seized power in 1969 and is now the longest-serving intelligence chief in the world. Charles de Gaulle, too, survived numerous attempts throughout the 1960s, one of which was brilliantly captured by Frederick Forsyth in his novel *The Day of the Jackal*. At the time, France was fighting a brutal colonial war in North Africa and there was no shortage of assassins, both from among the North Africans but principally from his own venomous far right-wing intelligence officers, who regarded him as a traitor. More recently, Presidents Mubarak of Egypt and Musharraf of Pakistan have survived numerous attempts by the Islamic fundamentalists who regard both men as traitors to their religion. Other politicians have also lived through near misses. Mrs Thatcher survived an IRA bomb, while both Presidents Ford and Reagan lived after being shot, as did Pope John Paul II and Vladimir Lenin.

Though the victim survival rate is much higher than might be imagined, many assassins do manage to complete their basic task of killing their target. However, virtually every assassin has another motive other than the simple removal of their victim. Most modern assassins believe, like Charlotte Corday, that their particular assassination will provoke very specific political change. However, most are disappointed and the number of assassins who actually achieve all their aims is remarkably low. The problem is this: it is often very difficult to predict which assassinations will succeed and which will fail as this is not an exact science, where there are fixed rules. There are some strong guidelines, but these have changed over time and as societies have become more complex so it has become increasingly hard to predict the repercussions which follow assassination.

In ancient empires, the assassins (or more often the people directing them) usually got exactly what they wanted, which was to come to power, though for many the occupation of the throne was only a transitory experience, as they were, in turn, removed by the next assassin.

As monotheism gradually took a grip, religious belief was added to the mix. Kings, queens and national leaders were also assassinated for their beliefs, as other rulers tried to impose their brand of religion. The Hashshashin changed all that, using assassination as a tool of political terror to subvert whole states to their will, though they only succeeded where the regimes they attacked were autocratic and brittle with all power focused on one individual. Kill the man, control the power structure. But, as assassins, they were unsuccessful against the Knights Hospitallers, which was a broad-based organization with power widely spread among a large number of individuals. Even if they assassinated the leader it had little impact as the Hospitallers just elected another.

The French Revolution then added ideology to the ingredients, all of which made assassination a more complex issue in the modern age but the basic principal of targeting the leader to effect political change remained. The effectiveness of the assassin was then decided by the degree to which the victim was synonymous with the state. If the victim was a monarch and all power was vested in the throne, then the effects were often seismic.

However, as soon as societies became more sophisticated, usually through the injection of even the most minimal pretence at democracy which in turn brought an instant media other than court-based gossip, the law of unintended consequences kicked in. The effects became surprising, unpredictable and often the exact opposite of what the assassin expected and hoped for.

In the case of Charlotte Corday, there was no popular democratic uprising in which the violent revolutionaries were removed by the public will. Instead, the exact opposite happened: the man she saw as 'a monster' became a martyr and busts of Marat quickly replaced crucifixes and other Christian icons. His death was just what the hard-line revolutionaries needed. The Jacobins redoubled their efforts, slaughtering the opposition in ever-greater numbers all over France. The assassination of Marat was the perfect excuse to abandon any pretence at the rule of law. New anti-terrorist laws were brought in by a ruthless and repressive regime, under the cloak of the revolutionary rallying cry *Liberté, Egalité et Fraternité.* There were purges in the army, federalism was destroyed, all power was centralized and foreigners were arrested. Even a young German man called Adam Lux, who wanted to put up a statue in her honour with the inscription 'Greater Than Brutus',[5] was sent to the guillotine as was a watchmaker whose only crime was making indiscreet remarks.

At her trial Charlotte Corday was asked by the judges, 'Do you imagine you have killed all the Marats?' She replied, 'No'.[6] It was a killer question that helped resolve the issue of whether assassins ever achieve their aims. In this case, the assassination was a total failure simply because there was a constellation of more powerful forces at work, far more powerful than a single assassin. The French revolution was not a one-man affair. Marat did not dominate like Lenin, Castro or Mao and there were other key figures involved, like Danton and Robespierre though they too would both meet violent and early deaths, executed the following year within three months of each other.

The French Revolution was a major hinge in history when a previously autocratic monarchical despotism was transformed into a republic virtually overnight and the removal of one man (no matter how influential) was never going to alter the tide. There was also a major class war in full swing. The aristocracy resented a monarchical system in which an intellectually derelict king had all the power but they got the bills, specifically the huge cost of supporting the American revolutionaries, which had almost bankrupted the country. The absence of any move towards power-sharing and political reform just made them more disaffected. The bourgeoisie, a dynamic and wealthy middle class of merchants and professionals, despised both the monarch and the aristocracy, seeing them as relics of a world long past its sell-by date. The *sans-culottes*, the mob of workers both skilled and unskilled, loathed everyone else. Add in an expensive and futile foreign war, an acute shortage of basics like bread, and the arrival of political ideology, and particularly the explosive power of new ideas, and all the necessary ingredients for a revolution were packed in Paris. No power on earth – least of all an assassin – was going to stop the meltdown of one world and the creation of a new one. In an atmosphere of profound communal fear, where death was rampant and commonplace, another murder was unlikely to have any effect. The assassination of a single individual was never going to make a difference. There were simply too many hands all competing to grab the levers of power.

But revolutions breed hard men, single charismatic figures who seize control of these forces (which had previously seemed uncontrollable) and bend them to their will. Once that happens the assassin can make a difference. Killing a man with genuine power, even in a world where death is part of the daily exchange, can make a significant difference. Had Charlotte Corday waited a few years until Napoleon held all the strings and killed him instead she would have made a huge difference to the subsequent history of France.

During the Second World War, the Allies used targeted assassination both against the Nazis and their key supporters. Taking a leaf from the Hashshashin assassination manual, they knew that assassination deep in the Nazi high command and close to the leadership could always shatter the nerves. An assassination in the heartland, just where they felt safe, could have profound effects. Here a single assassin could have a clear aim and succeed.

General Darlan, described by Churchill as an 'odious Quisling', was shot twice in the stomach at 3 o'clock in the afternoon in Algiers, the day before Christmas 1942. The assassin was a young French nationalist, Fernand Bonnier, but lurking deep in the shadows behind him were two men who got exactly what they wanted from this killing: Winston Churchill of England and General de Gaulle of France. Darlan was the Commander in Chief of the French Navy in 1940, the heir apparent to Marshal Petain and a key figure in the Vichy regime, who believed that the future of his country lay in it being Hitler's doormat, a compliant satellite of enthusiastic Nazis eating their croissants under the swastika. The US President Franklin Roosevelt was a keen supporter of Darlan, believing that a France which had learned to be compliant with the Nazis would be much more amenable to US influence after the war. On 12 December 1942, Churchill learned that Roosevelt intended to work with Darlan 'for a very long time . . . at least until the end of the war in Europe.' The reaction within the SOE, the Chiefs of Staff and the Foreign Office in London was sharp. Darlan had to be 'eliminated' and two weeks later he was dead. The Vichy regime was hierarchical and this assassination weakened it substantially. More importantly, it removed a compliant French leader and established Charles de Gaulle, with key British support, as the post-war leader of France. Churchill was happy too. He got a post-war independent France and not a US satellite just over the Channel.

In peacetime, it is often even harder for assassins to achieve their aims. While many assassins are attracted to the idea that the leader is all-powerful and therefore they can make a difference by removing them, this applies less and less the more complex a society becomes. Though the fundamentalists assassinated Sadat it did not change Egyptian society, which remained predominantly secular, though Muslim. But when the Egyptian secret police assassinated Hassan al-Banna, the Head of the Muslim Brotherhood, in 1949, it was a devastating blow. The Brotherhood was dominated by this one man, was very two-dimensional, and his assassination effectively de-capitated the organization.

Though the past was littered with failure, the Sadat plotters thought the moment was theirs. Like every revolutionary before them, they believed the conditions were ripe for a mass uprising leading to revolution. Looked at through fundamen-talist eyes all the evidence was there. Less than two years before, in February 1979, Ayatollah Khomeini had returned in triumph to overthrow the Shah of Persia and establish a hard-line Islamic state in Iran, a turnover of power which had not been foreseen by the CIA – their national intelli-gence estimate of the year before had concluded that the Shah was safe for another ten years. Later that year, in November 1979, an armed group of Islamic militants led by Juhaiman al-Utaibi, the grandson of an Ikhwan warrior, had seized the Great Mosque in Mecca to protest against the Saudi occupation of this holiest of holy shrines. Al-Utaibi and his followers charged the Saudi regime with being pro-Western and deeply corrupt. After several weeks (with the help of French special forces) they were crushed. The fundamentalists watched, horrified by the TV pictures of French soldiers trampling round the holiest of holy places with their boots on. Though the rebels were crushed, these two incidents sent a double shock wave round the Arab world.

The message on the temple walls was clear: from now on, no regime was safe.

The young Islamic radicals in Egypt believed their country was the next to fall. Just like Saudi Arabia and Iran, there was massive poverty and an almost vertical gradient between the small number of super rich and the millions of dirt poor. Once Sadat fell, they believed the other pillars of state would collapse and the whole edifice of the state, fetid and rotten with the stench of Western corruption, would come falling down. A new earthly paradise, where Islamic law prevailed, would then emerge. They believed that the single spark would ignite a mass uprising. But in revolutions, timing is everything.

They were not the only adherents of the single spark theory. The Minister for the Interior General Nabawy Ismail believed it, too, and he had a plan in place to deal with the immediate aftermath of a presidential assassination. It was called 'Code Ten'. Every police station in the country had been instructed that if he gave the code words 'Code Ten' they were to load live ammunition in their guns and take to the streets. Any revolt was to be crushed immediately. As soon as his president was shot, the general barked the two words into his radio set. Within twenty minutes, long before most people knew what had happened, Cairo, Alexandria and every town and village were closed down.

The Egyptian security services then brutally crushed every dissident response, no matter how small. In the coming weeks and months the members of Al Jihad were rounded up and systematically tortured. In many of the run-down houses of the plotters, the Egyptian security services found two objects, a compass to direct them to Mecca at prayer time and a torn photograph of Menachem Begin. Since then the Egyptian state machine has bulldozed its way through the fundamentalist groups, torture, imprisonment and hanging being the weapons of choice, and in the process have made the Egyptian state invulnerable to assassination.

Though there have been numerous attempts to assassinate President Mubarak, a successful attempt would not now make any difference. The army and the vast civil service which clogs every pipe in the state machine are so heavily intertwined that if Mubarak went he would simply be replaced by another figurehead chosen by the military and life would carry on as before. Even Al Qaeda has recognized this, announcing that they will not attack the Egyptian state as conditions are not ripe, which is revolutionary speak for saying *we would lose if we did.*

Few assassinations are spontaneous affairs. They are often preceded by lengthy discussions, when the pros and cons are fiercely argued. In the early 1960s the CIA discussed whether they should assassinate President Julius Nyerere of Tanzania but in the end decided against it, in the main because he was so obviously such a decent man that there were no volunteers.[7] But this case was exceptional. In general, the decision is taken round three key areas, which inform the discussions regardless of political creed or religious belief.

First, smart assassins only kill if they believe it will make a difference. Al Qaeda have made repeated attempts to assassinate President Musharraf of Pakistan as they know that his intelligence service and his army are both split between the secularists and the fundamentalists. They believe that if they can kill him that will give a huge boost to their supporters within the state and tilt the country towards the Islamic revolution they believe is theirs for the taking.

Second, if the purpose is to remove the leader as part of the process of change then there must be a reasonable chance that the replacement will be a weaker character so that the assassins can continue applying pressure with some long-term prospect of success. When the British diplomat Howard Smith put forward a plan to assassinate Lumumba in 1960, he did so after noting that he 'is not a leader of a movement within which there are potential successors of his quality and influence'. Once Lumumba had been removed, the British believed they could replace him with a leader who would be more compliant to the West, and in particular those Western companies which wanted to exploit the Congo for its vast untapped wealth.

Third, it is totally counter-productive if the target is going to be replaced by someone even stronger, which is why Al Qaeda have been very confused about their attempts to assassinate President Mubarak of Egypt. They know that he would be a huge prize and there would be great propaganda value in assassinating a fairly secular Middle Eastern leader. However, they also know that he fronts up for the Americans and his power is underpinned by the army and a very efficient security apparatus. After nearly a decade of heavy repression, the fundamentalists only have a limited grip in Egypt. If they were to assassinate Mubarak, they know they will set their cause back for decades.

But while assassins can succeed within traditional autocratic and hierarchical power structures, as soon as the circumstances become more complicated, the law of unintended consequences kicks in. Even when the assassins succeed, there are no guarantees as to the consequences. This applies in both peace and war.

In 1942, a group of young Czech nationalists decided to kill Obergruppenführer Reinhard Heydrich, the brutal and sadistic head of the Nazi security police. The planning was carried out in England with the help of the SOE but the assassination itself – in Prague – was a catalogue of disasters, feeble decision making and poor execution on both sides. On 27 May, Heydrich set off to work in the official car, sitting next to the driver in the front. As usual, there was no armed escort and the only weapons they carried were their 7.65 calibre pistols. The armour plate for his car was still on order and had therefore not been fitted. It was a delay that would prove fatal. As his car sped through Prague he was monitored by the Czech resistance. Shortly after 10.30 a.m. as he slowed down to round a corner, one of the young assassins, Josef Gabčík dropped his coat and raised his sten gun at point-blank range. He pulled the trigger but nothing happened. The gun jammed. Heydrich should have realized he was in an ambush and ordered his driver to get him to safety. Instead he stood up and drew his pistol, believing Gabčík to be the only assassin. At this point, the second assassin Jan Kubiš threw a grenade at the car but instead of it landing inside the car it exploded against the back wheel blowing shrapnel everywhere, including into the face of Josef Gabčík. In the confusion, Heydrich and his driver leapt from the car and fired at the fleeing assassins. Heydrich ran across the street but just like a really bad B-movie he suddenly fell down clutching his side and subsequently died in hospital of blood poisoning.

The consequences for the Czechs were horrific and un-predictable. As keen students of history, the Nazis knew exactly what this meant. The growing number of assassinations across Occupied Europe suddenly included one of their inner circle. Any one of them could be next. The Allies – just like the Hashshashin a thousand years before – knew the gut-wrench-ing, heart-stopping, panic-inducing fear an assassination can have, when it is hard-wired into the seat of power. The Nazi High Command simply lost it. The SS went on the rampage in Prague and the following month a special train marked AaH (*Attentat auf Heydrich*, Assassination of Heydrich) left Prague carrying the first one thousand Jews, followed by two more trains. But the Nazis were slaughtering Jews every day and this no longer had any shock value. A major gesture was needed. The following month they surrounded the tiny village of Lidice and murdered or arrested everyone, apart from eight children who were considered fit for Germanization.

The assassins were horrified. Instead of delivering a decisive blow against the Nazis, this assassination had backfired spectacularly, an outcome they had never predicted. It also backfired on the Nazis, delivering a huge propaganda coup to the Allies, for this was an act of unparalleled barbarism, which helped focus everyone's minds on why they were fighting the war.

The SOE and the Czech resistance were not the only ones to completely misread the signs. After generations of power building through assassination ('excellent cadavers' as they were called) the Italian mafia finally went an assassination too far. The consequences were not predicted either by the mafiosi themselves, who were obsessive and insightful observers of the Italian state, or their victims.

By the early 1980s, the Sicilian calendar was marked by saint's days, feast days and assassination anniversaries – the judges, senior government officials, police officers and prosecutors all murdered by the mafia to sustain their iron grip on the local economy. Overlaid on top of this were the family anniversaries, marking the assassinations which had kept score in the great mafia wars.

The legitimate heirs of the Hashshashin, the Sicilian mafia is a state within a state, a parasite deep within the belly of the government enforcing its will through bribery, corruption and assassination, both actual and threatened. For over a hundred years, the Italian government in Rome had optimistically sent down officials to Sicily without success. Few had gone with hope or optimism and many had returned in a locally made wooden box. After decades, the low-intensity conflict between state and organized crime had become an elaborate game, understood by the criminals and those trying to deprive them of their liberty. Shortly before he was assassinated in July 1983, General Alberto Dalla Chiesa, the prefect of Palermo, sat having dinner with some of the crusading anti-mafia judges and explained what he called 'the new rules of the game'. The mafia was assassinating men in power when there was a fatal combination of circumstances: men who became both too powerful, and at the same time isolated, and who were therefore vulnerable. The mafia meticulously watched the behaviour of the Italian government, reading the signs. As soon as the state equivocated and their support for a specific judge wavered, they knew it was either safe to assassinate them or that the government actively sought their removal.

After fifteen years, Giovanni Falcone was the most effective investigating magistrate. The greatest mafia defector, Tomasso

Buscetta, a boss in both Italy and the USA, defected after the mafia had murdered all his close relatives. Over the months, the two men talked and Falcone gained an intimate knowledge of the internal workings of Cosa Nostra which he used to devastating effect, arresting many senior members. As he applied ever-greater pressure, the mafia increasingly resorted to the assassination of those members who they thought might be traitors, which in turn led to more defectors breaking their vow of *omerta* (silence) because they would rather talk than die. Falcone was on a roll but after fifteen years he was still an assistant prosecutor. In contrast, his US counterpart, Rudolph Giuliani, had a small army of lawyers, prosecutors and investigators at his disposal and several federal agencies backing him up. This reflected something far greater: Giuliani had the power of the federal state behind him. Falcone had none.

When the position of Head of the Investigative Office became available, Falcone was easily and obviously the best candidate but after some very dirty politics, he was publicly snubbed, a clear cue to the mafia. A few days later he told his fellow judges, 'I am a dead man.' Despite his gloomy lack of optimism he survived for a while, leading the life of a heavily guarded recluse, but then his political bosses made their decisive move.

Even though he was operating – effectively behind enemy lines – in the mafia heartland of Sicily, his personal security arrangements were substantially reduced.

On Saturday, 23 May 1992 he returned to Palermo, as he did every weekend, leaving Rome on a military aircraft, landing in Sicily shortly before 6 p.m. The standard security arrangements for anyone as vulnerable as Falcone should have been a helicopter checking out the route shortly before he arrived. Had there been one, any counter-terrorist police officer would have noticed an unusual amount of unauthorized activity along the route and a gang of men loitering near a shack set back from the road. Standard protection would also have used a decoy car to check the route in advance of the judge. But Falcone, the most effective anti-mafia judge the Italian state had ever seen, had none of this. For a man who lived a hermetically sealed life there were few opportunities for even a semblance of normal existence. He could not go shopping with his wife, play with his kids or stroll to a restaurant for dinner. On that day, he enjoyed a tiny slice of everyday life and drove the car, rather than letting his bodyguard drive. It was a decision that cost him his life. As they sped along the road, the convoy was blown to pieces by a five hundred pound bomb, leaving a huge crater in the road. The three men in the lead car were killed, Falcone survived as far as the hospital before he too died. The driver, sitting in the back, survived. Hard-wired into their supporters in Rome, the Cosa Nostra knew that key politicians and civil servants were hostile to Falcone, knowing that sooner or later his investigations into the invisible tentacles of organized crime would lead to the very heart of the government.

But the assassination of Falcone was a major error for the men of honour. While they could control the politicians with the carrot of bribery and the stick of assassination, they could not control public opinion. There was a huge and immediate backlash against the mafia. A national strike was called in Sicily, while in Rome newspaper commentators wrote of the death of the Italian state. Suddenly the pressure was on the politicians as ever more mafiosi started talking. As a result of the Falcone assassination, his successor Paolo Borsellino suddenly acquired three new witnesses. But before he could bring any new cases to trial, he too was assassinated, blown to pieces by a car bomb outside his mother's flat. His security had asked for the area to be made a no-parking zone to protect against this sort of attack but the request was lost somewhere in the bureaucratic fog.

The public fury following Falcone's death now escalated. The papers were full of the latest revelations of massive corruption at the heart of government, with hundreds of politicians and officials named, all recipients of a transmission belt of bribes running right into the deepest recesses of government. Borsellino's widow was so disgusted with the Italian government that she refused a state funeral. When the politicians and government officials came from Rome they were attacked by the mob and the next day all the anti-mafia prosecutors resigned, demanding the removal of their boss, who had persistently blocked Falcone and Borsellino. The stock market fell, the lira weakened and the government panicked. Faced with imminent extinction, the government finally brought in all the measures which Falcone, Borsellino and the prosecutors had been demanding for years: a witness-protection programme, the transfer of Cosa Nostra bosses to remote offshore prisons from where it was harder to run their businesses and the dispatch of seven thousand troops to Sicily. The trickle of *pentiti*, men of honour willing to confess in return for a light sentence and a new life away from the threat of murder and violence, became a river. A new chief prosecuting judge was appointed. Every month banners condemning the mafia came out of the windows in Palermo and the prosecutors knew that they could move with public support. That autumn they captured the number two in the mafia, Giuseppe Madonia, a leading boss in the Neapolitan Camorra and arrested over two hundred in a joint operation with the FBI. The courts toughened their sentences. In the past, the mafiosi knew that their convictions and sentences would be overturned but this now stopped. The new reality was that suddenly they were confronted with a single chilling thought: they would die, old men in prison, never to smell the sweet mountain air of Sicily ever again. Those in prison opened up even more and they were joined by ever more mafiosi, all suddenly jostling to be heard.

It was clear that the mafia strategy of head-on confrontation with the Italian state underpinned by assassination had failed, even though its architect was still at large. But then, just nine months after the Falcone assassination, Totò Riina, the man who had ordered Dalla Chiesa's assassination a decade before, was captured in Palermo, travelling openly and unarmed as he had done for the previous twenty-seven years.

An era of open mafia defiance of the state was over. There was now a political will to destroy the mafia, in contrast to the past, where politicians, judges, police officers and civil servants had been happy to bathe in the warm current of easy money which flowed through the corridors of power. The two years which followed, 1992–4, were ones of enormous success as Falcone and Borsellino's successors made huge inroads into a criminal organization that had previously looked impregnable. Hundreds were arrested, not just mafiosi but those in government who had protected them. Billions of lire were recovered. Once these interrelated criminal gangs were focused on survival rather than making money even the assassination rate fell, with murders reduced by 42 per cent. Had they left Falcone and Borsellino trapped in the web of a corrupt, venal and supine state, it is highly unlikely that they would have suffered such a staggering reversal in their fortunes in such a short time.

Falcone's killing was also bad news for the seven times Italian Prime Minister Giulio Andreotti. Once Falcone was assassinated, his star witness, Tomasso Buscetta, opened up fully. Before this he had refused to talk about the mafia's relationship with the Italian state – but now he did, detailing Andreotti's intimate relationship with Cosa Nostra. Andreotti was eventually sentenced to twenty-four years in 2002 for his part in the assassination of an investigative journalist, Mino Pecorelli, though he was eventually cleared on appeal.

Assassination is a super virus. It is volatile, contagious, virulent and highly resistant to any form of antiviral treatment. The constant presence of death breeds paranoia and those in the business quickly discover that the toxic philosophy they embrace can quickly infect everyone, both victim and assassin. Once embedded in the body of any organization it is very difficult to eradicate and in some cases only disappears after it has killed every host.

Take the Abu Nidal organization. For nearly two decades, between 1974 and 1992, it was the world's most dynamic and effective terrorist group, responsible for nearly a hundred attacks in twenty countries, resulting in nearly a thousand deaths, including the assassination of two British diplomats in 1984 and a Jordanian diplomat ten years later. The organization sprang into life in 1974, when Abu Nidal (real name Sabri al-Banna) fell out with Yasser Arafat. Nidal wanted to assassinate internationally, while Arafat wanted to focus on Israel. Instead of agreeing to disagree, Nidal turned on moderate Arabs and these then accounted for half his victims. But killing became a habit. Life was discounted to an item of no value and assassination inevitably bred paranoia. A terrorist mercenary, Abu Nidal worked for Iraq, Syria and Libya (and maybe even for Israel as well) but he began to worry that with the continued failure of his global campaign his assassins would turn inwards and he ordered a major cull of his supporters, having over a hundred and fifty killed in one purge. He died in August 2002 in Baghdad. Though he had been suffering from cancer, his death was hastened by a reported three bullet wounds. At the end, he was the last man standing in what once was the world's most dangerous terrorist organization. A fitting end for one of the world's most prolific assassin masters.

This same pattern is seen in the great mafia wars of the 1980s. Paranoia breeds paranoia and Totò Riina, the boss of the Corleonesi, established their family dominance in Sicily through a policy of rolling assassination, virulent even by mafia standards. Riina confused the opposition and quickly established himself as one of the great post-war civilian killers by breaking the mafia code, which required men of honour not to lie to each other. But as the assassinations became transparent, mafiosi began to kill each other and worse still they turned themselves in and identified their fellow killers and then let the state do their dirty work for them. The internecine mafia wars only subsided when both sides began to run out of troops and there were not enough bodies left to run the business. Like the terrorists, there was no fear of death, as one of the mafiosi explained about the death of another, 'His thirty-seven years are like eighty years to an ordinary person. It's not a shame to die at that age. He didn't die tired and unsatisfied by life. He died sated by life.' Though the wars died down, the assassinations continued even in 'peace' time, as family feuds remained hereditary, though some were generations old and the original cause had long since been forgotten. The assassination virus is immune and untreatable with the result that many mafia family businesses are now run by women, their men either dead or in prison.

Though assassinations are unpredictable, there are those in the intelligence business who have learned from their history and who have used it in a highly targeted way to provoke shifts in policy or apply leverage to politicians to get them to do their bidding. As a strategy it is highly dangerous but can be devastatingly effective. This is the time when the assassins get exactly what they want.

In 1960, after a decade of failure and humiliation, the Russian Premier Nikita Khrushchev called a halt to the KGB programme of assassination. Over the previous ten years, the Soviets had made at least six attempts, had only succeeded twice and four of their assassins had defected to the West. But although he believed the Russians were out of the game, his intelligence service had very different ideas. They would seek – and get – their revenge against Khrushchev.

In September 1964, Horst Schwirkmann, a West German counter-surveillance electronics expert, was sent to the German embassy in Moscow to sweep it for bugs. This was a routine visit as most embassies in the world are regarded as legitimate targets by their host governments. The KGB was notorious for trying to bug and infiltrate every embassy in Moscow. The Russian attack was not just limited to bugging. As many Western embassies knew, since the early 1950s the Russians even bombarded the US embassy with a bizarre microwave signal beamed at the first-floor windows from across the street.[8]

After finishing his work, Schwirkmann and a small group of friends went to visit the spectacular Zagorsk Monastery, one of the holiest shrines of the Russian Orthodox Church and burial place of the sixteenth-century Tsar Boris Godunov. As he and his friends were looking at the magnificent paintings and gilded decorations, he suddenly felt a stabbing icy pain in his left buttock and his friends noticed the distinctive smell of rotting cabbage. They immediately rushed him back to Moscow where the German embassy wisely rejected the offer of a bed in a Russian hospital until they could get him back to Bonn. After numerous blood transfusions and intensive medical treatment he survived. It was a senseless assassination attempt, one which was guaranteed to fail and heap further embarrassment on the Soviets and which led to a major diplomatic rift between Moscow and Bonn.

The back story revealed that this was the KGB's purpose. In September 1964, Khrushchev had pulled off a huge diplomatic coup for himself when he announced the first ever visit by a Soviet premier to capitalist West Germany, a huge international triumph for the Soviet leader, who increasingly wanted to be seen as a modern world statesman. But the visit had met with massive internal resistance inside Russia and particularly from the KGB.

As Schwirkmann lay in the intensive-care ward of a German hospital, protected by armed guards, the details began to leak and Khrushchev's proposed visit to Bonn was put on hold, much to the joy of the communist party bosses in Moscow, who had got exactly what they wanted.

The Russians stayed silent in public but under huge pressure eventually had no choice and sent a statement to the German government, which was promptly leaked a month later on 13 October. According to the Germans, the Russians had expressed regret that 'such deeds have been done which are difficult to evaluate except as an effort to complicate the relations between our countries,' which translated as: this was an unauthorized operation by an intelligence service which is out of control and not under the political control of the government. And the only purpose was to sabotage

Khrushchev's visit, his desire for peaceful co-existence and the first ever Moscow/Bonn summit.

The same day, Khrushchev returned from a month's holiday on the Black Sea. He was met at the airport, where a fleet of limousines took him straight to an urgent meeting of the Presidium at which he was persuaded to 'resign' on the grounds of his advanced age and his poor health. The KGB had got what they wanted: the punishment and removal of their political leader, and they had used assassination to achieve their ends.

Khrushchev was not the first leader to discover that while he thought he had one agenda, his intelligence service had another. He would not be the last.

10

ALWAYS CONSIDER THE ALTERNATIVE

'They [the Kennedys] started on me with Diem, you remember,
saying he was corrupt and he ought to be killed – so we killed
him. We all got together and got a goddam bunch of thugs and
we went in and assassinated him.'[1]

President Lyndon Johnson, phone call to
Senator Eugene McCarthy, 9.20 a.m., 1 February 1966

Saigon, Vietnam, 11 June 1963 ...
A Buddhist monk, Thich Quang Duc, sits in the lotus position
in the middle of a busy crossroads and, with the help of two
other monks, burns himself to death with petrol. He never
moves a muscle, totally composed and spiritually secure. All
around him, a crowd of Vietnamese gathers, some stunned,
others weeping. The pictures flash round the world with
devastating effect. Vietnam and US support for the spectacularly corrupt and venal regime of President Diem is suddenly
catapulted to the top of the international agenda. As often in

the post-war world the Americans find themselves in a place
they do not want to be, with allies they neither like nor want
and no clear idea of how to extricate themselves other than
through regime change and assassination. Diem's sister-in-law,
Madame Nhu, embarrasses them even further, saying she will
bring the mustard to the next barbecue, a remark of staggering
insensitivity. According to one of the CIA officers there, this
prompts the USA to apply 'direct, relentless and table
hammering pressure on Diem, such as the United States has
seldom before attempted with a sovereign friendly government'.[2]

After the French, as the prevailing colonial power, are
outwitted and thrashed at Then Bien Phu in 1954 the country
is split into two, with the communist Vietminh controlling the
north and the non-communists, backed by the USA, with Ngo
Dinh Diem as prime minister controlling the south. Unifying
elections are promised in 1956 but the Americans, knowing that
the communist leader Ho Chi Minh will win, renege on their
commitment and there is to be no democracy for the
Vietnamese. Instead the Eisenhower administration props up
Diem, calling him 'the miracle man of Asia' who builds himself
a huge power base, underpinned by the military. Diem is the
worst kind of despot, capricious, autocratic and a firm believer
in nepotism and power for its own sake. He is also religious and
as a minority Catholic believes in his divine mission to
persecute the Buddhists, even though they make up the bulk of
the Vietnamese population.[3]

In 1960, he survives a military coup. Two years later, his own
air force pilots bomb and strafe the presidential palace but he
escapes assassination. The long-promised religious tolerance,
respect for the Buddhists and basic political reform all
evaporate. Back in Washington, the State Department convinces
President Kennedy that Diem is not really unpopular and the
attempts by his own people to assassinate him are only
happening because of the uncertainty caused by the ongoing
war with the communists in the north. The Americans pressure

him to clean up his act, but he knows that he can ignore their demands as he is their best bulwark against the communists and, as Vietnam is the frontline in the Cold War, that is more important than anything else.

By 1963, under President Kennedy, the US presence rises to sixteen thousand including soldiers taking part in combat operations. It is costing the American taxpayer more than one million dollars a day, money Kennedy is happy to pay as the military and the CIA are both feeding him a steady and optimistic portrait of Diem ('I have seen no one with the strength of character of Diem, at least in fighting communists' writes one general). The local military are just as bullish about the South Vietnamese army, telling the president they are 'confident' they will win the war and that the communists face 'inevitable' defeat. The self-immolation of Thich Quang Duc puts Vietnam on the international front pages but things had started falling apart a few months before.

This fantasy world, constructed by the military and the intelligence services, both of whom are on the prowl looking for new battlefronts in the Cold War, is then shattered on 8 May 1963 when the South Vietnamese army fires on a crowd of Buddhists celebrating the prophet's birthday. Their crime is flying banners other than the state flag, an illegal act under Vietnamese law. The Buddhists naïvely believe this will be all right as the local Catholic archbishop (one of Diem's brothers) has flown his religious flags shortly before. Though the Americans are fighting side by side with the South Vietnamese, pillaging and burning their way across the countryside, this is a step too far. Another monk[4] burns himself to death on 31 May 1963. Kennedy and his aides are genuinely horrified and put pressure on the Diem government to admit responsibility, pay compensation and provide some guarantees of future religious tolerance and equality. Diem infuriates Kennedy by simply ignoring him.

Firm, quick and decisive action is required. On 9 July 1963, the Director of the CIA John McCone briefs President

Kennedy, that 'a coup attempt is increasingly likely' and the Americans begin to get themselves alongside anyone who might be able to overthrow the government. Another monk dies in mid-August and Diem promises to clean up his act but then, shortly after midnight on 21 August, his brother Nhu orders troops to attack the Buddhists: fourteen hundred are arrested and their temples are sacked. For President Kennedy and the huge American presence in South Vietnam this is humiliation on a grand scale. Nhu has ignored their explicit instructions. Even more embarrassing, Diem and his brother are both Catholics, like Kennedy. A TOP SECRET cable (approved by Kennedy) is sent EYES ONLY to the US ambassador in Vietnam, Henry Cabot Lodge, instructing him to speak to 'key military leaders' (any generals who might be encouraged to start plotting against Diem and his brother) to tell them that 'immediate action' must be taken to stop Nhu becoming any stronger and that this will require his 'removal . . . from the scene'. The instructions are brutally clear: if they cannot get rid of the brother then 'Diem himself cannot be preserved' and he will have to go as well. Lodge is also instructed to tell the coup leaders that the USA will give them direct support in 'any interim period of breakdown of central government'[5] . . .

For the previous two years, assassination has always lurked round the top of the list of White House foreign policy options. The Kennedy brothers have continually kicked the US intelligence community to assassinate Fidel Castro, the Cuban leader, as well as Patrice Lumumba, so no one is in any doubt as to exactly what 'removal' means and just what is required here.

Three days later, at a 4 p.m. meeting in the White House, the previous (and recently returned) American ambassador from Vietnam, Frederick Nolting, disappoints Kennedy, telling him that a coup is unlikely to succeed as the other generals 'don't have the guts, determination and leadership capabilities of Diem and Nhu'.[6] This is simply not good enough for Kennedy: if they don't have the backbone then he will give them some. The issues now clarify in the White House: not only is the current leadership disobedient, but Kennedy and his advisers now believe they cannot win the war with Diem and his brother in charge.[7] Nolting, who had been the American man in Vietnam for the previous three years, describes the decision as 'stupid'[8] but he is ignored by a White House which already has a fixed policy which it is going to enforce regardless of any contrary intelligence it might receive. Diem and his brother have to go.

The White House turns up the heat, announcing they are likely to cut American aid to the Vietnam government, a move they know will provoke the collapse of the Diem regime. Nhu then inflames an already incendiary situation by publicly naming the local CIA station chief, John Richardson, a capital offence in the eyes of the Americans. The CIA is incandescent: no station chief has ever been identified in this way before and Nhu's days are now numbered, regardless of anything the White House might have wanted to do.

Shortly after this, one of the key CIA case officers in Saigon, Lucien Conein, makes fresh contact with the army plotters who tell him that their plans are well advanced but for the coup to be successful, they will need to assassinate both Diem and his brother. The local CIA response is typical of the circumlocutory language loved by the Agency bureaucrats, saying 'We do not set ourselves irrevocably against the assassination plot.'[9] The response from CIA headquarters in Langley is even more devious, drawing a fine line to make sure the assassinations happen but that their own fingerprints are not visible. The local CIA officers are told that while the Americans could not be seen to 'stimulate, approve or support' the assassination they could not be held responsible for failing to stop something about which they only had 'partial knowledge'. The local CIA officers are told therefore that they are not to engage in the coup plans ('believe best position is hands off'), but just so everyone is clear, Conein is told that the next time he talks to General Minh and his fellow plotters he is to tell him that the US will 'not attempt to thwart his plans'. Conein is also told that he can review the plans for the coup but should not vet or examine the assassination plans.[10] This subtle distinction allows the White House and the CIA to build a shield of plausible deniability to cover up their involvement when the inevitable assassinations happen during the inevitable coup.

Conein's boss, John McCone, a devout Catholic who is opposed to assassination on principle – and particularly the assassination of a fellow Catholic – cables Conein and tells him that 'We cannot be in position actively condoning such course of action and thereby engaging our responsibility,'[11] an expression of ambiguity which ensures that his fingerprints will not be on the smoking gun at least. Conein then meets General Big Minh to tell him that the USA is formally opposed to assassination. The general, a worldly man gets the message, saying, 'OK, you don't like it. We won't talk about it any more,' a reply that gives everyone what they want. Diem and his brother will be assassinated but there will be no formal evidence trail back to the Kennedy White House.

Three weeks later, on 24 October 1963, Conein draws three million piastres ($42,000) and puts it in the safe of his house.[12] Four days later, the plotters tell him that Henry Cabot Lodge, the American ambassador, should not go on holiday on 31 October. The day before the coup, Lodge tells Washington that Diem, his brother and their families would want to get out of the country as soon as the coup began, 'but we would certainly not commit our planes and pilots between the battle lines of the opposing forces.'[13] Lodge suggests a compromise: the Americans should say they are willing to take Diem and his relatives out 'during a truce in which both sides agree to removal of key personalities'. But if there is to be no truce there will be no escape, which only leaves the possibility of asylum and there the Americans have a problem. They have already offered sanctuary to the Buddhists so it will be difficult to refuse it to the Diems. The response from Washington to any asylum request from the family who had been their closest allies in Vietnam for nearly a decade is lukewarm at best. They 'may afford asylum' to anyone 'to whom there is any implied or express obligation of this sort,' but the basic instructions from Washington are that anyone seeking asylum should look elsewhere.[14] Washington has now closed down all the escape routes and the brothers are booked for a one-way trip to the nearest graveyard.

The day before the coup is about to happen, there is a bizarre loss of nerve in Washington and the White House tells the local CIA to stop it. At a National Security Council meeting in Washington, Bobby Kennedy warns against precipitate action (as he had done over the Bay of Pigs) as does the CIA Director John McCone and the Chairman of the Joint Chiefs of Staff, General Maxwell D. Taylor. For Bobby Kennedy the issue is not morality (removing and causing the assassination of a close ally who was also the head of a sovereign state) but simply one of deniability. The only question is: would they get caught? 'I mean it's different from a coup in Iraq or South American country. We are so intimately involved in this . . .' he said. In a panic, the White House cables the US ambassador instructing him to tell the plotters to back off. When the White House is told this is now impossible they tell the ambassador they do not believe that they do not have the power to stop or discourage it, an instruction of staggering arrogance. By now it is way too late and they might as well have told the ambassador to go and stand on the beach and stop the incoming tide.

The official version of events is that the following day the US embassy is given just four minutes' notice, but the CIA officer closest to the plotters, Lucien Conein, has time to set off home to collect the money from his safe to pay the leaders so they can buy food for their troops and pay compensation to anyone killed on their side during the military action, which is by now underway.

Once the coup is well advanced, Diem rings the American ambassador to ask about the US attitude. Lodge dissembles, saying 'I do not feel well enough informed to, be able to tell you.'[15] On the face of it, this looks like a bare-faced lie but his confusion is understandable. His instructions were to stop the coup but if it happened (which was as certain as night following day) then 'it is in the interest of the US government that it should succeed.'[16] Having just received a suitcase of cash, the plotters have no doubts about the actual level of the American support they are receiving and tell Diem to surrender or be 'blasted off the face off the earth'.[17] Diem offers to surrender if he is given safe conduct to the airport. When this is not given he surrenders anyway.

The following morning between 6 and 7 a.m., the coup plotters, Generals Minh and Don, ring their CIA paymaster, Lucien Conein, to ask him for a plane so they can fly Diem and his family out of the country. Though the original request for it had been made three days earlier, Conein is now told that there will be no plane available for the next twenty-four hours. The signal to the local CIA officers and the army generals could not have been clearer: the USA has washed its hands of its former allies. Cutting off this last chance of escape is the signature on their death warrant. Exactly what happens next is unclear, but both brothers are dead within a couple of hours, maybe less. Like Thomas Becket, Diem and his brother are seized in church. General Minh claims they were then locked up in an army vehicle, but 'due to an inadvertence there was a gun inside the vehicle'[18] which they used to commit suicide, a claim which Conein does not believe as both men were Catholics. The preposterous nature of this claim is confirmed two weeks later when the local CIA officers are shown pictures of the bodies. Both men had their hands tied behind their backs and had died from being stabbed and shot, making this one of the more imaginative 'suicides' in assassination history.[19] An ironic end for a Catholic who as a minority leader had routinely persecuted Buddhists.

Throughout, Kennedy was in no doubt that once there was a coup (which he had green lit and encouraged) Diem and his brother would be assassinated. He knew this both from the

CIA on the ground and his advisers back in Washington, but he went ahead anyway, even sending a private emissary to Diem shortly beforehand telling him to get rid of his brother and seek asylum in the American embassy. The alternative which Kennedy offered Diem was *a coup d'e'tat*, in which he faced certain death.[20] Diem ignored this and Kennedy condemned him to his fate. At the time, one US diplomat mused about what would have happened if the Vietnamese leader had ordered Kennedy to get rid of his brother Bobby but these were just idle thoughts.

There was further damning evidence against Kennedy, from his successor President Lyndon Johnson. It came in a taped phone call the president had with Senator Eugene McCarthy, early on the morning of 2 February 1966, when he was trying to handle the growing hostility to the Vietnam war. The conversation started very jovially with Johnson and McCarthy sharing jokes about their long-suffering wives but then quickly moved on to the important business of the day: the bombing of Vietnam and McCarthy's opposition to it. This was not the warmonger Johnson as he was widely portrayed but a desperate president willing to do virtually anything to get out of a futile war by getting the Viet Cong to the negotiating table. He made it clear that this was not his mess and the particular target of his venom was the Kennedy administration and its supporters in the Senate ('that damn crowd'). Johnson's beef was that Capitol Hill supported Kennedy getting into the war but now refused to give him their support in continuing it, a betrayal which infuriated Johnson as he could not see any way out other than a humiliating withdrawal, which would certainly cost him the presidency. 'They [the Kennedy administration] started on me with Diem, you remember,' saying 'he was corrupt and he ought to be killed' and then Johnson confirmed what many had long suspected, 'so we killed him. We all got together and got a goddam bunch of thugs and we went in and assassinated him.'[21]

Johnson continued this refrain in his next call, when he spoke to General Maxwell D. Taylor, the recent US ambassador in

Vietnam (though not the ambassador at the time of the coup) to ask him to do 'a labour of love', which was to go and see McCarthy to explain why they were bombing. He told the general, 'They [the Kennedys and their supporters] started out and said "We got to kill Diem, because he's no damn good. Let's, let's knock him off," and we did.' The general, who as chairman of the Joint Chiefs of Staff had opposed the original *coup d'état* agreed, replying, 'Yeah, that's where it all started.' Johnson continued, 'That's exactly where it started! And I just pled with them at the time, "Please don't do it" but that's where it started – and they knocked him off.' Johnson's tone is matter of fact and his objection is that this assassination solved nothing but only dragged the US deeper into a war from which he could not escape.

However, he was not morally clean here. Under Johnson, the CIA ran their largest ever assassination programme, part of the daily routine of a squalid war. Over twenty thousand Vietnamese were killed under Operation Phoenix,[22] a programme of assassination and terror initially run by the CIA but then taken over by the military. As in Guatemala, lists of suspects were drawn for 'neutralizing'. The programme talked of 'Protecting People from Terrorism' which in reality meant brutal torture and extra-judicial assassination. The lessons of the 1954 CIA assassination manual ('Assassination can seldom be employed with a clear conscience. Persons who are morally squeamish should not attempt it') were not forgotten. Phoenix's architect, William Colby, who would go on to became Head of the CIA, sent out a memo saying 'If an individual finds the police-type activities of the Phoenix program repugnant to him, on his application, he can be reassigned from the program without prejudice.' As with Guatemala, the intelligence was poor and in the words of one CIA analyst, Sam Adams, 'they assassinated a lot of the wrong damn people.'[23]

Kennedy was assassinated three weeks after Diem and some commentators have linked the two, arguing that Kennedy's murder was revenge, adding southeast Asian drug lords to the

CIA, the mafia, the KGB and the Cubans in the lengthy queue of potential assassins. But the final irony was that, whoever killed him (and there was no shortage of powerful groups with a motive) the assassination he called for had had a far more profound effect on American society than his own.

The assassination of President Kennedy was one of the most iconic events of the twentieth century. It was one of the great clichés that everyone can remember where they were when they first heard the news. It sent a shock wave through American society, the reverberations of which are still being felt. But the assassinations of Diem and his brother, which condemned the USA to a decade of futile war, were far more significant.

Crucially, the war Kennedy had started in Vietnam continued and escalated, destroying a generation and leaving a legacy of pain at every level of American life. The Vietnam War is the most significant defining event in post-war American society, affecting everyone from Oklahoma City bomber Timothy McVeigh, the Christian militia and the other disaffected patriots to the heroin addicts dying in the projects from an international drug business which began in Vietnam with opium smuggled back to the USA in body bags. All are casualties of a whole series of movements in American society, whose foundations were laid in southeast Asia in the 1960s.

Kennedy's motives for the assassination were highly suspect. The good reason was he wanted to remove Diem and his brother and replace them with leaders more capable of winning the war, but the real reason was that he was worried they were trying to negotiate peace with the communists. Under this deal, which was an open secret in Saigon at the time, the American special advisers and soldiers would all have been kicked out of Vietnam, a humiliating reverse for Kennedy. The odds on peace were high. The North Vietnamese had been to the United Nations, whose Secretary General U Thant had condemned the South Vietnamese government as one of the world's most corrupt. At the end of August, General De Gaulle had thrown his considerable weight into the debate, calling for a united Vietnam, 'independent of outside influences'. Nhu too had been busy meeting members of the North Vietnamese government, men he described as nationalists first and communists second. He then met British, French and Polish diplomats to tell them of these meetings. They believed that the North Vietnamese were serious and had a high possibility of success. One of those Polish diplomats, Mieczyslaw Maneli, even went as far as having talks with Ho Chi Minh and other North Vietnamese leaders.

The outlines of a deal were put together. The north would export goods to the south which would pay for them with rice. Postal, economic and cultural relations would begin and reunification would follow. The north agreed that no Chinese or Russian troops would be allowed on Vietnamese soil and they even conceded that Diem could head up a coalition government. So desperate was the north to get the Chinese and the Russians off their backs that they even offered them a deal which would split Vietnam in two and allow free exchange and trade between the two countries. It was not just the Poles who believed that peace was possible. Following Ho Chi Minh's public suggestion of a ceasefire in August, Brigadier Robert Thompson from the British Advisory Mission to South Vietnam (BRIAM) told the Americans at the Saigon embassy that the communists were prepared to pay almost any price for American withdrawal, a view also echoed by local French and Indian diplomats who were talking to the north.

By mid-August, Nhu was effectively running South Vietnam and he knew that his relationship with the Americans was at an end. The British told their American counterparts that Nhu's only move was an alliance with North Vietnam. Both north and south had a lot in common: above all, both sides were fervent nationalists and the communists in the north were just as worried about becoming the pawns of the Chinese as the capitalists in the south were worried about living in the pockets of the Americans.

The North Vietnamese had a further problem, which had brought the situation into even sharper focus. They had less fertile land than the south and had just experienced their worst drought for a decade, compelling them to accept food aid from both China and the Soviet Union, neither of whom they ever wanted as allies. The North Vietnamese were smart and realized that the Americans would reject any deal that smacked of defeat so they offered a gradual reunification and the establishment of a Western-style democracy in a neutral and independent Vietnam. Nhu himself was so keen on this deal that he and his wife agreed to send their children to school in Hanoi as a gesture of friendship and respect.

But there was one element they had missed in the equation: American domestic politics. Kennedy was worried that any such deal would cost him re-election. He told a close friend, Charles Bartlett, that he could not let South Vietnam go and then ask ordinary Americans to vote for him. 'Somehow we've got to hold that territory through the 1964 election,'[24] even though he knew that De Gaulle was right: there was no military solution in Vietnam, the only settlement was going to be a political one.

Kennedy also told Bartlett that the USA had no future in Vietnam and that at some point they would 'kick our asses out of there'. While there was no guarantee that Diem and his brother could have negotiated a lasting peace with the north, there were plenty of others who believed this was possible, including the British, the Poles and the French. Furthermore, a negotiated peace had been managed in Laos. Had Kennedy added his considerable weight to the international push for peace he could have made it happen. Instead, he had the two men crucial to the deal assassinated and all chances of peace died with them. The cost was huge.

These two assassinations did not just replace one set of corrupt South Vietnamese leaders with another, substituting 'one puppet for another' as the Viet Cong claimed,[25] they set the United States on course for a decade of war which would

leave 75,000 Americans severely disabled and take the lives of a
further 58,000, nearly two thirds of whom were under the age
of 21. But these figures, though appalling, are tiny compared
with the millions of Vietnamese, Laotians and Cambodians,
many of them civilians, who were slaughtered by the relentless
American bombing.

Before the coup, Brigadier Bob Thompson (who was
reporting directly to Kennedy), a very smart British army
officer in Vietnam and a keen student of history, had warned
that – after a coup – there could be 'a complete mess and the
whole structure might collapse'. More specifically he argued
that government ministries 'would be dazed and cease to
function for a critical period'. This is exactly what happened, but
worse. On top of the numbing effects of the coup there was the
assassination of two long-serving leaders, which – as always –
sent a shock wave through the government machine amplifying
the negative effects of the coup. Thompson rightly predicted
that whoever replaced Diem would have all his failings and none
of his authority, be seen as an American puppet and be quickly
replaced in a further coup, which is exactly what happened.[26]
The new government was ineffective both as civil leaders and
military commanders. They failed to deliver prosperity in the
south or win the war in the north. The new leader, General 'Big'
Minh, was popular with his US paymasters, playing tennis with
them and entertaining them with fanciful war stories but he was
a hopeless figure, preferring to play *mah jong* than fight the Viet
Cong or run the country. He was replaced and over the next
decade the Americans shuffled their puppets, eventually settling
on General Nguyen Van Thieu, though Minh returned to
surrender to the Viet Cong in 1975.

Thompson had rightly identified the other long-term effect
of assassination: it traumatizes and paralyses governments.
Politicians and civil servants simply lose confidence and
become frightened and distracted as they become ever more
fearful for their lives. Assassination carries a huge social cost,
bringing instability and preventing the state from ever deliver-

ing those sustained periods of relative peace and prosperity, when civilization flourishes. The absence of stable central government means that people are even more vulnerable to the key drivers which generally govern their lives: climate, trade, disease and wars with their neighbours.

Apart from the suicidal who do not care if they are identified, there is a very good reason why those who order assassination want to cover their tracks: it is highly contagious. President Kennedy, who with his brother ordered more assassinations than any other US president, was careful to cover his tracks outside the internal group he could trust. In 1961, he and his brother talked to Tad Szulc, a highly influential journalist working for the *New York Times*. President Kennedy tested the waters by asking him 'What would you think if I ordered Castro to be assassinated?' Szulc gave Kennedy two reasons why he should not: first, that it was unlikely to make any difference to the Cuban regime; the second reason was that it was morally wrong for the US to be in the murder and assassination business. The brothers then enthusiastically endorsed Szulc's view, Kennedy lying to him by claiming that he was resisting pressure from his advisers 'to okay a Castro murder'.[27] This was a direct lie as the Kennedy brothers were kicking the CIA all over Washington to assassinate Castro. At the end of the briefing, Kennedy revealed the real reason, saying, 'we can't get into that sort of thing or we would all be targets'. In the end both were assassinated, with a long queue of suspects, the final confirmation that Kennedy's worry about becoming a target was highly prescient.

Assassination simply rips the heart out of the body politic. Thompson argued that with Diem in control the US had the option of winning or losing. Without him, there was only one option, the latter. After a humiliating decade the Americans withdrew, Nixon and Kissinger agreeing basically the same terms that had been offered to Kennedy back in 1963.

* * *

For Vietnam, read many other post-war conflicts, where the assassinations of passionate and talented nationalist leaders have left a power vacuum from which many countries never recover. The Congo has been brutalized by civil war and genocide ever since the assassination of Lumumba and tens of millions have died. Much of Latin and South America has been force fed the US diet of assassination, military coup, more assassination, as one corrupt military dictator has replaced another. The palaces of tin-pot dictators get ever larger and so do the graveyards.

This pattern is now so well established that the vast majority of political assassinations in the twenty-first century are trade unionists, human rights lawyers and journalists. The political cycle of repression, oiled by assassination, destroys all who are touched by it. The CIA's own internal history of the Guatemala operation (1952–4) pointed out that the lesson of intervention was that it produces 'allies' who are 'stubborn, aid hungry and corrupt'. As the author pointed out, it was a lesson the US would have to re-learn in Vietnam – and it is one that every subsequent administration has also had to re-learn ever since.

The corollary is that the absence of assassination helps underpin political stability and that in turn tends to deliver prosperity. Though there was constant tension at court, the ancient Egyptians did not resort to the routine use of assassination as a means of resolving family disputes. This delivered lengthy periods of powerful dynastic rule, which in turn provided a platform for what was then the world's most advanced civilization.

The same pattern is even clearer in imperial Rome, where much of the dynamic growth took place in the second century CE when just five rulers ran the empire for nearly a century.

Trajan (98–117 CE) secured the loyalty of the governing class of senators by promising not to execute any of them on his personal order alone. It had to be a joint decision, effectively replacing the use of quasi-official assassination with something approaching the rule of law. A smart and able administrator, he adopted an inclusive liberal attitude to governing with the emphasis on the quality of life: general prosperity underpinned by new roads, public buildings, libraries and bath houses, earning him the title *Optimus Princeps*, Best of Emperors.

His successor Hadrian ruled for twenty-one years,[28] securing the imperial borders, which again enhanced the general level of peace and prosperity. When he returned from securing the Danube frontier he discovered that four Senators had been executed. He immediately claimed that he had not ordered the killings, promised it would not happen again and used generous tax breaks and a conveyor belt of gifts to the ruling classes to help cement his peace with the Senate. Unlike many of his predecessors he knew that assassination (even if done in the name of the state) is both corrosive of the delicate fabric of state and highly contagious. By denouncing these acts of dubious state execution he stopped the disease spreading, further securing his position by delivering peace and prosperity.

Hadrian was succeeded by another long-serving emperor, Antoninus Pius, who ruled for twenty-three years.[29] Unlike Hadrian, he stayed in Rome, was both generous and a good administrator, centralizing bureaucratic control, delivering stability by leaving civil servants in position and promoting local growth through public building and the use of financial grants.

His successor Marcus Aurelius ruled for nearly two decades, until 180 CE. As well as fighting wars to secure the empire he worked hard at home to enhance the quality of life for all. The rule of law was reinforced by a new system of circuit judges and permanent officials were given new responsibilities to ensure the proper distribution of food and the proper care of children. A near century of stability had provided the platform for the thousands of soldiers, engineers, civil servants, inventors and technologists to do what they were best at: delivering an ever-improving life experience for those who lived during the golden years of one of the world's greatest imperial civilizations. But all that was about to end.

The wars Marcus Aurelius fought, combined with the plague, crippled the state. Romans then living had only known relative peace and prosperity, but now that was quickly replaced by economic stagnation and bankruptcy. The new emperor Commodus abandoned the rational and inclusive practices of his predecessors and put capricious decision-making back into the heart of the state. He became joint ruler with his father when he was fifteen and emperor when he was eighteen. Within two years, his sister tried to assassinate him but failed. He turned on the Senate, executing his enemies and injecting massive corruption into the state machine, which had previously been a largely egalitarian organization. Impulsive, cruel, narcissistic, venal, ostentatious and egotistical, he was a ruler without a single redeeming characteristic. He was assassinated by his mistress, who first tried to poison him, but when this failed sent a wrestler in to strangle him in his bath.

Assassination generally takes a couple of generations to clear the political DNA but the strangling of Commodus spliced it right back into the genetic structure. No Roman ruler would feel safe for the next century, when the empire would get through just over thirty emperors. No single one of these assassinations significantly changed the course of history, as few of these emperors were around long enough to make their mark, some only lasting weeks. But collectively, this endless round of killing injected a sickness into civil life. After Commodus, Rome quickly slid into the traditional ancient pattern of monarchical despotism, punctuated by assassination, with the pace and frequency of the killing increasing, regardless of whether the emperor was any good or not. In one period, 275–84 CE, there were no fewer than seven emperors, all assassinated. Aurelian was a brilliant soldier who, in the space of four years, defeated Rome's empires in both the east and the west, earning him the title *Restitutor Orbis*, Restorer of the World. His reward was to be assassinated by his secretary Eros and a small platoon of his soldiers. His successor, a seventy-five year old senator called Tacitus, lasted a year before he too was killed, almost certainly by his own troops. By now the Roman army had a taste for regicide and assassinated his successors,

Florianus (276 CE) and Probus (282 CE). The army then installed Carus. But what the Roman army gave they could also take away. He lasted a year before he too was assassinated in an army putsch led by his prefect Arrius Aper. Carus was succeeded by his sons Numerian and Carinus, but neither lasted long. The next year Aper assassinated Numerian, even though he was his son-in-law. The army then elected Diocles as emperor, who then became known as Diocletian. A survivor, he immediately had Aper executed and then went to war against Numerian's brother Carinus, who was assassinated by his own troops, leaving Diocletian as the sole leader. He then stopped the endless rash of assassination by broadening the government base. Instead of just one emperor who was an easy target for an army grown restless he devolved power to four rulers, each of whom had a deputy. Overnight he increased the number of targets from one to nine and a period of relative stability followed.

Diocletian understood that it was possible for sole autocratic rulers to survive, but the odds were always going to be poor. All empires, whether ancient or modern, are uniquely vulnerable to assassination, which has an unerring ability to be able to find the hidden fault lines, which often lie concealed deep beneath the surface. The US, for all its unassailable military power, was shattered by the war that followed the assassination of Diem. Fifty years earlier, two 9 mm bullets from a Browning pistol, serial number 19074,[30] were enough to open up the vast subterranean crevasses concealed under the highly polished veneer of European civilization.

In 1963, relatively few had heard of Diem. In 1914, even fewer had heard of the Archduke Franz Ferdinand and his wife Sophie. Gavrilo Princip, Nedeljko Cabrinovic, Trifko Grabez, Vaso Cubrilovic, Cetres Popovic and Mehmed Mehmedbasic are even less well known (even now), yet the assassination they carried out in Sarajevo on 28 June 1914 was the spark that started the First World War.[31] Cabrinovic threw the bombs but

missed [one of the many historical precedents informing the
CIA advice to would-be assassins not to use this method of
attack], only injuring the occupants of the carriage behind.
Princip was an untrained nationalist who was already in the
advanced stages of tuberculosis, yet he dispatched the Duke and
Duchess with just two shots from a Browning pistol, making
him much more effective than many of the highly trained KGB
assassins who would follow. This precipitated a chain reaction
of events, in which previous diplomatic alliances served to drag
most of the advanced world into war. Even though the archduke
was not that popular, the Austro-Hungarian government argued
that the Serbian government was implicated in the Black Hand
gang terrorists and gave the Serbians an ultimatum they couldn't
possibly meet. The Serbians did not want war, were placatory in
their response, but this was not enough. The assassination was
little more than a pretext and exactly a month later the Austrians
declared war. The assassins killed the archduke in protest against
Austrian persecution of their fellow Serbs. What should have
been a localized playground brawl spread across Europe faster
than the plague. As Serbia's long-term allies, the Russians were
then brought in, which brought in the Germans, as they were
allies of the Austro-Hungarians. France, which was bound to
Russia by treaty, then joined in declaring war against Germany,
as did Britain, which was allied to France. Once Britain signed
up for war so did Australia, Canada, India, New Zealand and
South Africa. Japan had a military agreement with Britain and so
they too got involved. From assassination to world war took less
than three months. Italy and the USA managed to stay out of the
initial round but both were subsequently sucked in – Italy in
1915 and the USA in 1917.

In all, this assassination brought down three empires,
initiated the collapse of two more, provoked the mass slaughter
of eight and a half million and caused the greatest ever
redistribution of wealth from the major combatants (Germany,
UK, Austria, France, the Balkans and Italy) to the rest (the
USA, Japan, Spain and Argentina).[32]

Some historians have argued that the First World War would probably have happened anyway and there is some virtue to this argument. The Austro-Hungarians were desperate to go to war against the Serbs and would have found an excuse sooner or later. In the nineteenth century, Otto von Bismarck had predicted that 'some damn fool thing in the Balkans' would trigger the next European war. He was right on the money. That damn fool thing, the charge in the dynamite keg, was the assassination of a pair of minor royals, who were not liked inside their own country and unheard of outside their borders. Despite Austro-Hungarian protestations, there was no evidence of any Serbian involvement in the assassination and none has ever been found since. The very public murder of the archduke and duchess simply gave them the pretext they needed to attack Serbia then all the other countries fell into the conflict as a result of their previous treaty obligations, which – it should be said – were underwritten by a fair degree of mutual loathing and suspicion. Even after thousands of years of political killing, the capacity of assassination to shock had not lost its potency.

This shock value of assassination is so great that it can easily confuse. All sides involved take the moral high ground, propaganda replaces clear reporting and logical thought loses the battle to be heard.

Take the case of the shooting of three Provisional IRA members – Daniel McCann, Sean Savage and Mairéad Farrell – in Gibraltar by an SAS patrol in March 1988.

At the time, the IRA propaganda machine effectively spun it as a very public assassination by British trained killers so consumed with bloodlust they were prepared to shoot Republicans in a public street in front of witnesses, a view which was then helped by the much-publicized and highly controversial television programme *Death on the Rock*.[33]

If it had been pre-scripted, the whole incident could not have turned out to be more positive publicity for the IRA. The car the Provisionals were using was supposed to be full of high explosives, but it turned out to be empty. When the dead bodies were searched they were found to be unarmed; Mairéad Farrell carrying nothing more dangerous than a handbag. The eyewitnesses described how the terrorists were gunned down at very close range, accounts which were subsequently confirmed by the forensic evidence.

At the inquest it emerged that the British soldiers opened fire when they were less than two metres away from their victims. They then shot the terrorists repeatedly until they were dead. The inquest revealed that Mairéad Farrell was shot eight times, three times in the back at a range of three feet and a further five times in the neck and face, some of these bullets being fired when she was facing her killer. Daniel McCann was shot three times in the chest as he was down or going down and then twice in the head. Sean Savage was shot sixteen times, five times in the back and seven times in the head and chest. The strike marks made by the bullets on the pavement suggested that Savage had been shot in the head while lying on his back, the gunman standing above him, pointing towards his feet. Professor Watson, the pathologist who carried out the post-mortem examination, agreed under cross-examination at the inquest that Savage was 'riddled with bullets' and that it was like a frenzied attack'. This prompted a vicious joke which appeared in *Private Eye*: 'Why did you shoot him sixteen times, soldier?' 'Ran out of bullets, Sir!'

On the surface, it looked as if the SAS patrol had executed them in a state-sponsored assassination. Since the early 1970s, the IRA had claimed that the British government had been running a shoot-to-kill operation against them.[34] These shootings – very public and at such short range – only seemed to confirm what they and many others – on all sides in the Troubles – believed.

The Gibraltar inquest jury decided by a majority of nine to two that these were lawful killings, an understandable verdict as the three IRA members would have detonated a huge bomb on their streets a couple of days later if they had not been stopped. The European Commission of Human Rights in Strasbourg in 1995 then reversed this, deciding by ten votes to nine that Britain had used excessive force in breach of Article 2 of the Convention. This article gives all citizens a right to life under the law and restricts the use of unnecessary force. The parents of the three Provisionals (who brought the case) were awarded a nominal contribution towards their costs.[35] Their claims for damages and other costs were dismissed. But this was never about money. It was about headlines and the IRA won this skirmish, even though they subsequently lost the armed struggle to the British.[36]

But as often in these incidents, little was as it seemed at the time – or more importantly how it was reported. Afterwards, there was a huge but unreported row between the SAS and MI5, which reverberated round Whitehall for months and fractured relations for years to follow.

This operation against the IRA, code-named FLAVIUS, is a classic example of cock-up or conspiracy. The SAS soldiers shot the Provisional IRA members after a briefing from MI5, which was completely inaccurate in every crucial detail. To this day, those closest to this operation in the SAS believe they were deliberately misled so that they would assassinate three hard-line, experienced terrorists.[37] If they are right then this was a conspiracy by MI5 to set up the SAS. If it was a cock-up, then MI5 was guilty of criminal negligence and incompetence. The evidence suggests that MI5 was guilty on all counts. The British were therefore guilty under Article 2 of the Convention but it was the wrong people on trial. On the basis of what they were told, the soldiers were completely innocent and the wrong people were put in the dock.[38]

The story began early in 1988 when the British discovered from an intelligence source that the IRA was planning a major attack on Gibraltar. The specific target was Ince's Hall on 8 March. On that day there was to be a ceremonial changing of the guard by the Royal Anglians, a British regiment which was a long-term IRA target as they had opened fire on the crowd at Bloody Sunday in Derry in 1972, an iconic moment in Republican history. At this stage, the operation was a closely guarded secret within the inner circles of the IRA. The British took the threat very seriously as their source was almost certainly Stakeknife, a high-ranking Provisional and the major source of human intelligence from within the IRA.

A group from MI5, the SAS and the Gibraltar Police Special Branch was formed to advise the Gibraltar Police Chief Joseph Canepa. At the end of February, SAS soldiers flew to Gibraltar and started work with the local police on a joint operation in which control would be passed to the SAS who would then arrest the IRA members once they reached Gibraltar. On 4 March 1988, the IRA team was spotted in Malaga. The next day, in the best SAS tradition of careful planning, they began rehearsals for the arrests in which they planned to get up close to them and then shout 'Stop. Police. Hands up!' But then at midnight on 5 March, a senior MI5 officer briefed the SAS. After this, everything changed.

He told them four key facts, all of which would turn out to be untrue. First, the IRA members would be armed and if confronted would use their weapons. Second, the bomb would be in a car and brought across the border. A blocking car (to reserve the parking space) would not be used, as the terrorists would drive in either the night before or the morning of the parade. Therefore whichever car turned up would have the bomb in it. This was a surprising claim as the local police chief inspector (who was not at the briefing) said subsequently that parking places were always at a premium and finding a place would have been difficult. Third, the IRA would be using a remote-control device, a single button which any of the terrorists might be carrying. The possibility that they might use a timer was dismissed as 'highly unlikely'. And finally, he told them that the attack would be in three days' time on 8 March 1988. The Gibraltar police therefore put together an evacuation plan for that date.

The following day the SAS soldiers began patrolling the town, with MI5 officers watching at the border. One member of the IRA active service unit slipped past them and was not picked up until 12.30 p.m. when a car was seen being parked in the area under observation. According to one of the MI5 watchers, the driver took a long time getting out and fiddled with something between the seats. However, neither he nor another MI5 watcher was able to identify him. Finally, ninety minutes later, another member of the MI5 surveillance team spotted Savage in the town. Half an hour later, at around 2.30 p.m., Daniel McCann and Mairéad Farrell crossed the border from Spain into Gibraltar, past the MI5 watchers who initially failed to clearly identify them as well. Twenty-five minutes later, the three IRA members were seen looking at the suspect car and were positively identified. An arrest was considered, which meant handing control over to the soldiers. But when the police asked if the identification was certain they were told that it was only 80 per cent. During this crucial delay – while the MI5 team tried to decide whether the three people under observation were some of Northern Ireland's most prominent terrorists – the IRA team left the area. Thankfully for the security services who had just lost the most dangerous IRA team operating that day, the three returned half an hour later at 3.25 p.m. to have another look at the car. At this point their identities were finally confirmed. After they left the area, a bomb intelligence officer had a quick look at the Renault and confirmed that it was a 'suspect car bomb,' the telltale clue being a rusty aerial, out of place for the age of the car. Fifteen minutes later, at 3.40 p.m., the Gibraltar police formally signed over control to the SAS.

Knowing that transport would be needed, the order was then sent down the line to recall the duty police car but it was stuck in traffic so the driver put on the siren. At that very moment and just a short distance away, two SAS soldiers were approaching McCann and Farrell who were both walking briskly in front of the Shell petrol station on Winston Churchill

Avenue. As the soldiers approached from behind, McCann was freaked by the sound of the police sirens. He turned and there was an instant moment of recognition. McCann knew that the man following him was a soldier and the SAS man knew he knew. According to four witnesses, the first SAS man, known as Soldier A, shouted 'Stop! Police!' but McCann moved aggressively and – fearing that he was going to press the button and explode the bomb – Soldier A opened fire and shot him in the back. Seeing Mairéad Farrell suddenly move her handbag across her body he shot her as well – again in the back – before then shooting McCann once more in the body and twice in the head. He fired five shots in all, from a range of three feet. Soldier B shot immediately afterwards, first at Farrell, then at McCann and then back to Farrell. He fired seven shots in all, only stopping when Mairéad Farrell's hands were away from her body.

A short distance away, the two other members of the four-man SAS unit were closing in on Savage. According to one of the surveillance team, Soldier C shouted 'Stop!' when he heard the police siren. Savage spun round and his hand went down to his side. Both soldiers fired rapidly and Sean Savage went down in a hail of bullets.

The soldiers then put on their berets so they were clearly identifiable to the local police.

It was only afterwards that the true story began to emerge. Inside Farrell's handbag was a set of keys for a red Ford Fiesta (registration number MA9317AF) which the Spanish police then found just across the border. Despite having said that the terrorists were under surveillance, MI5 knew nothing of this vehicle. Inside it, the Spanish police found the keys to another Fiesta (registration number MA2732AJ). Inside the boot of this car were five packages of Semtex weighing 64 kg, two hundred rounds of ammunition packed round the explosive, along with two timers, one marked 10 hours 45 minutes and the other set for 11 hours 15 minutes. These were huge bombs and had the IRA team been successful the death toll would have been enormous.

As soon as these timers were found there was fury at SAS headquarters, as they believed they had been duped by MI5. Clearly the car in Gibraltar was a blocking vehicle to reserve the space, something that was a standard tactic by the IRA and terrorists round the world. They had shot the IRA team having been told they were armed and dangerous (not) and that this was a 'button job' and that any of the terrorists could have activated the bomb (again not). In fact the timers were set to go off two days later. The SAS anger only intensified when it became increasingly apparent that even if it had been a bomb which could be triggered by a remote control the aerial on the car was unsuitable for the job.

When the SAS investigated they discovered that the aerial on the 'suspect' car was the wrong length for the expected frequency. Furthermore, it was pointing along the roof when it should have been standing up. Simply put, if there had been a receiver attached to a bomb it was highly doubtful whether it could have been detonated from a distance.[39] The aerial would have worked had the IRA team had line of sight to the car, but by the time they were shot they were not close enough. Either way, the technical evidence was not strong enough to underpin a briefing which was effectively an order to the SAS to carry out a very public assassination, especially when one expert told the inquest that – had there been a bomb in the car – it could have been deactivated by simply ripping the aerial from the roof.

As it was, MI5 retreated back to the shadows and the SAS took the heat. Given the briefing they had received, the SAS team had no choice but to kill the terrorists. Their specific orders said, 'You and your men may only open fire against a person if you or they have reasonable grounds for believing that he/she is currently committing, or is about to commit, an action which is likely to endanger your or their lives, or the life of any person, and if there is no other way to prevent this.' Once they had received the briefing they did at midnight on 5 March 1988, the only question was when the IRA team would die.

* * *

The big argument in any conflict is how far a democratic state goes in protecting the thin veneer of civilization against an enemy which is not bound by any restraint, which can lie, make false charges and use the media for propaganda purposes. The formal position is that expressed by French writer Albert Camus, which is that 'it is better to suffer certain injustices than to commit them'. Many military thinkers also argue that it is not just a matter of ethics but one of practicality and that it is counterproductive to try and brutalize the local population. If by torturing thirty suspects an occupying army creates fifty terrorists, then this is counterproductive. There is no doubt that in the early stages of the Troubles, particularly round about the internment period, IRA suspects were brutally treated and this was a disaster for the British. However, most terrorists captured after that claimed that they too had been tortured, their badge of honour in a war where there were no medals, only full military funerals. Many were not but the damage had been done[40] and the IRA was able to capitalize on this after the Gibraltar shooting and secure a propaganda victory against the British.

While some assassinations have profound epoch-changing effects, the converse is also true. There are many instances where the failed assassination has had just as powerful an impact. Had Hitler been assassinated in the 1930s the history of the twentieth century would have been very different. The British tried to assassinate Robert Mugabe shortly after he became the Zimbabwean leader but missed him. It is impossible to predict what would have happened if they had been successful but the history of this battered country could not have been worse.

But even more significant than the failed assassinations, there are those instances where the conscious decision not to assassinate has had a profound and beneficial effect.

There were numerous attempts to assassinate Hitler, but by 1944, the British decided that he was of more value to the Allies alive rather than dead. Churchill argued that his assassination would be 'positively counterproductive'. An SOE officer went further arguing that 'As a strategist, Hitler had been of the greatest possible assistance to the British war effort.' There was a further long-term argument against assassination. If the Allies killed him he would become a martyr, spawning the myth that Germany would have been saved had he lived. It was a very good call, but not for all the right reasons. Had the SOE tried to assassinate him they would have failed, as they believed he was at Berchtesgaden but in fact he had left there several months before. More importantly, the British did not know with any certainty about the desperately poor state of the Führer's health. By 1944, he was deranged, suffering from a type of Parkinson's disease. His hands shook, his eyes were bloodshot, he had lost the use of his left arm and could no longer sign his name, read a map on a wall or draw a straight line with a pencil. A doctor described him as 'senile',[41] a palsied, physical wreck, his face puckered like a mask, all yellow and grey. His decisions were increasingly erratic and frequently damaging to the Nazi cause. His deputy, Martin Bormann, signed all crucial papers and undermined him in every way. What no one knew – neither the Nazis nor the British – was that Bormann had been a major KGB asset since 1941.[42] He had completely negated the Nazi war effort by briefing Stalin on a daily basis, giving away all the crucial details of the German advance in the east. Crucially, he gave away the German plans for the Battle of Kursk, the world's biggest ever tank battle and a massive defeat for Hitler,[43] which effectively ended the German war in the east.

While the British considered the assassination of Hitler, the Americans were discussing whether they should commemorate the anniversary of Pearl Harbor by assassinating Emperor Hirohito by bombing his palace. Lauris Norstad, the Commander of the 20th Air Force, put the idea to his boss, General Henry (Hap) Arnold, who turned down the proposal, as he was worried about Japanese reprisals against American prisoners of war. He wrote 'Not at this time' on the memo and instead, he

ordered the American air force to continue bombing factories
and docks but added, 'Later destroy whole city.'[44] What Arnold
could not predict was the valuable role Hirohito was to play,
less than a year later. When the Japanese politicians were split
over whether to accept the Allied conditions for surrender in
August 1944, it was Hirohito who intervened and ordered the
Cabinet to accept. Had he been assassinated, his successor
would not have carried the same authority and the war would
have dragged on.

And finally, there are those instances where the operational
incompetence of the assassins, and particularly the intelligence
services standing behind them, has had a positive and beneficial
effect.

In 1986, American F111 bombers flew from RAF Mildenhall
in East Anglia and dropped bombs on the tent of Colonel
Qaddafi of Libya but missed him as he was elsewhere, having
been tipped off by both the French and the Russians. Ten years
later in 1996, the British were involved in another attempt to
assassinate him, a botched MI6 operation, in which they
worked closely with a fundamentalist Islamic group with
close links to Osama Bin Laden. Again the bomb missed him.
Had either attempt been successful then Qaddafi's unique
brand of predominantly secular Islam would not have survived
and Libya would have become vulnerable to the onset of
Islamic fundamentalism, which has engulfed both Algeria and
Morocco. Instead Qaddafi has been a powerful bulwark for the
last forty years preventing his country being seduced by the
combative Islam preached by Osama Bin Laden.

That has not been his only value to the West. Since 1999,
long before Prime Minister Tony Blair's very public rapproche-
ment with Muammar Qaddafi in March 2004, the Libyan
Intelligence Service has worked closely with both MI6 and the
CIA, providing vital intelligence on the activities of Al Qaeda
to both the British and the Americans. But this programme has
not been confined to intelligence-sharing. According to one
source close to the operation, as well as identifying key

fundamentalists the Libyan intelligence service and MI6 have worked together since 1999 to hunt down key members of Al Qaeda and assassinate them. Qaddafi's specific reason for helping the West: he wants revenge on Osama Bin Laden for trying to assassinate him in the mid-1990s.

In the assassination business everyone ends up with strange allies at one time or another.

11

THE UNBROKEN CHAIN – FROM SADAT TO THE WORLD TRADE CENTRE

'I will be assassinated – but never by an Egyptian.'
President Sadat, to friends, a week before his death

Cairo, Egypt, 6 October 1981 ...
On the Giza plateau just outside Cairo, the pyramids shimmer, their triangular peaks pushing up through the haze. The morning calm is suddenly ripped apart by a flight of Mirage jet fighters approaching at speed, low over the sands. Straight off the production line, the jets perform complex aerial acrobatics, slicing the desert sky in close formation, carving patterns with plumes of smoke, red and blue. These latest jet fighters from the French manufacturers, Dassault, made their debut flight less than three years earlier – and here they are flying in the colours of the Egyptian Air Force. Captured by the television cameras to be packaged for the nightly news, the jets are just part of a

show of patriotic force with the world's best-known monuments as the backdrop, uniting the glory days of Egypt's past with the present.

Just seconds away from the aerial acrobatics is a crowded stand, where the elite of Egyptian society is assembled for a full-scale military parade. In pride of place in the centre of the podium sits their president, Anwar Sadat. A few feet away an Egyptian police general, Nabawy Ismail, the Interior Minister in charge of all of the country's internal security and intelligence services, watches anxiously, expecting an assassination attempt at any moment.

His judgement is impeccable. For weeks he has been arresting and interrogating the country's Islamic fundamentalists, many of whom are members of a loose alliance called Al Jihad. He now knows three critical facts about them. First: unlike the other Muslim groups, they encourage their members to penetrate the state by joining the army, the security and intelligence services and the civil service, a strategy that the Egyptian security services know about but have been unable to prevent. Second: they have declared a *fatwa* (a death warrant) against Sadat and it is now open season on the president. Third: though two assassination attempts have already failed, many of the key activists are still on the loose and some of them are sleepers, buried deep in the armed forces.

General Nabawy Ismail has specific intelligence that the Islamists have recruited at least one pilot in the Egyptian Air Force, though he does not know the assassin's identity. And just to quicken the blood, he has discovered that there is a plan to assassinate Anwar Sadat by flying a jet into the stand exactly where he is sitting next to the president and the rest of the Egyptian governing class. With film crews and photographers everywhere this occasion would provide the Islamists with the global media platform they so desperately seek, an image far more potent than any recruiting poster. But two days before, the Egyptian Air Force shuffles the pilots and by a complete fluke, they manage to transfer the killer pilot to other duties and the world will have to wait for another two decades before a suicidal terrorist will use a jet plane as a terrorist weapon of mass destruction.

But Nabawy Ismail suspects that after several failures the assassins will have learned the value of a good back-up plan. What he does not know is that their contingency plan is sitting just a few hundred yards away. Crouched in the back of an army truck, cradling his automatic rifle, is the man who will lead the assassination team. First Lieutenant Khalid al-Islambouli is just twenty-four years old.

Eight years earlier the Egyptian army had caught the Israelis unaware on Yom Kippur, for Jews their holiest of holy days. Though the Israelis survived and the war was not won, today is still a proud day for Sadat, a personal triumph and a vindication of his policies, as he believes it has brought about peace, no matter how fragile, in the Middle East.

While Nasser had looked east to Moscow for international support, Sadat turned west to embrace Washington – despite the initial opposition of the US Secretary of State, Henry Kissinger, who did not believe that Sadat's overtures to the West were genuine, even after he had kicked the Russians out of Egypt. As one of the largest African countries, which controls the Suez Canal, Egypt was a key piece in the game of Cold War chess being played out between the USA and the Soviet Union, a game where national leaders were pawns and major countries were reduced to the status of knights and bishops, pieces to be played and sacrificed as part of a much bigger game plan.

Turning to the West alienates the hard-line religious fundamentalists back home for whom Sadat's crimes are easy to see. He enjoys a celebratory Western lifestyle, is pro-American and proud of it. If that is not enough, Sadat's prodigious use of cannabis is an open secret. The CIA and other intelligence services know about it as do the media and many in government and therefore in fundamentalist circles. In 1977, Sadat is invited to give a speech at the Knesset, the Israeli Parliament, the first (and last) Arab leader ever to do so. He tells the Israelis they can have guaranteed peace and security if they leave the Arab lands they have occupied since 1967 and recognize the rights of the Palestinians. He invokes Salah-din, the greatest ever Arab commander who hammered the crusaders into submission and then (much to the chagrin of his hard-line supporters) enforced a policy of religious tolerance and mutual respect throughout Palestine. Sadat's speech is clearly written for the ears of President Carter in the White House. It does not play equally well everywhere, hard-line Jews and Arabs alike being united in their distrust and contempt. The Islamists believe he has sold out and their suspicions are confirmed when they see photographs of the Israeli leader, Menachem Begin, touching Sadat's wife, which for them is a sacrilege – a Jewish man with Palestinian blood on his hands touching the pure flower of Islamic womanhood.

The following year, in 1978, Sadat spends twelve days at Camp David with Menachem Begin and Jimmy Carter, where they thrash out a blueprint for peace in the Middle East. For Sadat, there is the Nobel Peace Prize and immediate promotion to statesman status in the marbled halls of international diplomacy. For his country, the Camp David Accords bring immediate financial rewards. Before the ink is dry, a tidal wave of dollars comes rolling in over the desert sands. Egypt begins to receive around $2 billion a year from the USA, making it the second largest recipient of American military and economic aid, after Israel, the country which has long been their favoured client nation in the Middle East. Two thirds of the American money is earmarked for military spending. Twenty million dollars (at 1981 values) alone goes on Sadat's personal security entourage and a special unit to combat international terrorism, both provided and trained by the CIA, keen to be seen protecting their Egyptian asset.

What is left of this American generosity is theoretically earmarked for social reform. The money is desperately needed. Just a month before, a major riot in the slums of Cairo between poor Muslims and Coptic Christians leaves at least seventeen dead. Despite the riots, as Sadat watches the parade of military might in front of him, he has good reasons for believing he is safe. Immediately after the riots, he had reacted quickly, his security service rounding up thousands of the usual suspects, including more than fifteen hundred fundamentalists, mostly from the Islamic Brotherhood. By the time of the parade, most of Sadat's enemies and critics are either in prison, being tortured by his secret police or crushed. The Coptic Pope Shenudah III is banished to a desert monastery, while 170 of his bishops and priests have joined their Muslim brothers in prison, along with critical journalists and politicians. For good measure, Sadat has also closed *Ash Shaab* (The People) newspaper. A stage-managed referendum on the purge shows 99.5 per cent of the electorate approve, but no one believes the result, least of all the president himself. Sadat is trapped and he knows it. Believing that democracy is the way to transform Egypt into a modern state he has allowed dissent and encouraged criticism and pluralism. But he is now fighting for his survival, desperately trying to hold together a nation heavily fractured by internal discord – and the only way he can achieve this is to return to the traditional ways of his predecessors and buy himself some breathing space through repression. The plan is to take the dissidents out of circulation for six months while he tries to cement peace in the Middle East. They can then be released back into a more stable world, where prosperity will undermine fanaticism.

In his eyes (and those of his supporters) he is a hero and a very resplendent one, too. His new dress uniform has arrived from his English tailor a few days before, crisp and beautifully cut. The very image of a modern warrior statesman, his knee-length leather cavalry boots shine in the morning sun and the broad Sash of Justice swoops down from his right shoulder to his left hip. Like many leaders of developing countries he is ostentatiously decorated. He has big hands but they cannot cover the medals on his left breast.

In the weeks before the parade, there has been only one hot topic both on the streets of Cairo and in the inner circles of the presidential retinue: assassination. It's in the air and everyone expects a major attempt, at the very least. Just a few days before, Sadat has chatted with some of his closest supporters throughout the afternoon going on into evening, at one point talking in Pharaonic terms about his life after death. He tells them that his efforts to bring peace to the Middle East have brought him many enemies who he believes would like to assassinate him, but he reaffirms his confident belief that the killer will come from abroad, not from Egypt. The night before the parade, the general calls up pleading with Sadat to cancel it, but he is rebuffed. In a fatal mixture of arrogance and optimism, Sadat reverts to the refrain which has sustained him over the previous weeks, saying 'These are my children, they will not kill me!' . . .

It is a fatal decision and a strange one given the history of Egypt over the previous four decades where violent death for the country's leaders had long been a local Egyptian tradition. In the period immediately after the end of the Second World War, it became a common political event. Sadat's predecessor, the socialist President Gamel Nasser survived numerous assassination attempts. Though his enemies came from every area of the political spectrum they were united by one common factor: breath-taking incompetence. In 1954, the Muslim Brotherhood shot at him during a speech but missed. He immediately abolished their organization and cracked down on Islamic fundamentalists, taking the country in the direction of Arab socialism, aligning his government with the Soviets, much to the horror of the West. MI6 concocted a plan to assassinate him by pumping cyanide gas through the U-bend of his toilet, a plan long on ingenuity but short on practical application. The CIA asked one of their agents, Miles Copeland, to kill him, but he refused, telling his bosses that Nasser was his friend and he could not therefore kill him. He then told Nasser of the US plot against him, though Nasser was already well aware of the Western desire to assassinate him. Despite surviving these different attempts, when he died of a heart attack in 1961, many in the Arab world believed he had been murdered by the Americans – a belief which still persists to this day.

Nasser himself rose to power during a period in which the Egyptian state and the Muslim Brotherhood, the main Islamic fundamentalist movement with around two million members, traded assassination. After 1945, Egypt was still under the control of the British, whose frontman King Faruk was nicknamed 'the thief of Cairo,'[1] a hedonistic monarch on the grandest scale, who ruthlessly plundered the country's wealth. He compiled one of the largest ever collections of pornography and squandered much of the rest of his huge fortune in Europe's most expensive casinos and nightclubs, while the poor (of which there were many millions) got steadily poorer. These were classic revolutionary conditions and the Muslim Brotherhood carried out the prescribed strategy of revolutionaries everywhere: arson, riot and assassination, specifically targeting those Egyptians it regarded as traitors or more precisely, pro-British. The first post-war Prime Minister, Ahmed Maher, was shot dead at point-blank range in parliament. His death was publicly described by Churchill as 'a serious loss to his king and his country,'[2] even though Maher was one of the defendants acquitted in the trial which followed the assassination of Sir Lee Stack, the British Commander in Chief of Egyptian forces, who was murdered as he walked home from the War Office in Cairo in 1924.[3] Another politician, Amin Osman Pasha, knighted by the British for his war efforts but hated by the Islamists, was assassinated in 1946 (a killing in which Anwar Sadat was implicated).[4] The Muslim Brotherhood, whose founder and spiritual leader was Hassan el-Banna, had a paramilitary wing (called the Secret Apparatus) and they assassinated a senior judge, Ahmad al-Khazindar, whose crime was handing out a harsh sentence to one of the Islamic brothers. His sentence, carried out on the orders of Hassan el-Banna, was six bullets at close range. As well as assassinating prominent politicians, the Brotherhood also took the other predictable Islamic fundamentalist route of attacking Jewish businesses and households, killing twenty in one bombing alone.

After three years assassination was becoming firmly embedded in Egyptian post-war politics, and in 1948 the Muslim Brotherhood moved even further against the state, assassinating the police chief Amin Zaki with a hand grenade while he was visiting the university. When the university president protested he was denounced as a 'European' and narrowly escaped assassination himself. By now, Hassan el-Banna's assassins had taken out a judge and a police chief and he decided to raise the stakes even further.

Taking his cue from the Hashshashin handbook, he recruited a twenty-three-year-old student, Maguid Ahmed Hassan for the next and even-higher-profile killing. The target was the prime minister, Mahmoud Fahmy el-Nukrashy Pasha, and the indoctrination was flawless. First an Imam told the young assassin that the Quran sanctions the assassination of the 'enemies of Islam' after which he retired for ten days of contemplation and prayer. Fixed in his mind, he then set off, in exactly the same way as the followers of Hasan ibn el-Sabah had done nearly a thousand years before. He put on a police uniform and casually strolled into the Ministry of the Interior. The security only saw the uniform and waved him through, where he merged easily with the other police officers and shot the prime minister dead, even though his guards surrounded him.

This was a killing straight out of the Hashshashin handbook. The assassin had donned the garb of his target, easily infiltrating himself before murdering his victim, knowing that he would be captured immediately afterwards but certain in the belief that he had just booked a one-way ticket to heaven. Assassinating in this way causes panic and widespread fear by hitting the enemy in their heartland where they feel safe. Subversion and terror then creep silently, hand in hand, and no one can feel secure. It is the quintessential terrorist crime, far more devastating than an anonymous bomb.

The man who ordered the assassination, Hassan el-Banna, was a hard-line fundamentalist, a genuine prototype for Osama

Bin Laden. He believed passionately in the totalitarian Islamic state, ruled by the Imams and governed by strict *sharia* law. 'We aim to smash modernism in government and society,'[5] he told one Western journalist, which also inevitably included the Jews. 'We must crush Zionism, which is Jewish modernism. It is our patriotic duty. The Quran commands it,' he continued.

The Egyptian security services then took matters into their own hands. At 8.30 p.m. on 12 February 1949, as Hassan el-Banna left the Young Men's Muslim Association, officers from the Egyptian secret police shot him five times as he went to get into the taxi. It was a devastating blow against the Muslim Brotherhood, a decapitation from which they never recovered.

Even though Sadat himself had been intimately involved in his own country's recent assassination history, he believed he was safe among his own and declined the bulletproof vest, despite the pleas of his security services, though this was not the only reason. A vain man, he had recently re-watched the television coverage of his visit to Jerusalem. Not trusting the Israelis, he had worn it but now regretted it as he thought it made him look fat. But on this day, in the end, it would not have made any difference whether he'd been wearing a bulletproof jacket or not.

In an Egyptian army truck, four young Islamists, members of a secretive underground Islamic fundamentalist movement called Al Jihad, were also wearing unfamiliar clothes. Two days before, as their president was admiring his new uniform, they shaved their beards and slipped into the army barracks, staying with the young Lieutenant Khalid al-Islambouli. They left their *jelabia* behind, exchanging them for the boots and uniform of the regular soldier. No one recognized them and, given the intensely bureaucratic and secretive nature of the Egyptian army, they were not questioned about their arrival, everyone assuming they were covert members of military security, infiltrated into the army to weed out dissidents.

Resistance to Sadat was widespread. Egyptians of all classes felt betrayed by a president who promised wealth and prosperity for all but only delivered it to a few. Sleaze and greed defined political life and Sadat himself was a very rich man, injecting new levels of sleaze into an already spectacularly corrupt government machine. Entrepreneurial Egyptians, of which there were many in a country with a small but dynamic middle class, routinely made donations to 'charities' which were close to Sadat. These donations (usually 10 per cent) rang the cash register in time with the granting of import licences and government contracts. Sadat himself did not just draw the presidential salary. He had been travelling first class on the CIA gravy train for well over a decade, his reward for re-aligning Egypt with the West.

Though the Egyptian intelligence services were efficient, they had not picked up everyone. The arrests in early September focused on the Muslim Brotherhood and other activists, most of whom were already well known to the authorities, and they were all safely tucked up in prison by the time of the parade. But throughout 1981, in the months before the assassination, the Egyptian intelligence services also targeted a newly emerging and shadowy group, Al Jihad (the Holy War), the faction which Nabawy Ismail, the Interior Minister identified as 'easily the most dangerous group operating in Egypt'.[6]

Through technical intercepts and spies, Egyptian counter-intelligence identified and arrested many of their members, including Ayman al-Zawahiri, at this time a young doctor from a good family. Though he did not register on anyone's radar, by the turn of the century he would be a household name as Osama Bin Laden's right-hand man in Al Qaeda and the chief architect of the attack on the World Trade Centre. Zawahiri, like the others, was subjected to brutal torture. In his case, he was bent backwards over a door, tied and left for three days,[7] after which he – like all the rest – gave up the names of his fellow Islamists.

But counter-terrorism is a slow business and by October 1981 there were still members of Al Jihad at large and several of them were in the Russian-built army truck which was now part of the parade trundling towards the presidential podium.

Once inside the military, the Al Jihad cadets were instructed to lie low as sleepers until they were called on. Just two weeks before, one of these sleepers, Khalid al-Islambouli, was activated after being told that he would be leading a detachment towing twelve field guns in the 6 October victory parade. Next to him in the truck, now inching towards the podium, was Hussein Abbas Mohammed, an instructor at the Civil Defence School and for seven years the Egyptian army's champion marksman. In the near distance, they could see Sadat taking the salute.

As a matter of general practice, Sadat's CIA-trained security officers ensured that no live ammunition was ever issued on occasions like this. To be doubly certain, the firing pins were also removed from all weapons. But today was different. As First Lieutenant Islambouli stroked his Kalashnikov assault rifle, he knew – as did his comrades – that the magazine was loaded with live rounds and the grenades attached to his belt were not for show.

The truck carrying the assassins crawled ever closer and suddenly stopped. Everyone's heart skipped a beat – the politicians in the podium, the assassins in the parade and the security services everywhere else. In front of them all a tank had broken down and everyone had to wait until it was towed away. Outside the perimeter fence, at that very moment, a young intelligence officer, with vital information for the general, was trying to get through the presidential security cordon. That morning one of their spies inside Al Jihad discovered that there was to be an assassination attempt on the president during the parade. At great personal risk to himself he got this priceless information to his control, who immediately passed it on. Despite being told this was a matter of life and death the soldier in the presidential guard had his orders and was adamant: no one enters after the president. While they argued, inside the cordon, the broken-down tank was towed away and the parade restarted.

As the planes passed by overhead the elite of Egyptian society craned their necks to get a better look. Nabawy Ismail breathed a sigh of relief. There was no suicide bomber in the Egyptian Air Force on that day, though he would subsequently discover just how close he had come to losing his life when he interviewed the pilot who had been chosen for what would have been the world's most spectacular terrorist attack. As the Russian-built Egyptian army truck arrived opposite the podium, the young First Lieutenant Khalid al-Islambouli pulled his pistol and held it to the driver's head, ordering him to stop. The driver panicked and slammed on the brakes, causing the vehicle to slew round. According to one of the press photographers there, Makram Gad Al Karim,[8] Sadat spotted them immediately and shouted at them, telling them not to be stupid. But Hussein Abbas Mohammed, the army's champion marksman, stood up on the top of the truck and fired. The plotters had chosen their assassin well. A good fifty yards from the podium, he shot Sadat with his first bullet, which ripped through the president's neck.

Islambouli and his fellow assassins then jumped down from the lorry and ran towards the president and his entourage, throwing their grenades. Hussein Abbas Mohammed and Khalid al-Islambouli aimed at the podium, their fellow conspirators providing covering fire. The film crews fled for cover, as did many of the press photographers. A few stayed behind and photographed the horror in front of them, though their films were confiscated immediately afterwards. The pictures that emerged for the world's press were taken by a quick-witted photographer who handed blank films over to the security services, slipping the rolls of shot film into his socks.

Vice President Hosny Mubarak, who had been standing on Sadat's right, dived behind the chairs and survived, as did a young Coptic diplomat, Boutros Boutros Ghali, who later went on to become General Secretary of the United Nations. When he was just a few metres from the podium, the young First Lieutenant saw Mubarak cowering under the chairs and

ordered him: 'Get out of my way. I only want this son of a
dog!' Islambouli then stopped to shoulder his weapon and
opened fire, shooting continually into Sadat's chest and
stomach. A senior intelligence officer was killed, along with five
others. Twenty-eight were injured.

As Sadat lay dying, Islambouli (whose Al Jihad code name
was 'Zafer' meaning victorious) shouted out 'I have killed the
Pharaoh', a reference to the fact that he and his accomplices did
not regard Sadat as a true Muslim leader but as an autocrat.
Ironically, the Sadat monument (which now stands opposite the
podium where he was shot) is a huge concrete pyramid,
engraved with the names of the Egyptian soldiers who died in
the 1973 Yom Kippur war. Even in death his tomb is protected
by armed guards, twenty-four hours day, as is the podium
where he was killed.

There was no popular Islamic uprising and nothing was
achieved at the time. The relatively secular Egyptian state
survived untouched. The military and the security services
cemented their positions in the state machine and a leader who
had been relatively tolerant towards the fundamentalists was
replaced by one who crushed them without mercy. Despite the
spectacular failure of the assassination, at his trial the following
year, Islambouli declared, 'I am guilty of killing the unbeliever
and I am proud of it.' He was shot by firing squad, along with
the other two military conspirators. The two key civilian
plotters were hanged. The remaining plotters were given prison
sentences of up to twenty-five years. Towards the end of their
sentences, several of the conspirators repented, condemning the
rise in Islamic fundamentalism worldwide, a movement they
had done much to create.

Whereas a number of Western leaders, including three former
United States presidents, attended Sadat's funeral, only one
member of the Arab League was represented by a head of state,
Egypt's southern neighbour Sudan. Only two, Oman and
Somalia, sent representatives. In Egypt 43 million people
carried on with the celebration of *Id al Adha*, the Feast of

Sacrifice, as if nothing had happened. There were no throngs in the streets, no public grieving and lamenting, as there had been when Nasser died. There was little forgiveness for his attempted deal with the Israelis and in much of the Arab world, Sadat's death was greeted with jubilation.

Some assassinations change the course of history, though often – like earthquakes – their primary fallout is domestic rather than international, a temporary blip in the great sweep of politics, not a global shock. The assassination of Sadat was of a different order of magnitude to any other killing of a major political figure in the last fifty years, far greater in its long-term global effects than the assassination of President Kennedy and more significant in Middle East politics than the murder of Israeli Prime Minister Yitzhak Rabin. For thousands, it was the beginning of a lifetime's commitment to the cause of Islamic fundamentalism, the incendiary effects of which are still reverberating around the world and will continue to do so for decades to come.

Unnoticed at the time, what looked like a localized Middle Eastern affair began a seismic shift in one of the major fault lines of modern civilization, splitting east and west, Christian and Muslim, the secular enlightenment of the West and the profoundly religious combative fundamentalism which now pollutes much of the Arab world.

At the time, the leader of the assassination group, Lieutenant Khalid al-Islambouli, was dismissed by the world's press as a religious fanatic, a lone nut (like every other assassin of a major political figure). The killing of Sadat was explained away by many commentators as little more than a domestic tiff between the emerging Egyptian state (modern, democratic and western) and a few Islamic fundamentalists (backward looking, undemocratic and essentially medieval in outlook). The belief was that these Islamic fanatics would inevitably wither in the bright lights of a vibrant capitalist economy.

Nothing could have been further from the truth. The assassination of Sadat gave the Islamic fundamentalists an unshakeable belief in their ability to change the course of history to their own will through asymmetric warfare, the notion that a tiny group can inflict long-lasting damage and even win substantial victories against a vastly larger, better financed and better equipped enemy. They were simply putting into practice the strategies first defined by the Hashshashin nearly a thousand years before.

There is an unbroken chain from the assassination of Sadat to the attack on the World Trade Centre in 2001, which involves the same characters on both sides of the equation. The secular Western intelligence services on one side and the fundamentalists on the other.

Just twenty-four years old, First Lieutenant Khalid al-Islambouli had risen quickly in the Egyptian army, privately rejecting the comparatively moderate politics of the Islamic Brotherhood for the seductive simplicities of the more hard-line religious fundamentalism of Al Jihad. The sect's spiritual mentor was (and still is) a blind cleric, Sheikh Omar Abdel Rahman, a professor at the University of Al-Azhar, who was therefore qualified to interpret religious laws and issue the occasional *fatwa*. Islambouli and others in Al Jihad had been worried whether they could justify killing Sadat under Islamic law, which enshrines a very strict code of warfare. The Quran quotes God speaking to the Prophet Mohammed, 'Fight in the cause of Allah those who fight you, but do not transgress limits for Allah loveth not transgressors.' But where did the limits lie? The plotters approached Sheikh Omar Abdel Rahman to ask whether it was permitted to shed the blood of a ruler who did not obey God. In a fateful religious ruling, he pronounced that killing a leader who was not a good Muslim was sanctioned by religious law.

For lovers of irony, it is worth noting that ultra-orthodox rabbis in Israel revived a similar piece of archaic theology to pronounce their own death warrant against President Rabin. *Din rodef* is the duty to kill a Jew who threatens the life or property of another Jew and the argument was that Rabin was a *rodef* for giving up land to the Palestinians and should therefore die.[9] Both assassinations, Rabin and Sadat, were underpinned by an archaic religious principle from a completely different age, dusted off and dragged into the twentieth century by religious zealots looking for a moral justification for murder.

In clarifying the theoretical issue, Omar Abdel Rahman effectively signed Sadat's death warrant.[10] The only remaining questions to be answered by the faithful were two: where the deed should be done and when.

The Sadat plotters defined a way of operating that has confused Western intelligence services ever since and made the fundamentalists relatively impervious to traditional counter-terrorism operations. As far as Khalid al-Islambouli was concerned, he was a member of a small group of like-minded fundamentalists. These groups, which constantly formed, split and reconstituted themselves in new combinations were scattered throughout the mainstream of Islamic fundamentalist thought, the *gama'at el-islamiyeh*. In Arabic, these groups were called '*anquds*, which means bunch of grapes. The theory is that each grape is self-contained and can be plucked without affecting the others. It is not a traditional terrorist cell structure but loose groupings, constantly shifting, all separate but sharing the same aim, united by their absolute belief in an idea, not bound by any management structure and never stable long enough for traditional intelligence analysis to get a serious triangulation on them.

As well as being conspirators in Sadat's murder, all these men were united by their veneration for the spiritual leadership of one man, Islamic theoretician Sayyed Qutb. Unknown in the West, Qutb was hanged by the Egyptian government in 1966 but not before he had written two books which define the ideology and approach of every Islamic-based terrorist group now operating anywhere in the world. Qutb's key message, which pops up continually in Al Qaeda material and which inspired Islambouli to assassinate Sadat, is the fundamentalists' rallying cry: 'Brother, push ahead, even though your path is soaked in blood. Do not turn your head right or left but look only up to heaven.'

Qutb's two books, *In the Shade of the Qu'ran* and *Signposts* are the equivalent of Marx's *Communist Manifesto*, Lenin's *What Is to Be Done?*, Tom Paine's *The Rights of Man* or Mao's *Little Red Book* for the fundamentalist Muslim world.[11] Together they offer a complete reinterpretation of the Quran, ignoring both its progressive messages and its specific prohibitions against any terrorist activity, which might result in the death of non-combatants. Instead, Qutb replaced the prophet's message of peace and respect for others with a hard-line call to arms where every terrorist action can be justified in the name of God, whose transcendental spiritual desires now coincided exactly with the temporal strategy being followed by the fundamentalists.

Qutb argued that the modern world was the equivalent of *jahiliyya*, the state of ungodliness, which existed before the Prophet Mohammed. He argued that the true Muslim must break completely with the modern world, destroy it and build a new Islamic empire on the ruins, an earthly paradise governed by the law of *sharia*. This idea underpins every Islamic fundamentalist movement and is the cornerstone of Al Qaeda theology. For Qutb and his followers the ungodly are easily identified as they consist of all those who oppose them – whether they are Christians, Jews or Muslims who have strayed from the path. For them, Sadat and Nasser stand alongside Colonel Qaddafi and Saddam Hussein as the enemy, just as evil (if not more so) than Western leaders like George W. Bush and Tony Blair. When asked why he killed Sadat, Islambouli replied 'because he did not rule in accordance with the *sharia*, because he concluded *sulh* [conciliation] with peace, and because he insulted the scholars of Islam.' The same reasoning underpinned the Al Qaeda attempt on Colonel Qaddafi's life in 1996, an attempted assassination which was financed in part by Britain's MI6.

The fundamentalist assassins in Egypt did not just appear and grow spontaneously and organically. They were also sponsored, nurtured and financed from outside, initially by Egypt and the USA and then, after Sadat's death, by the Americans alone.

There is a wealth of evidence to suggest that the CIA, resurgent and combative under its new boss Bill Casey,[12] was complicit in Sadat's death. After the spectacular failures of the past there was little enthusiasm in Washington for a directly contracted hit as discovery would destroy the US in the Middle East for generations, but there was plenty of support for a proxy assassination, one where – for once – there would be no CIA fingerprints. The White House knew beforehand that an assassination was planned (as one CIA officer remarked at the time, 'We've got the country wired from top to bottom') and they then created the conditions in which it became inevitable rather than making sure it did not happen. The fundamentalist terror groups then did what the US wanted – which was to assassinate a leader the White House no longer supported and who they wanted to replace with someone who would be both more reliable and more compliant. The evidence for this is complex but compelling.

In order to counteract the rise of the communists during the 1970s the Egyptian government promoted and encouraged the rise of Islamic fundamentalism. By the late 1970s Sadat admitted to his colleagues that this had been a mistake and the Egyptian government started to pull away and move against them, but his close allies in the CIA took the opposite view. For them, the fundamentalists were essential cannon fodder in the only war that mattered, the Cold War against the Soviet Union. They dabbled energetically in the murky world of Islamic fundamentalism, getting ever closer to these groups, telling their counterparts in the Egyptian intelligence services that this was necessary in order to understand what was happening.

After the fall of the Shah of Iran in 1979, Sadat gave him asylum in Egypt to the fury of the religious fundamentalists.

The Ayatollah Khomeini, now installed at the head of the Islamic revolution in Iran, denounced Sadat as 'a pot smoking CIA stooge'. Though this was true, Khomeini did not know that the stooge's paymasters at CIA headquarters in Langley, Virginia were becoming restless. In April 1981, just six months before he was murdered, Sadat went to Washington to see President Ronald Reagan and his CIA Chief William Casey. He presented them with a dossier of evidence, detailing the activities of the Islamic fundamentalists who were plotting to assassinate him. One of those named in the files was Omar Abdel Rahman, the spiritual mentor to the fundamentalist groups. The Americans promised help but – in actuality – did the opposite. After he returned to Egypt, Western newspapers were briefed that Sadat had lost the plot and was suffering from the paranoid delusion that he was going to be killed. Crucially, either before this date or subsequently, the Americans put Omar Abdel Rahman (the cleric who signed Sadat's *fatwa*) on the payroll, a decision that would backfire spectacularly when he tried to blow up the World Trade Centre in 1993 – providing the inspiration for the second, devastating attack on the World Trade Centre in 2001.

After Sadat's visit to Washington, the Americans saw Egypt as part of the problem, no longer a key element in their solution to peace in the Middle East and a frontline state in the Cold War. The CIA analysts got down to work. Their TOP SECRET assessment of Egyptian foreign policy (in early 1981) was worried that Sadat would try and put 'distance between Egypt and the US'. If he did, their multi billion-dollar investment would have to be written off. For the CIA, the key issue was Sadat's instability. The report noted that Sadat was always searching for 'ways to be unpredictable', a man who listened to many, confided in few and took advice from none, least of all his American paymasters. Instead he now saw himself as a global philosopher king, dispensing advice to all, not all of which was high quality. Among the recipients of his generously given free advice was President Carter, who was given instructions by Sadat on how to get re-elected. Whether he took it or not, Carter was ambushed at the polls by Reagan and was only a one-term president.

By mid 1981, the CIA, the rest of the American intelligence community and the White House believed that Sadat could no longer be trusted and they wrote him off in favour of a man they could do business with: his deputy, Hosny Mubarak. In the days just before the parade, Mubarak was invited to Washington to talk to the men who would become his closest international allies for the next twenty-five years, the mandarins of the US State Department and their paramilitary counterparts in the CIA. Shortly before Mubarak set off, a group of young Islamic fundamentalists in Egypt were treated to the local brand of US generosity. Two weeks before Sadat's assassination, they were given a deep background briefing from a rogue ex-CIA case officer turned international arms dealer, Ed Wilson. The subject on the agenda: Sadat's security arrangements. Wilson's motives (as in everything he did) were cloaked in mystery. He was pro-Libya (his biggest client) which was involved in a low-scale war with Egypt at the time and he was also trying to cosy up to his former bosses in Washington. And finally, just to shorten the odds even further, on the day he was assassinated, the CIA-trained guard which was supposed to protect Sadat was stood down and marshalled sixty metres behind the podium, where they could do nothing to protect the president.

All this can be explained away as a series of unrelated events, but after the killing of Sadat, the CIA cemented its relationships with many of the key figures in the assassination and then worked closely with them, in some cases for the next decade, in others for the next two.

On the government side, Sadat's deputy, Hosny Mubarak, became America's marionette in the Middle East, a compliant hardman who could be guaranteed to stick to his brief. Before Sadat's death, the US focus had wandered and the White House had become increasingly obsessed with Afghanistan, following the Russian invasion at the end of 1979. Afghanistan was just one of many Cold War battlefields and, though it was in their backyard, the Russians were overstretched, perfect conditions for the CIA and MI6 who were not too fussy about who they had as bedfellows.

Mubarak quietly folded Egypt into a bizarre coalition of the rich and the opportune (the USA, Saudi Arabia, the UK, China and Pakistan) all lined up against the Soviets. The coalition also included the Islamic fundamentalists and some of the key figures were graduates of the Sadat assassination, fanatics who would go on to form Al Qaeda. Egypt's role was to ruthlessly crush the fundamentalists at home but allow the US to use Egypt as a frontline station for their proxy war against the Russians.

The Afghanistan war had the feeling of a medieval contest in which both generals met for dinner beforehand and agreed the time and place. The Russians invaded believing the Americans were already there and were met with the inevitable response as the CIA poured money, arms, military know-how and matériel into the inflammatory cauldron of a country which had traditionally been the graveyard of imperialist hopes and dreams. The war against the Soviets in Afghanistan in the 1980s quickly became the largest CIA paramilitary operation since Operation Mongoose against Cuba in the 1960s. Their conveyor belt of cash kept the focus on defeating the Russians but it was a messy war, which inflamed the already volatile tribal and religious divisions in the country. Like Cuba it was quasi-covert at best. It was no secret that the CIA Director William Casey shared President Reagan's world view that Russia was the 'evil empire', which needed to be confronted and defeated.

The Afghan crisis began in 1978 (as these things often do) with assassination. After ruling the country as a republic for five years, Sardar Mohammed Daoud Khan was assassinated in 1978 in a coup which installed the communist party in Kabul and gave the country a new name, the Democratic Republic of

Afghanistan, which then quickly became the frontline in the clash of civilizations. The Soviets met resistance straight away, both from the tribes who resented being controlled by an outsider and from the Islamic fundamentalists who hated the secular Soviet programme of reform, particularly equal rights for women. The ghost of Stalin was not far away and the newly installed communist party purged the middle class, completely removing the governing elite and replacing them with a rigid Soviet bureaucracy, a centralized party structure all wrapped up in an enduring fantasy that a happy-socialist-anthem-singing industrial proletariat would fill the vacuum and build a workers' paradise. When the revolution did not happen they began to plot with the president to murder the prime minister and once assassination was injected into the mix, chaos was not far away.

On 14 February 1979, the US ambassador to Afghanistan, Adolph 'Spike' Dubs, was kidnapped and then assassinated by government forces after a gun battle. With a pro-Marxist government sitting on top of a fractured religious and tribal country it was not clear who was responsible for the killing but all fingers pointed to the Soviet-backed government. This single death sent a shock wave through the body politic and everything fell apart very quickly.

The following month[13] the Politburo met in Moscow to discuss the 'urgent' and deteriorating situation in Afghanistan. According to their intelligence reports thousands of 'religious fanatics, saboteurs and terrorists' were swarming in from Pakistan and disrupting the peace. The issue for the Kremlin was simple. As far as they were concerned, Afghanistan was their southern neighbour with whom they had enjoyed stable relations for sixty years. They also knew that the US had just lost one of its major allies in the Middle East, Iran, where their puppet, the Shah, had just fallen to a fundamentalist coup. Their fear was that the Americans would seek a substitute and their country of choice would be Afghanistan. They simply could not give it up and agreed to supply weapons and a hundred thousand tons of bread and – just like the Americans in Vietnam – they slid into a war that they would inevitably lose. Just like Vietnam it started with advisers and assassinations, but the soldiers and the major divisions soon followed. And just like Vietnam, they would be defeated by the conditions abroad and hostile public reaction at home.

As the Soviets desperately tried to control a rapidly deteriorating situation they quickly realized that their placemen were not heroes fit for the revolutionary struggle. The Soviets then decided to resolve matters through selected assassination. They helped Prime Minister Comrade Noor Mohammad Taraki to try and assassinate President Comrade Hafizullah Amin but despite several attempts he failed and instead Amin got his retaliation in first. Taraki was assassinated in September 1979. The official version was that he died of poor health, though this was exacerbated by palace guards suffocating him with a pillow and then shooting him. Comrade Amin himself did not last much longer. He tried to prevent the further clash of civilizations by attempting to mollify the Islamic groups, promising more religious freedom and even invoking the Quran in his speeches. This was all way too much for the Soviets back in Moscow, who also suspected that he was trying to cut a backdoor deal with the CIA. Two days after Christmas, several hundred Spetsnatz (Russian Special Forces) stormed the presidential palace in Kabul, assassinating President Amin. The internal Kremlin report was a gem of Soviet self-deception: 'Broad masses of people met the announcement of the overthrow of H. Amin's regime with unconcealed joy . . . the situation is normalizing.'

Ten years later the Soviets withdrew, having lost an estimated 15,000 dead and 37,000 wounded. The Afghan losses were between one and two million dead and the country had been smashed. Both the Soviets and US had spent billions of dollars on a war which neither could win.

Though the Americans had one agenda: combating Soviet influence, the fundamentalists had two: to get the Russians out of Afghanistan and – more importantly – to wage holy war against all those who did not support their hard-line Islamic agenda. When the Russians pulled out in 1989 the Americans reneged on all their promises to support the Afghans and instead of investing in some serious nation rebuilding they simply walked away. It was a foreign policy disaster of catastrophic proportions far worse than the intelligence failures before 9/11. They left a country in meltdown where Year Zero was somewhere in the Middle Ages. There was no government or political structure, just a lawless power vacuum, where war lords ruled supreme and the main source of income was opium. The only victors in this proxy war were the fundamentalists. Out of this festering crucible the Taliban emerged and established some level of country control but concealed within their number was the most devastating terrorist group the world has ever known: Al Qaeda. As far as Bin Laden was concerned, Afghanistan was 'the kitchen' out of which would come a steady army of Islamic revolutionaries, willing to die for the cause. Once again, the Hashshashin had provided the template for modern life.

In all, five key Al Qaeda members, who first served their terrorist apprenticeship in the assassination of Sadat, would graduate through Afghanistan and go on to form the nucleus of Al Qaeda. Together they would wreak devastation on the West and especially against their Afghanistan paymasters and allies – the USA.

At the time of Sadat's assassination, Mohammed Shawky al-Islambouli, was already in prison, jailed for being one of the hard-line fundamentalists gathering against Sadat. As his brother Khalid was the man who led the assassination squad, he acquired instant celebrity status in fundamentalist circles. As soon as he was released he joined the Afghan struggle against the Soviets at Peshawar, the Mujahadeen's base in eastern Pakistan. He quickly became a significant figure as he had close links to Tehran, where his brother is celebrated as a great martyr and has a street named after him. He too was venerated by the

Iranian hard-liners and became the trusted conduit for their funds to Afghanistan. But Mohammed al-Islambouli never forgot that his brother was dead, hanged for the killing of Sadat. He tried to assassinate Mubarak and other Egyptian leaders in 1992 and was sentenced to death in his absence by an Egyptian court.

Two other members of Al Jihad both fled immediately after Sadat's assassination. Mohammed Ibrahim el-Mekkawi evaded the secret police and fled Egypt immediately afterwards for Pakistan, from where he joined the Afghan war. A key member of Al Qaeda, he became Bin Laden's security chief. A former Egyptian army colonel, he then used his experience to help train the Somalis who killed US soldiers at Mogadishu. Western counter-terrorist experts also believe he is linked to the bombings of the US embassies in Kenya and Tanzania as well as training the 9/11 hijackers in the use of explosives.[14]

Another member of the Sadat assassination team was Mahmud Abouhalima, who then went on to another assassination, this time in New York. Nine years later, on 5 November 1990, he was the driver of the getaway car. On this night, two young Palestinians, one wearing a red leisure suit and white patent leather shoes, went into the Marriott Hotel where Rabbi Kahane, fifty-eight, one the founders of the Jewish Defence League, was holding a meeting. An Israeli fundamentalist firebrand preacher, he had just been exhorting his fellow Israelis to return to the homeland.

The man in the red suit and the white shoes, Al-Sayyed Nussair, walked up to him, a .357 Magnum under his coat, and shot him dead. Outside, Abouhalima was waiting in his cab. But the doorman moved him on and Abouhalima drove off into the traffic, just as Nussair ran out of the hotel. After a short exchange of fire, Nussair was shot and injured.

That night, the New York police raided a house in New Jersey, where they found Abouhalima, another man, Mohammed Salameh, and a trove of terrorist materials. To their amazement, here were training manuals from the Army Special

Warfare School at Fort Bragg, TOP SECRET documents to the Joint Chiefs of Staff, bomb-making manuals, maps and photographs showing the Statue of Liberty, Times Square, Rockefeller Centre and the World Trade Centre, with notes written in Arabic and a manifesto exhorting Muslims to topple the 'tall buildings of which the Americans are so proud'.

The police took away sixteen boxes of materials and wanted to arrest Abouhalima, but the FBI arrived and removed the evidence. Apart from Nussair, no one was arrested and the chief of police announced that Nussair acted alone. There was no conspiracy. He told journalists, 'it was the work of a lone deranged gunman ... he acted alone ... he didn't seem to be part of a conspiracy or any terrorist organization.'

Interestingly, eighteen months before this, the FBI had secretly photographed Abouhalima, Salameh and Nussair at the Calverton Shooting Range on Long Island, New York. Over four successive weekends, they were photographed firing AK-47s, semi-automatic handguns and revolvers.

At trial, Nussair had an unusual benefactor paying his legal fees – Osama Bin Laden.

Two years later, Abouhalima was arrested in New York, following the first attack on the World Trade Centre. The FBI suspected him of being the main bomb-maker. The formula used to make the bomb matched one in the boxes of materials taken away from Abouhalima's house. His capture then led them to the Farouq mosque in Brooklyn, where the key Imam was Omar Abdel Rahman, the cleric who signed Sadat's *fatwa*.

There had been a brief power struggle inside the mosque and the old Imam was murdered so that Omar Abdel Rahman could take over. As a magnet for Islamic terrorists, it instantly became an FBI target. Many at the centre were given weapons and ammunition training at secret terrorist camps all over the US. The key trainer was a former US Marine, Siddig Ali, who had served two tours in Vietnam and taught martial arts. He trained them in mock night-time assaults on a nearby electric power substation. The FBI put a phone tap on Siddig Ali and heard him say, 'Our goal is that these people get extensive and very, very, very good training, so that we can get started at any place where *jihad* is needed.'

The FBI learned all about one of these training camps from an informant, but after two days they suddenly cancelled their surveillance.

The mosque was being partly financed by the CIA, part of a deep cover operation raising paramilitary militia to fight the Russians in Chechnya and elsewhere. The key figure here was Omar Abdel Rahman, the blind cleric who signed Sadat's *fatwa*.

By 1990, Omar Abdel Rahman had become an important American asset as a result of his work in Afghanistan – even though Sadat had warned Reagan and his CIA boss, William Casey, a decade before that he was one of the most dangerous terrorists in Egypt. When Rahman wanted to enter the USA in 1990, his visa was originally refused by the American embassy in Cairo who recognized him for what he was: a life-long terrorist, an enemy of the Egyptian state and a hard-line terrorist for whom America was 'The Great Satan'. The embassy bureaucrats were overruled by more powerful interests in the State Department in Washington who let him in. Once in the USA, Rahman's mosque in New York quickly became a hotbed for revolutionary Islamic fundamentalism. Two years after he had made the USA his new home, he organized the first – and unsuccessful – attack on the World Trade Centre in 1993. He is now in prison in the USA, unrepentant and regarded by the faithful as a major Islamic martyr.

In CIA parlance what happened is called a 'Frankenstein' and it is every intelligence officer's nightmare. Thousands of hours and millions of dollars are spent cultivating a significant intelligence asset who then outgrows his creator and turns into a monster. First the CIA teams created Sadat, who had turned into a Frankenstein, out of control, unpredictable and dangerous. But he in turn – along with the CIA and MI6 – created a far more dangerous monster, uninhibited global Islamic terror-ism, a movement which was initially encouraged, financed, promoted, guided and advised by the Western intelligence services.

Though Mubarak has clung to power and Egypt is a predominantly Westernized Islamic state, fundamentalism re-mains. The Sadat exiles have always been on the fringes chewing away at the fabric of the Egyptian state, always spicing up their campaign with assassination.

In 1992, the militant Islamists launched a major campaign of terror, assassinating a secular commentator, Farag Foda, attack-ing tourists, intellectuals and Coptic Christians, even killing a group while they were praying in church. Two years later, they attempted to assassinate the Nobel prize-winning writer Naguib Mahfouz and a year after that they tried to take out Mubarak himself, just one of several assassination attempts against the president. In 1996, they gunned down eighteen Greek tourists outside a Cairo hotel. The Egyptian security services fought a classic low-intensity war both against Al Jihad and another loose group of militants, the Gama'a al-Islamiyya, killing them in large numbers. In a desperate attempt to shore up the tourism industry, the government then announced a victory in its war against the terrorists, but in a fractured society like Egypt, the prevailing conditions of mass poverty, ignorance and religion will always produce an annual crop of fresh recruits, for whom terror, assassination and the glorious death of the martyr is taken as a given. In September 1997, two 'brothers' opened fire on German tourists outside the Cairo Museum, killing nine and the driver. The authorities claimed they were not part of an organized group but two months later, a highly organized Islamist hit squad attacked a tourist bus at the temple of Hatshepsut at Luxor in southern Egypt, machine-gunning down sixty unarmed and defenceless tourists, mostly Swiss, Japanese, German and British. The Gama'a al-Islamiyya left a leaflet behind saying the attack was in homage to Mustafa Hamza, one of their exiled leaders who was on the run after failing to assassinate Mubarak. Other leaflets venerated Omar Abdel Rahman.

The fifth graduate of the assassination was Ayman al-Zawahiri, one of the members of Al Jihad jailed beforehand and the man who was now even more significant in Al Qaeda than Bin Laden himself. He was interviewed while in prison by General Nabawy Ismail who remembered him as 'a very quiet man, a young doctor from a good family, with no leadership qualities at all.' Egyptian prison clearly released his hidden management potential. He is now effectively the joint leader of Al Qaeda and number two on the FBI's list of most wanted terrorists.

Born in 1951, Ayman al-Zawahiri, like many revolutionaries, had a classic bourgeois upbringing in a rich Egyptian family of doctors and academics. As a teenager he joined militant Islamic cells and earned his first stripes when he was arrested, aged fifteen, for being a member of the Muslim Brotherhood, the Arab world's oldest fundamentalist group but one he later condemned for being too moderate. According to his unpublished auto-biography, he was tortured in prison, a claim which is true. What is not in his book is the claim of the Egyptian secret service that he betrayed his comrades, turning their names over to save himself.

In prison he studied the works of the ultimate philosopher-terrorist behind Al Qaeda theology, Sayyed Qutb, describing him as 'the most prominent theoretician of the fundamentalist movements'. The diet of hard-core fundamentalist theology and brutal torture changed the man utterly and by the time he was released, he had hardened his position. He left Egypt for Saudi Arabia, Pakistan and inevitably Afghanistan to join the war against the Russian invaders. There he established a local branch of the Egyptian Al Jihad, first meeting Bin Laden in the late 1980s.

The year after the Luxor attack, he signed a motion with Bin Laden, calling for a *fatwa* against American 'civilians'. He then merged his Egyptian Islamic Al Jihad group with Bin Laden's Al Qaeda ('the base'). Bin Laden had global reach and tens of millions of dollars at his disposal, Zawahiri brought military expertise and planning, a working knowledge of asymmetric warfare as well as two sons who were by now both veteran military commanders in Afghanistan. Once they merged their two groups, the level of global terrorism increased dramatically. The bombings of the US embassies in Tanzania and Kenya followed and a year later, in August 2000, Zawahiri and Bin Laden sat together for a video-taped celebration to honour the men who had carried out the attacks. They sat together under a banner naming the man who had set Zawahiri on a lifetime path of global terrorism: Omar Abdel Rahman, who was picked out for special praise by both Bin Laden and Zawahiri as the great hero of their cause. On 15 April 2002, an undated videotape of Zawahiri was released on Al Jazeera, the Arabic satellite news channel. He described the September 11 attack as 'a great victory', though his natural modesty prevented him from adding that much of the plan and its execution was his own.

The day of Sadat's assassination, Mohammed al-Islambouli wrote in a book for his brother, who was about to lead the assassination squad against Sadat: 'The greatest prize for a believer is salvation, and to kill or be killed in the cause of God', a thought echoed by every suicide bomber since and central to the thinking of the World Trade Centre attackers, four of whom were Egyptian. All four were inspired by the example of their role model from twenty years before, the young Egyptian army First Lieutenant, Khalid al-Islambouli, who emptied his Kalashnikov into the freshly tailored bespoke uniform of his president, Anwar Sadat, a hero to some but a traitorous dog to others.

The ironic result is that the USA is now in the public assassination business, with huge cash rewards ($25–50 million in the currency of your choice) for the capture or assassination of Osama Bin Laden and Ayman al-Zawahiri.

The cynical advice given to torturers is that if you break a man as badly as the Egyptians broke Zawahiri then you had better kill him, otherwise he will come back and destroy you.

When the planes flew into the World Trade Centre in 2001, many commentators looked for significance in the date, but none spotted the crucial link. It was exactly twenty years to the month since Zawahiri, the key planner of the attack, had been arrested, tortured and broken.

EPILOGUE

The story of assassinations is not one thickly populated with heroes. For the most part it is a series of interlocking tales of morally bankrupt politicians, self-seeking intelligence officers, terrorists strapped by their obedience to a corrupt ideology, and criminals of every type. It is a business where the pathologically disturbed, the emotionally crippled, the paranoid and the egomaniacal all roam free, united in their flawed belief that the assassination of a particular individual will fundamentally change the world and make it a better place.

There is one man who tried to make a partial claim to heroic status, standing aside from the moral cesspit and refusing to take part in the assassination programme going on around him.

In October 1960, Michael Mulroney, a senior CIA officer and the Deputy Head of what is described as an 'extraordinarily secret unit' in the Directorate for Plans, is called in to see his boss, Richard Bissell, one of the agency's high-flyers and, at that time, the man in charge of all CIA Covert Operations everywhere in the world. His orders to Mulroney are simple: go down to central Africa and kill Patrice Lumumba, the democratically elected leader of the Congo.

Mulroney is a bizarre choice as assassin-in-chief. Just a few years earlier, in 1955, he was withdrawn frotn Thailand where he was briefly CIA Station Chief.[1] As a Catholic, Mulroney was a robust critic of the corruption and drug dealing of the local police chief, Colonel Phao Siyanon,[2] a man with blood on his hands who had assassinated many of his opponents while consolidating his power base in the military dictatorship that ran Thailand after the end of the Second World War.[3] But Phao and his fellow military leaders were much liked by the power brokers in London and Washington, who did not share Mulroney's moral objections to doing business with one of the country's leading criminals. Phao was a loyal foot soldier in the Cold War, a minor bulwark against the communists in South-East Asia and, as far as Mulroney's political masters in Washington were concerned, that was enough to give him licence to pursue his criminal endeavours, unfettered by the state.[4]

In a brave and career-threatening move, Mulroney informs the Senate Committee investigating the CIA's assassination programme that he refused to kill Lumumba; his objections being both philosophical and legal. He tells the senators he is 'morally opposed' to assassination and believes that intelligence officers should be both scrupulous and moral. He tells them that when he was first ordered by his superiors to commit murder he was also worried about the criminal consequences, warning his boss that 'conspiracy to commit murder in the District of Columbia [where the CIA was and is headquartered] might be in violation of federal law',[5] a complaint 'airily dismissed' by Bissell. However, Mulroney accepts a compromise: he agrees to go to the Congo to 'neutralize' Lumumba 'as a political factor'. As his boss told the committee, although Mulroney had expressed a 'negative reaction' to the assassination of Lumumba and was therefore not under assignment to do this, he was there 'merely to make plans for such an operation'.

When Mulroney reaches the Congo, Lumumba is being kept under UN protection. His mission is to try to get him turned over to the Congolese authorities, so he can 'be tried by a jury of his peers'.

This is little more than the tiniest moral fig leaf. Lumumba had committed no crime and the 'peers' who were to 'try' him were not an elected government but his enemies, a bunch of brutal psychopathic killers, who can be guaranteed to assassinate him as soon as they have him in their control, that is, doing exactly what the West, and especially the CIA and the White House, require. Mulroney knows this. Under cross-examination, he admits there was a 'very, very high probability' that Lumumba would be executed by these rebels, without even the pretence of a show trial. The Senators can be in no doubt as to the end game here. Among the thousands of CIA cables they have examined is one that gives the game away, describing the view of the UN Special Representative in Congo, who portrays this plan as 'JUST A TRICK TO ASSASSINATE LUMUMBA'.[6]

When Mulroney arrives in the Congo, he meets a fellow CIA officer who tells him that a lethal virus, which he knows is not 'for somebody to get his polio shot up-to-date',[7] has already been delivered by diplomatic pouch and is safe in the Embassy, ready to be used on Lumumba. Having established what for him is a morally unassailable position, from which he can send Lumumba to his death with clean hands, Mulroney begins the delicate task of prising him away from the protection of the United Nations and into the murderous clutches of his enemies.

Shortly after Mulroney's arrival, the first CIA assassin arrives, under the code name QJ/WIN, reporting directly to Mulroney, followed by a second assassin, WI/ROGUE,[8] regarded even by the local CIA as one of the most unscrupulous men they have ever worked with. Other CIA officers describe these two men as part of 'an execution squad' though Mulroney claims they are there for counter-espionage, members of the team who will spring Lumumba from UN protection. This is an extraordinary claim to make, given that Mulroney admits he knows QJ/WIN to be a man of few scruples, capable of anything 'including assassination'.

QJ/WIN is a bit of a celebrity in CIA circles. Even the top boss, Richard Helms, knows about him. When asked about QJ/WIN's capability, he tells the senators, 'if you needed somebody to carry out murder, I guess you had a man who might be prepared to carry it out'.[9]

Mulroney's mission is successful and in a feat of magic worthy of Harry Houdini, one of the world's most heavily guarded political prisoners manages to escape. The CIA deny they are involved but the paper trail gives the game away. In a TOP SECRET cable sent the day after Lumumba escapes, the CIA in the Congo tells Washington they are working with the government [sic] to get the troops out and the road blocked, a tactic which succeeds. Lumumba is captured by his arch rival, Mobutu, one of the most evil, corrupt psychopaths ever to run an African state. Lumumba's fate is sealed. Not surprisingly, there is no American pressure from the US Embassy for 'a trial of his peers' and instead it is secretly agreed in TOP SECRET cables that QJ/WIN, the contract killer who works directly for Mulroney, will go to Stanleyville to kill him. The only CIA concern is whether their assassin might be caught and how close this might 'place the United States to the action'.

Mulroney excuses his actions and that of all his fellow CIA officers, telling the senators, 'All the people I knew acted in good faith. I think they acted in the light of maybe not their consciences but their concept of patriotism. They felt that this was in the best interests of the US. I think that we have too much of the "good German" in us, in that we do something because the boss says it is okay. And they are not essentially evil people. But you can do an awful lot of wrong in this.'

Mulroney's professed philosophical reservations were little more than a tiny side step round the law, the thinnest patina of plausible deniability. The USA (who knew that 'drastic steps' were needed to prevent Lumumba's return to power), the UK and Belgium had all helped turn Lumumba over to his enemies. The 'trial by his peers' which Mulroney said he wanted, never happened. A totally predictable 'awful wrong' was then done to Lumumba who was savagely beaten over days and then executed by a Belgian firing squad.

Despite his self-portrayal as an honourable man, Mulroney was no moral guardian. In fact, unlike many other CIA officers at the hearings, he did not even testify under his real name. His real name was Justin O'Donnell, a man who told the American senators investigating the CIA's assassination programme in five countries, Cuba, the Congo, the Dominican Republic, Chile and South Vietnam, 'murder corrupts'.[10]

APPENDIX I

GENERAL PRINCIPLES IN ASSASSINATION SCIENCE

ALWAYS:

- Start with the basics: go back to the original documents and find out what actually happened.
- Discount the impossible. The basic laws of physics and chemistry always apply and if they say something is impossible then it is. Bullets – especially over short distances – only ever travel in straight lines.
- If possible, visit the site.
- Put together a timeline of what happened and source every entry.
- Read the footnotes and appendices of all official investigations. This is where the interesting evidence is often parked.
- Ignore all comment from pundits, especially anything of the 'what would have happened' school of journalism. Unless the writer was actually there or has done the hard research, then they have nothing to contribute. The comment of pundits is cheap and its sole value is essential insulation for fish and chips.

- Ignore anything written by someone who starts off by saying 'I only believe in cock-up . . .' This is nonsense and anyone who claims to understand this world should know better. Anyone who says this already has a fixed mindset and is therefore unfit to carry out a serious empirical investigation. Generally, pundits who preface their remarks this way are the worst kind of conspiracy theorists. Their problem is that they do not like anyone else's theories.
- Check out the background of everyone, especially the 'experts'.

NEVER ASSUME:

- That things are what they seem or appear to be.
- That any organization (particularly one connected to the security and intelligence services) is monolithic. They are always fragmented and split by faction.
- That there is only one thing happening. Assassinations are like three-dimensional chess, with many interlocking zones of influence.
- That any organization or individual is behaving rationally or is acting in their own best interests.
- That because the conclusions of an official investigation say there is nothing suspicious, the evidence will support this. In many investigations the evidence points to only one inescapable conclusion – foul play – but the opposite conclusion is then reached.

ALWAYS ASSUME THAT:

- Coincidences do happen but they are nothing more than random chance.
- Cock-up and conspiracy will go hand in hand.

AND FINALLY:

- Never underestimate the venality and moral corruption of political leaders or the lengths to which the supine and the ambitious will go to advance themselves and their careers.

APPENDIX 2

'CONFERENCE ROOM TECHNIQUE' FROM CIA ASSASSINATION MANUAL

(1)	(2)

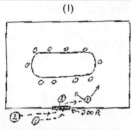

(1) Enters room quickly but quietly.

(2) Stands in doorway.

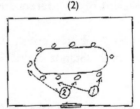

(2) Opens fire on first subject to react. Swings across group toward centre of mass. Times burst to empty magazine at end of swing.

(1) covers group to prevent individual dangerous reactions, if necessary, fires individual bursts of 3 rounds.

(3)	(4)

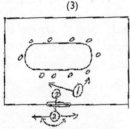

(2) Finishes burst. Commands 'shift'. Drops back through [sic] door. Replaces empty magazine. Covers corridor.

(1) On command 'shift', opens fire on opposite side of target, swings one burst across group.

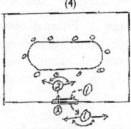

(1) Finishes burst. Commands 'shift'. Drops back through [sic] door. Replaces magazine. Covers corridor.

(2) On command 'shift', re-enters room. Covers group: kills survivors with two-round bursts. Leaves propaganda.

(5)	(6)

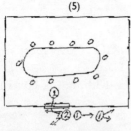

(2) Leaves room. Commands 'GO'. Covers rear with nearly full magazine.

(1) On command 'GO', leads withdrawal covering front with full magazine.

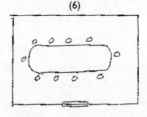

Conference room technique

Transcript of 'Conference Room Technique'

1

Gunman 1   Enters room quickly but quietly

Gunman 2   Stands in doorway

2

Gunman 2   Opens fire on first subject to react. Swings across group toward center of mass. Times burst to empty magazine at end of swing.

Gunman 1   Covers group to prevent individual dangerous reactions, if necessary, fires individual bursts of 3 rounds.

3

Gunman 2   Finishes burst. Commands 'Shift.' Drops back thru [*sic*] door. Replaces empty magazine. Covers corridor.

Gunman 1   On command 'shift', opens fire on opposite side of target, swings one burst across group.

4

Gunman 1   Finishes burst. Commands 'shift'. Drops back thru [*sic*] door. Replaces magazine. Covers corridor.

Gunman 2   On command, 'shift', re-enters room. Covers group: kills survivors with two-round bursts. Leaves propaganda.

5

Gunman 2   Leaves room. Commands 'GO'. Covers rear with nearly full magazine.

Gunman 1   On command 'GO', leads withdrawal, covering front with full magazine.

6

[Conference terminated.]

The Guatemala 1954 Documents, Document 2 'A Study of Assassination', The National Security Archive, Washington, D.C.

NOTES

Introduction

1. White House spokesman, Ari Fleischer, briefing to journalists, 1 October 2002. He was asked about the cost of going to war and said that the Bush administration would welcome the assassination of Saddam Hussein by his countrymen, arguing that 'one bullet' would be the most effective way.
2. President Ford issued executive order 11905, which prohibited political assassinations. This order said, 'No employee of the United States Government shall engage in, or conspire to engage in, political assassination.' President Carter amended this, removing the word 'political'. In 1981, President Reagan issued the exact same executive order, 33314.
3. Throughout I have used the classification CE, Common Era and BCE, Before Common Era, rather than AD (Anno Domini) the year of our lord and BC (Before Christ). The vast majority of people on the planet are not Christian and global measure of time is therefore the fairest.
4. *The Times*, 23 March 2004.
5. The full statement read 'Israel is not entitled to go for this kind of unlawful killing and we therefore condemn it. It's unacceptable, unjustified and it's very unlikely to achieve its objective.' 22 March 2004.

6. BBC News, 24 July 2003. Straw said they had been given 'every opportunity' to leave Iraq but made their choice when they decided to stay. This is a variation on the old ploy, 'now see what you made me do!'

7. CNN, 22 July 2003.

8. See the report of the investigating French magistrate by Judge Stephan.

9. The first blood test was taken by scooping a sample from out of his chest with a spoon, a test which runs an obviously high risk of contamination.

10. His blood test results were acquired by the author and released in a television documentary *Diana: The Secrets Behind the Crash*, made by Fulcrum TV for ITV in June 1998.

11. Professor Alastair Hay, Leeds University, *Diana: The Secrets Behind the Crash*.

12. The Paris crash is dealt with in much greater detail in Chapter 9.

13. Plutarch, *Life of Caesar*.

14. These papers were discovered by Matthew Jones, a Reader in international history at Royal Holloway University, University of London.

15. de Witte, Ludo, *The Assassination of Lumumba*, Belgium 1999, London 2001, passim.

16. 'Alleged Assassination Plots Involving Foreign Leaders', An Interim Report of the Select Committee to Study Governmental Operations with respect to Intelligence Activities, 1975. Known as the Church Committee this extraordinary investigation examined the American government's role in the assassination business. It interviewed many witnesses at all levels within the intelligence apparatus, from junior officers through to the Head of the Central Intelligence Agency (CIA). The cases they examined included the many attempts on Fidel Castro and his brother, Raul. The committee also looked at the assassinations of Patrice Lumumba (Congo 1960), Rafael Trujillo (Dominican Republic 1961), Diem and his brother Nhu (Vietnam 1963) and General Rene Schneider (Chile 1970). The testimony about the presidential order to assassinate Lumumba comes from Robert H. Johnson, a veteran member of the National Security Council (NSC), p. 55.

17. The document is at the British Public Records Office, FO371/146650, 28 September 1960.

18. De Witte, Ludo, *The Assassination of Lumumba*, Belgium 1999, London 2001: passim.

19. Lumumba repeatedly argued that 'the exploitation of the mineral riches of the Congo should be primarily for the profit of our own

people and other Africans.' The Washington view was that this would pave the way for a communist takeover 'with disastrous consequences for the prestige of the UN and for the interests of the free world generally.' This telegram sent by CIA Head Allen Dulles on 26 August 1960 went on to order that Lumumba's removal 'must be an urgent and prime objective'. Dulles was a former lawyer to the Rockefellers, who were major investors in the Congo. Allen Dulles and his brother John Foster Dulles, were partners in the law firm of Sullivan and Cromwell. This firm was legal adviser to the Anglo-Iranian Oil Company (AIOC), whose commercial interests were protected in the CIA-sponsored coup in Iran in 1953. Allen Dulles had also been a director of the merchant bank, Henry J. Shroeder, one of the consortium behind the Industrial Bank of Persia, financiers to the AIOC. Their law firm also represented the United Fruit Company in South America, whose interests were protected by the CIA *coup d'état* against another democratically elected leader, Jacabo Arbenz Guzmán in Guatemala 1954. His brother John Foster Dulles, who was the US Secretary of State at the time, had served on the company's trustees board. As often is the case, intelligence policy followed commercial interests, though for the Dulles brothers this was spiced up by having their own wallets on the line.

20. Thyraud de Vosjoli, P. L., *Lamia.* Boston, 1970, pp. 263–6. Lamia was the code name of this SDECE (Service de Documentation Extérieure et de Contre-Espionage) officer. He was intimately involved in the French government assassination programme in the late 1950s and early 1960s. The major targets were African nationalists in French colonies but this programme spilled over to take in their non-Africa supporters as well, including academics who made contact with these groups.

21. Wise, David and Ross, Thomas B., *The Espionage Establishment*, London 1968, pp. 53–6. It should be noted that both these 'nationalists' had suspect war records having fought with the Nazis in the Second World War.

1. Never Write Anything Down

1. Cullather, Nicholas, *Operation PBSUCCESS*, 1994, p. 109.
2. Schlesinger, Stephen and Kinzer, Stephen, *Bitter Fruit, The Untold Story of the American Coup in Guatemala*, Doubleday, 1982, pp. 108–29.
3. *A Study of Assassination*, CIA 1954. The most likely author is Rip Robertson himself as he was the man in charge of all training.

4. This was a highly prescient forethought. The assassination team, which was hired by a shadowy anti-Qaddafi organization, Al Burkan, to come to Britain in 1984 and murder his supporters was caught with three Walther PPK handguns. Their claim that they were acting in self-defence collapsed when the judge asked them why they needed silencers as well.

5. This was the case in many of the Provisional IRA bombings in Northern Ireland as well as the Cosa Nostra assassination of Judge Giovanni Falcone in 1992 when radios were also used to track the movements of his car.

6. Ranelagh, John, *Agency: The Rise and Decline of the CIA*, London: 1986.

7. Blum, William. *The CIA: A Forgotten History*, p. 77.

8. William Prescott Allan, the publisher of the *Laredo Times* and a friend of President Eisenhower, telegrammed his friend after visiting Guatemala to tell him that 'Yes, Guatemala had a small minority of communists, but not as many as San Francisco', quoted in Richard H. Immerman, *The CIA in Guatemala*, Austin, Texas, USA 1982, p. 183.

9. 2.2 per cent of the landowners own 70 per cent of the land and the annual income of agricultural workers is $87. Blum, William, *The CIA: A Forgotten History*, p. 79.

10. Immerman, Richard H., *The CIA in Guatemala*, Austin 1982, pp. 80–1.

11. Thomas Corcoran, the UFCO lobbyist, saw Thomas Mann, the Deputy Assistant Secretary for Inter-American Affairs, on 15 May 1950 to suggest action to remove the Guatemalan President, Juan José Arevalo, six months before Arbenz was elected. Cullather, Nicholas, *Operation PBSUCCESS*, 1994, Appendix A.

12. Allen Dulles met Mann to solicit State Department approval for a coup on 10 July 1952. The land distribution started on 7 August 1952 and PBFORTUNE was approved 18 August 1952. PBSUCCESS started the following year.

13. Ranelagh p. 134.

14. Haines, Gerald K., *CIA and Guatemala Assassination Proposals 1952–4*, CIA History Staff Analysis, June 1995, p. 11, footnote 32.

15. CIA MEMORANDUM To All Staff Officers, SUBJECT: Selections of individuals for disposal by Junta Group, 31 March 1954.

16. Haines, Gerald K., *CIA and Guatemala Assassination Proposals 1952–4, CIA History Staff Analysis*, June 1995.

17. Ibid p. 3.

18. *Strange Fruit* p. 207–10.

19. Ibid p. 219.
20. Quoted by Mike O'Brien, MP, Minister of State, Foreign and Commonwealth Office, speaking at a RUSI Conference, 19–20 September 2002. These proceedings were subsequently published under the title *War and Morality*, edited by Patrick Mileham, p. 7.
21. 'Alleged Assassination Plots Involving Foreign Leaders', an Interim Report of the Select Committee to Study Governmental Operations (also known as The Church Committee), 1975, Chairman Frank Church.
22. Ibid pp. 72–3.
23. MacDonald, Callum, *The Killing of SS Obergruppenführer Reinhard Heydrich*, p. 182.
24. SOE War Diary, Public Records Office, HS/212, 10, 26 January 1941. I am indebted to Dr Saul Kelly of Joint Services Command and Staff College, who very kindly provided me with a guide through these records and whose advice and guidance was invaluable.
25. SOE War Diary, Public Records Office, HS7/214, 7, 19 March 1941.
26. SOE War Diary, Public Records Office, HS7/215, 18 April 1941.
27. SOE War Diary, Public Records Office, HS7/216, 27/28 May 1941.
28. SOE War Diary, Public Records Office, HS3/154 2 May 1941.
29. SOE War Diary, Public Records Office, HS7/217, 5, 8/9,12/13, 16/17 June 1941.
30. Memo written 20 August 1945 to Lord Pethick-Lawrence, the Secretary of State for India.
31. Lt Colonel J.G. Figgis was sent to investigate but his report is little more than a second-hand account and he never got anywhere near any first-hand evidence, SACSEA Telegram, SAC 12782/INT, copy in the British Library, London.
32. Dorril, Stephen, *MI6: Fifty Years of Special Operations*, Fourth Estate, 2001, p. 57.
33. Young, G.K., *Masters of Indecision*, p. 15. Young argues that the men in the Arab lands had not evolved 'from a tool making animal' whose greatest joy was destruction. 'While the European has been building, the Arab has looted and torn down.' He vilifies the Arabs as suffering from a 'perpetual neurosis' in which concepts like truth are meaningless.
34. Knightley, Philip, *The Second Oldest Profession*, p. 389.
35. This was the same reasoning behind the assassination of Sir Lee Stack, in 1924. The Egyptians objected to him being the head of what they perceived as their army.

36. Dorril, p. 613. When he wrote his book, Nutting toned down Eden's comments saying that he had called for Nasser's 'removal', but subsequently recanted, saying that Eden had in fact called for Nasser to be 'murdered.'

37. Dorril, p. 586.

38. In 1957 Macmillan and Eisenhower approved a joint MI6–CIA plan to assassinate Abd al-Hamid Sarraj, the Head of Military Intelligence in Syria; Afif al-Bizri, the Chief of the General Staff; and Khalid Bakdash, the Leader of the Communist Party.

39. This document is in the British National Archives at Kew, London. The reference is FO371/146650.

40. A career diplomat and MI6 officer, Baroness Park became Principal of Somerville College, Oxford and a Governor of the BBC. Interviewed for the *Daily Telegraph* in April 2003 she was still an unapologetic colonialist demanding strong action against Robert Mugabe of Zimbabwe. 'The government is too worried about speaking out because they think they will be accused of being colonialist. Well I don't think that's such a terrible crime.' Some beliefs die hard.

41. Ludo de Witte, p. xvi.

42. Sudoplatov, Pael and Anatoli, *Special Tasks*, USA/Canada: 1994, pp. 32, 58.

43. Andrew, Christopher and Mitrokin, Vasili, *The Mitrokin Archive*, London: 1999, p. 757.

44. Testimony of Deriabin, Senate Committee 1965. Wise, David and Ross, Thomas B., *The Espionage Establishment*, p. 60.

45. Wise, David and Ross, Thomas B., *The Espionage Establishment*, p. 55.

46. Seymour Hersh, *The New Yorker*, 23 December 2002.

47. US DOD briefing 3 December 2002.

2. Be Careful When You Choose Your Assassin

1. According to the *Biographic Directory of the USSR*, he was recalled in March 1953. The exact date, the 10, is contained in Wise, David and Ross, Thomas B. *The Espionage Establishment*, footnote, p. 51.

2. Samadoghlu, Vagif, *Stalin's Personality Cult: Three Times I Changed My Mind*, Azerbaijan International, Autumn 1999.

3. Brent, Jonathan and Naumov, Vladimir. *Stalin's Last Crime*, London: 2004.

4. *The Splendid Misery: The Story of the Presidency and Power Politics at Close Range.* Contributors: Jack Bell. Doubleday, New York, 1960. When Truman referred to him as SOB Pincushion, it prompted the question from his Chief Protocol Officer, Stanley

Woodward, 'My God, how am I going to translate that into diplomatic language?' pp. 179–80.

5. *Biographic Directory of the USSR*. Contributors: V. S. Meretisalov, Institute for the Study of the USSR; Institut zur Erforschung der USSR. New York: Scarecrow Press; 1958, p. 473.

6. Ibid.

7. Other accounts suggest a tank.

8. CIA assassination manual, p. 4.

9. Sudoplatov, Pavel and Anatoli, *Special Tasks*, pp. 249, 252–3 Sudoplatov names Khrushchev as the man who ordered this killing. Professor James Mace, a consultant to *The Day*, a Ukrainian newspaper, named Stalin and Lazar Kaganovich as the men who ordered it, 3 October 2000.

10. Rositzke, Harry, *The KGB: The Eyes of Russia*, Sidgwick & Jackson, 1982, p. 138.

11. This phrase is quoted by a former CIA Case Officer, Harry Rositzke in his book, *The KGB*, p. 138.

12. Heilbrunn, Otto, *The Soviet Secret Services*, Frederick A. Praeger, 1956 pp. 84–5.

13. Ibid.

14. Andrew, Christopher and Mitrokin, Visali, *The Mitrokin Archive*, paperback edition, p. 467.

15. Ibid, p. 466.

16. US Office of Naval Intelligence (ONI) Review, December 1954.

17. Khokhlov, Nikolai, *In the Name of Conscience: The Testament of a Soviet Secret Agent*, New York, 1959, p. 233.

18. Andrew, Christopher and Mitrokin, Visali, *The Mitrokin Archive*, paperback edition, p. 467.

19. Heilbrunn, Otto, *The Soviet Secret Services*, Frederick A. Praeger, 1956 pp. 84–5.

20. Wise, David and Ross, Thomas B., *The Espionage Establishment*, p. 52.

21. Khrushchev was reported to be just 5 foot 1 inch tall.

22. Dorril, Stephen, *MI6*, London: 2000, p. 409.

23. Ibid. p. 417.

24. Ibid. pp. 226, 227.

25. Rositzke, Harry, *The KGB*, p. 139.

26. CIA assassination manual, 1954, Guatemala.

27. Rositzke, Harry, *The KGB*, p. 135–6.

28. After the defections of Philby, Burgess and Maclean, the British security and intelligence services inevitably turned inwards, chased their own shadows and began to see Russian spies everywhere. One

internal audit suggested that the Russians had recruited over three dozen agents but the evidence was often elusive. But even if it had been cast-iron there was little appetite for a series of public trials. The ones who had escaped had already caused enough damage.

29. Khokhlov, Nikolai, *In the Name of Conscience*, Chapters 2 and 3.
30. Ibid. p. 54.
31. Though different names have been suggested over the years, he is the best candidate to be QJ/WIN, see De Witte, Ludo, *The Assassination of Lumumba*, p. 188 and was named by Richard D. Mahoney.
32. Memo to CIA Finance Division, re: payments to QJ/WIN, 1/31/1961, quoted in Church Committee report, p. 43.
33. Church Committee report, p. 43.
34. CIA Inspector General's report on 'Plots to Assassinate Fidel Castro', 23 May 1967, pp. 39–40. The contents of this memo were so secret that the front cover instructions were 'Destroy the one burn copy retained temporarily by the Inspector General.' President Johnson, who had asked for the report, was not allowed to see it and it was withheld from his successor, Richard Nixon, as well. The contents are explosive, highly damaging to the CIA even now. Had it been released in 1967, the damage would have been immense. As it was, some of the subject matter was leaked by the veteran investigative journalist, Jack Anderson. It was, of course, denied at the time.
35. CIA cable, Africa Division to Leopoldville, 27 October 1960, Church Committee, p. 46.
36. CIA Cable, Africa Division to Leopoldville, 27 October 1960, Church Committee, p. 46.
37. Church Committee, p. 183.
38. When Venezuela broke off diplomatic relations with Cuba he went to the Mexican embassy. Castro refused to give him a safe conduct pass until 1964 when he left for Mexico City. He emerged in Miami in 1965.
39. $4 million in 2001 and $5 million in 2002. Source: Human Rights Watch.
40. CIA World Fact Book, Yemen.
41. Hellfire is derived from an acronym, Heliborne-launched, Fire and Forget.

3. Assassinate One, Terrify a Thousand

1. Hazard, H.W., *The History of the Crusades, The Fourteenth and Fifteenth Centuries*, volume III, p. 53.

2. This is traditionally ascribed to a well-known priest called Brocardus. But the key text *Directorium as passagium faciendum transmarinum* was believed to have been written by Guillaume Adam or Raymond Etienne. Hazard, H.W., *The History of the Crusades, The Fourteenth and Fifteenth Centuries*, volume III, p. 51, footnote.

3. Ayatollah Ali Khamenei attacked George W Bush's 2002 State of the Union address as being that of someone 'thirsty for human blood'.

4. Although Abraham Lincoln visited the tiny theatre in Washington, D.C. where he was assassinated, the obvious question is why the President did not have armed guards on the door to his box. As it was, his assassin, John Wilkes Booth, had no problem going through the door, shooting Lincoln in the head before escaping.

5. Yasser al-Sirri was arrested for his role of providing the letters which allowed the assassins to slip through the Afghan defences but the charges were thrown out.

6. For a more detailed account there is an excellent article by Jon Lee Anderson in the *New Yorker*, 10 June 2002.

7. 'Brocardus'.

8. Gibbon, Edward, *The History of the Decline of the Roman Empire*, volume 7, London: 1896, pp. 12–13.

9. Since their demise there have been numerous explanations of where the word assassin comes from. Writing in 1331, an Arab historian Abul Fida argued that because the Assassin headquarters were on a mountain called *Jabal Al-sikkin* this was the root, *sikkeen* meaning knife and therefore this was the Mountain of the Knife. Writing in 1700, Thomas Hyde argued incorrectly that the root word is *hassas*, meaning to exterminate or kill. Other explanations followed – that it came from al-Sasani, the family of a man called Sasan, which is also an Arabic term meaning adventurer. Alternatively, it was argued that this was the name of a family who were renowned adventurers. Others have argued that it derives from their founder Hasan ibn el-Sabah or that it was a corrupt form of Arabic words meaning rock or fortress. More recent explanations suggest that Hasan ibn el-Sabah's faithful disciples were those who were faithful to the *assass*, the foundation of the faith. However, the dominant and most recurrent theory has Hashish as the root.

10. Quoted in Bernard Lewis, *The Assassins*, p. 130, 2003 paperback edition.

11. Rowan, Richard Wilmer, *33 Centuries of Espionage*, p. 43.

12. Quoted in Bernard Lewis, *The Assassins*, pp. 58, 59.

13. For a fuller account of this phenomenon, Loretta Napoleoni has produced a devastating account of the terror economy in her book, *Modern Jihad, Tracing the Dollars Behind the Terror Networks*, London 2003.
14. Quoted in Bernard Lewis, *The Assassins*, pp. 115–16.
15. Ibid. p. 117.
16. Irwin, Lieutenant General Sir Alistair, *Military Power*, edited by Professor Brian Holden Reid, quoted in 'The Ethics of Counter Terrorism', RUSI Conference September 2002.
17. Napoleoni, Loretta, *Modern Jihad*, London 2003.
18. This is a hugely controversial subject but there can be no doubt that it happened. There are various estimates of how frequently it happened and some suggest at least two hundred times. After the Abu Ghraib incidents, there was a fear in the US High Command that the army would unravel once again.
19. This is a very controversial subject and the estimates of the number of suicides among American and other troops who served in Vietnam vary enormously, depending to some extent on political viewpoint. However, the feeling of helplessness amongst the troops and the long-term destabilizing effects is well recorded.
20. This account comes from Arnold of Lubeck, a German historian writing around 1200.
21. It is also seen in the Palestinian suicide bombers.
22. There is no literature for Project BIZARRE and its existence is formally denied. My source is one of those who worked on it.
23. Wood, Frances, *Did Marco Polo Ever Get To China?* London 1995. She argues, very convincingly, that Marco Polo never made the trip but that his book, *Description of the World*, was constructed from previously existing sources, plus a large slice of imagination. Its value therefore is as a distillation of what was believed at the time, a cocktail of fact and myth, not a journal of record.
24. Dante, *Divine Comedy*, Book XIX.
25. 'Io stava come it frate the confessa.
    Lo perfido assassin . . .'
26. It was the lotus flower.
27. Jonnes, Jill, *Hep-Cats, Narcs and Pipe Dreams*, New York 1996, quoted p. 128.
28. Walton, R.P., *Marijuana, America's New Drug Problem*, Philadelphia 1938, quoted in *Marijuana Reconsidered*, Lester Grinspoon, Harvard University Press, Cambridge MA, 1971, p. 16.
29. Ibid. p. 17.

30. For a fuller account see Jonnes, Jill, *Hep-Cats, Narcs and Pipe Dreams*, New York 1996.

4. Keep it Tight

1. This account is based on that given by Plutarch, *Life of Caesar.*
2. There are a small number of exceptions, but there are few examples where a group of plotters get together in peacetime to collectively get rid of a leader.
3. There is one video in which he allegedly boasts about his role but this is of doubtful provenance.
4. He describes the assassination as 'safe, simple, and terroristic.' Safe meaning the assassin escaped afterwards [which was not true], simple meaning the subject is unaware and terroristic meaning it needed publicity to be effective. The trainer does get some parts right, remarking that 'in safe assassinations, the assassin needs the usual qualities of a clandestine agent. He should be determined, courageous, intelligent, resourceful, and physically active. If special equipment is to be used, such as firearms or drugs, it is clear that he must have outstanding skill with such equipment.'
5. The Head of the Assassins was known in both Arabic and non-Arabic legend as 'The Man of the Mountain'.
6. This manual was discovered by the British police on 10 May 2000 in a raid on the house of Nazih al Wadih Raghie in Manchester, England.
7. For a full account of this read Reeve, Simon, *One Day in September*, London 2000, a brilliant book.
8. Others say he was the PLO representative in France.

5. Get Someone Else to Do Your Dirty Work

1. Robin Robison, who worked for the Joint Intelligence Committee (JIC) in the mid-1980s saw two in three years. Another MI6 officer told the author he had seen just one in the previous year.
2. Interview with one of the students on the coach. For obvious reasons, he has not been named. Even now, the Qaddafi regime is not that stable and the assassination of dissidents is still not off his agenda.
3. Pitt the Elder, Edward Stanley and William Gladstone.
4. Interview by Fulcrum TV for *Dispatches*, Channel 4.
5. Hugh Thomas 'at thirty yards, you'd expect the bullet to go almost straight though anybody standing in front of it.' Lt Col George Styles confirmed this saying he did not believe she could have been shot from the submachine gun, because the bullet was travelling comparatively slowly.

6. Tom Peile, the Security Manager for the building, Channel 4, *Dispatches*.

7. MI5 redeemed themselves with Mrs Thatcher by running the dirty tricks campaign against the National Union of Mineworkers and its president, Arthur Scargill. She then understood how useful it is to have a secret lever of the state to carry out the will of the prime minister outside the formal political structure.

8. In late February 1984, Nagler took apart a gold-coloured Mercedes, number plate BNY604, in one of Hein's workshops at 32 Kleinstrasse, Berlin. He wrapped three Walther PPK pistols in plastic and hid them in the sump. On the 28, he drove the car to Britain, his ticket shows he stayed in Cabin 307, deck C; just one of several trips to Britain.

9. It is available at the National Security Archive website, www.qwu.edu/~nsarchiv/.

10. There are other good reasons for believing this was not the work of the Provisional IRA. It was the same time as Warrenpoint, their single biggest attack on the British army when they killed eighteen British servicemen in a bomb attack. The purpose of this was to deliver a great propaganda coup to their troops. Instead, they lost the PR war through the cowardly assassination of a pensioner. Though the IRA always liked to punch above its weight, the fact is that it was never more than a few hundred strong and the number of skilled operators was a fraction of this. The internal British Army view was that they did not carry out two major operations on the same day and furthermore did not have enough skilled bombers to do both.

11. Zeigler, Philip, *Mountbatten: the Official Biography*, London 1985, p. 528.

12. Personal interview.

13. These details are contained in an affidavit written by Jock Weir, one of the most extraordinary documents to come out of Northern Ireland.

6. Get Your Cover Story Straight

1. For an interesting analysis of Becket and Henry see *The Age of Faith: A History of Medieval Civilization – Christian, Islamic and Judaic – from Constantine to Dante AD 325–1300*, Will Durant New York 1950.

2. The Constitutions of Clarendon was signed by all sides in January 1164.

3. Benedict of Peterborough's description of the scene after the murder of Thomas Becket, in *English Historical Documents*

volume II, 1042–1189. Edited by David C. Douglas and George W. Greenaway, 1991, pp. 820–1.

4. Church Committee Report, p. 316.

5. Interview with Richard Bissell Junior, quoted in John Ranelagh, *The Agency, The Rise and Decline of the CIA*, 1986, London.

6. Church Committee Report, p. 334.

7. Memo written by George McManus, Executive Assistant to Richard Helms, 19 January 1962, Church Committee Report, p. 141.

8. The CIA assassination manual from 1954 says, 'It should be assumed that it [assassination] will never be ordered or authorized by any US Headquarters, though the latter may in rare instances agree to its execution by members of an associated foreign service. This reticence is partly due to the necessity for committing communications to paper.'

9. Harvey's testimony to the Church Committee, 25 June 1975, quoted p. 316.

10. President Reagan did the same with Colonel Oliver North who then ran an illegal arms and drug network to finance the Contras in Latin America. More recently, President George W. Bush did the same in the preparations for the invasion of Iraq, completely bypassing the CIA and the traditional Washington intelligence network.

11. Church Committee Report p. 335, evidence given 17 July 1975, pp. 44–45.

12. Church Committee Report p. 336, memo written January 30 1962.

13. Church Committee Report p. 142, the quote comes from Parrott.

14. CIA Inspector General's Report on Plots to Assassinate Fidel Castro, 23 May 1967.

15. She has told her story in an autobiography, *My Story, with Ovid Demaris*, 1977. The Church Committee referred to her as a 'close friend' of the President who was also a 'close friend' of two mafia bosses, Johnny Roselli and Sam Giancana. There can be little doubt that this story is true. The White House phone logs show seventy phone calls between her and Kennedy.

16. Sam Giancana was shot at his home in Oak Park Illinois on 18 or 19 June 1975 with a .22 handgun with silencer. There were no signs of forced entry implying that he knew – and trusted – whoever shot him.

17. Richard Helms.

18. Church Committee Report, p. 149, evidence given on 13 June 1975.

19. Carroll, Lewis, *Through The Looking Glass*, 1871.
20. Lansdale never went public with this story. The source is Daniel Ellsberg, who worked with Lansdale in Vietnam. Ellsberg was a contract analyst with the Rand Corporation and leaked what became known as the Pentagon Papers to the *New York Times*, a collection of memos, telegrams and minutes of meetings which provided a definitive account of the US slide into war. For a fuller account see Seymour Hersh's brilliant account of the Kennedy years, *The Dark Side of Camelot*, New York 1997, pp. 426–8.
21. Presidential Order 12333.
22. There was another much more cynical view in the CIA, articulated by Vincent Canistraro and others. The really danger-ous countries in the Middle East, like Syria, were too big for the US to tackle so whenever anything went wrong they attacked Libya, 'kicking the cat' in his phrase. The great advantage was that Qaddafi liked being attacked by the Americans as it enhanced his credibility in the Arab world. Everyone benefited but it had little reference to anything that was actually happening.
23. Woodward Veil, Bob, *The Secret Wars of the CIA*, London 1987, p. 186.
24. The details are contained in a classified Soviet report by Air Force Marshal Koldunov, US aggression against LIBYA, 20 April 1986. A translation is available at the website of the Cold War International History Project. According to this report, three US aircraft flew into Libyan airspace at 12.00 hours on 24 March 1986. Two Russian VEGA anti-aircraft missiles were launched and 'the target disappeared from the monitor'. The American search and rescue helicopters were then immediately deployed, suggesting they were looking for wreckage. Two more aircraft were seen in Libyan airspace later that day, at 18.00 hours and again the Libyans fired missiles, in all claiming five hits.
25. United Nations Charter, Article 51: 'Nothing in the present Charter shall impair the inherent right of individual or collective self-defence if an armed attack against a member of the UN, until the Security Council has taken measures necessary to maintain international peace and security.'
26. Craddock, Sir Percy, *In Pursuit of British Interests*, London 1997, p. 74.
27. This whole incident was brilliantly investigated by John Goetz, a producer for *Frontal*, the current affairs flagship programme for ZDF television in Germany. The programme was transmitted in August 1988.

28. The details are contained in a classified Soviet report by Air Force Marshall Koldunov, US aggression against LIBYA, 20 April 1986. A translation is available at the website of the Cold War International History Project.
29. This was an off-the-record conversation with one of the officers involved, who cannot be named for obvious legal reasons.
30. Vincent Canistraro, interview for PBS/WGBH Frontline, 2001.
31. The phrase is from Craddock, Sir Percy, *In Pursuit of British Interests*, London 1997, p. 76.

7. Whenever You Can, Set Up a Patsy

1. There is a very good analysis of this in Michael Karpin and Ina Friedman, *Murder in the Name of God*, London, 1998, Chapter Four.
2. These were the two criteria identified by General Dalla Chiesa, who was assassinated by the Italian mafia.
3. A Beretta 84F semi-automatic pistol, .380 calibre, serial number D98231Y.
4. Shamgar Report p. 89.
5. Nachman ben-Yehuda, *One More Political Murder by Jews*, Nachman ben-Yehuda, Chapter Two, 'The Assassination of Yitzhak Rabin', edited Yoram Peri, Stamford, California, 2000.
6. *Jerusalem Post*, 5 November 1995.
7. Legal cross-examination of Amir.
8. Chamish, Barry, *Who Murdered Yitzhak Rabin?* Venice, CA 1998. Although this is a highly controversial book, the core information contained is accurate. Barry Chamish very kindly provided me with photocopies of the key documents, Dr Gutman's note and the transcript of Gladstein's evidence. But you do not need to be a pathologist to work out that Yigal Amir, standing behind Rabin, cannot possibly have shot him in the chest.
9. Raviv was on trial as at August 2004.
10. Robert Kennedy, post-mortem, page 1, with more details on p. 2.
11. Wecht, Cyril, *Cause of Death*, New York 1993.
12. There is a vast literature on this. It had various project names, ARTICHOKE, MK-ULTRA, and involved some of the most exotic Cold War science – on both sides of the Iron Curtain.
13. Taking the measurement of the newspaper, which is known, and extrapolating it gives a man who is five foot four and a half inches tall, a good five inches shorter than Lee Harvey Oswald was in real life.

14. He was arrested by Superintendent Tommy Butler, of the Metropolitan Police Flying Squad.

15. One of the tapes sent to Johnson and his Attorney General Robert Kennedy was King making a highly questionable joke about the sex life of Jack Kennedy that involved the funeral and Mrs Kennedy. Edgar Hoover knew how to hurt a guy. Richard Gid Powers, *Secrecy and Power: The Life of J. Edgar Hoover*, p. 417.

16. The FBI war against the black civil rights movement was part of a much wider operation against political dissidents, which went under the code name COINTELPRO (counter intelligence programme) and ran from 1956 to 1971. The targets were predominantly left wing and black and the US government used harassment, intimidation, violence, fraud, forgery, theft, false arrest, encouraging gang warfare and falsely labelling activists as police informers knowing they would be assassinated. See 'Supplementary Detailed Staff Reports on Intelligence Activities and the Rights of Americans, Book III, Final Report of the Select Committee to Study Governmental Operations with respect to Intelligence Activities', 23 April 1976.

17. Even Gerald Posner, who believes that Ray was the killer and therefore bears the ultimate responsibility for King's death, argues that 'Whilst it may not have pulled the trigger, the government did however, by such outrageous conduct, create an atmosphere where racists thought it was safe to shoot a black leader in the south and think they could get away with it. To that extent, the government bears moral responsibility for the death of Dr King', *Killing The Dream*, New York 1998.

8. Beware the Powers at Work

1. The dress, designed by Christina Stambolian, subsequently sold for $74,000 at auction.

2. It is not clear whether they had a sexual affair. Prince Charles' cheerleaders, like the writer Penny Junor who is one of his inner circle, have tried to protect him by smearing Diana and blaming her for the collapse of the marriage because of her sexual affair with Mannakee. However, there is no evidence of such a relationship and if there were, Charles' long-standing affair with Camilla Parker Bowles, his life-long mistress, predates it.

3. There can be no doubt about this as she spent days away at Hewitt's house in Devon, with her royal protection guard with her, her every movement reported back to London.

4. The former MI6 officer, Richard Tomlinson, received the same threat when he refused to sign a contract guaranteeing his silence. After this threat, he reached for the pen ...

5. There are several accounts of these threats. Hewitt first broke the story in *Death of a Princess*, Fulcrum TV for ITV. Charles Wardle, a Conservative MP, gave a full account of them in a speech to the House of Commons, 22 June 1999.

6. The member of the royal family has been identified to me along with the regiment concerned. For obvious legal reasons he cannot be named, however there is no doubt that such an exchange took place.

7. In one case a paparazzo chased her as she drove across West London shouting at her that she was a 'cunt' and 'a whore' to try and force her to cry.

8. Rob Evans and Richard Norton-Taylor, *Guardian*, 26 August 1999.

9. These were the two conditions identified by General Dalla Chiesa, the prefect of Palermo, see Chapter Nine, p. 22.

10. At Le Bourget were Romuald Rat and his driver Stephane Darmon (on a dark blue Honda 650, registration 302 LXT 75), Fabrice Chassery (black Peugeot 205, registration 5816 WJ 92), David Oderkerken (driving a beige Mitsubishi Pajero 4 × 4 (S20 LZP 75), Alain Guizard (driving a grey/blue Peugeot registration number 3904 ZR 92) and Laurent Cahuet (blue BMW motorbike).

11. Police statement, 3 September 1997.

12. Alain Guizard drove a grey/blue Peugeot registration number 3904 ZR 92 and was the driver of the only dark Peugeot 205 at Le Bourget.

13. I met him in Paris and apart from being a genuinely nice man he is an exceptionally gifted driver. I asked him if the paparazzi had modified their behaviour since the crash and he replied no, 'It does not matter if you have Sharon Stone or Princess Diana, it is always the same!' He also confirmed that when the Paris paparazzi do not get the picture they want they punish the drivers and frighten the stars by firing their camera flashes in the driver's eyes.

14. Alain Guizard, working for the Angeli Agency, told police that he was called between 12.30 and 1 p.m. and told that the couple were on their way to Paris from Sardinia.

15. Apart from the false claim about Henri Paul's remarks to the journalists, he planted two other rumours, neither of which were true. He claimed the Mercedes sped off, though again he was the only one who saw this and he also claimed that a Ritz Hotel security manager had told the police that Henri Paul was drunk. In fact, he told police the exact opposite.

16. The four are Serge Benamou, Jacques Langevin, Fabrice Chassery and Alain Guizard. This is confirmed in the judge's report who remarks that 'he [Lucard] alone described it'.

17. Professor Murray Mackay, one of the world's leading car crash experts believes that these were the two speeds. The official crash report has a range but the median figure is close to Mackay's.

18. Letter to police dated 31 August 1997, plus statement 24 September 1997. He says the registration of the scooter/motor-bike was 75, making the most likely candidates Serge Benhamou (who drove a green Honda scooter, registration 884 LCD 75) or Romuald Rat, who was travelling pillion with Stephane Darmon (on a dark blue Honda 650, registration 302 LXT 75).

19. The most likely candidate for this was Alain Guizard, a reporter who was working for the Angeli Agency. In his statement to the police on 3 September 1997 he said he moved his car back at the lights to allow Martinez to go behind the Mercedes.

20. The source is Jean Louis Bonnin. He gave a statement to the police on 24 September 1997 and to the judge on 27 April 1998.

21. The presence of the motorbike blocking the exit is suggested in the technical papers used to advise the judge.

22. French police source.

23. A confidential source who has seen the original statements and was shocked both at the virulence of the anti-American racism and the fact that the internal police culture is so indisciplined that a detective could feel confident enough to write this without fear of being disciplined.

24. Final report by Paris Prosecutor's Office. The judges were Hervé Stephan and Christine Devidal.

25. Mobile phone records contain a lot of data: the time (which is accurate to the second), the number called, whether it was sent or received and most crucially of all where the call was made from. In this instance there are three cells: the Place Vendome (where the Ritz is located), the Place de la Concorde (where the paparazzi surrounded the Mercedes) and the Alma tunnel (the crash site).

26. Rees-Jones, Trevor, *The Bodyguard's Story*, p. 75.

27. Police statement 3 September 1997.

28. Philippe Dourneau, Statement, 3 September 1997, p. 3.

29. He names them as Martinez, Rat, Oderkerken and Benhamou.

30. Identified as D22 in the evidence.

31. The details are in his affidavit, which is now widely available on the Internet. The three-page plan was written by Dr Nicholas Fishwick, the MI6 officer in charge of Balkan operations, and was

circulated to Maurice Kendwrisk-Peircey, John Ridde, the SAS liaison officer, Richard Fletcher and Alan Petty, the personal secretary to the MI6 Chief, Sir Colin McColl. It is not clear why the plan was not operated upon.

32. *Diana: The Secrets Behind the Crash*, ITV.

33. The arguments for not returning them have constantly shifted. In September 1999, the judges refused to return them in case they should be needed for other expert appraisals. The Court of Appeal in October 2000 then said (despite case law to the opposite) that the samples were not objects under the criminal code and could not therefore be returned. The next court said it could only be decided by the first judge and the Supreme Court then ruled they could not be returned. Having been assured that the samples had been properly preserved the parents were then told that any analysis of blood levels would not now be accurate, but despite this, the court refused to return them in case they were needed for further analysis. A wonderful legal contradiction, which makes no sense at all. The Paul family then brought a suit against the doctors for falsifying the data, quoting the poor paperwork. The French courts got round that one by refusing to hear the case. All of which misses the point: the parents want the samples back to carry out a DNA test to see whose blood it is.

34. Others joined in including Madonna, Arnold Schwarzenegger, Sean Penn, Tom Hayden and Jane Fonda.

35. The explanation given by Mules was that this was a pre-recorded paragraph on the computer, which was accidentally inserted. However, there is no such paragraph in Diana's post-mortem.

36. It is normal practice for a pregnancy test to be carried out on any woman of child bearing age who dies suddenly and most British coroners would expect this to be done with any British national dying abroad. There is no mention of such a test in her post-mortem, though many believe it was carried out and left unreported. Bizarrely, Diana's body was embalmed, which made any decent pathology impossible. Dodi's father, Mohammed Al Fayed, commissioned research to discover what happens if a standard pregnancy test is carried out on an embalmed body. The results were astonishing, but unhelpful. Urine samples from both men and non-pregnant women were analysed. Regardless of sex, the vast majority of both male and female subjects tested positive, as if they were pregnant.

37. Confidential source. MI6, who knew Aitken well, wanted to know exactly what was going on in Paris.

9. Decide What You Want to Achieve

1. *The Death of Marat* is currently in the Musées Royaux des Beaux-Arts de Belgique, in Brussels.
2. New Annual Register 1793, 186, Quoted by Deborah Kennedy, *Philological Quarterly*, vol 73, 1994, 'Spectacle of the Guillotine: Helen Maria Williams and the Reign of Terror'.
3. Church Committee Report, p. 71.
4. See the Inspector General's Report 1967.
5. Quoted by Deborah Kennedy, *Philological Quarterly*, vol 73, 1994, 'Spectacle of the Guillotine: Helen Maria Williams and the Reign of Terror'.
6. Thompson J.M., *The French Revolution: A History*, OUP 1945, p. 401.
7. The source for this is a CIA case officer who took part in the discussions. One of the key factors in Nyerere's favour was that he was a devout Christian.
8. The Americans set up a committee of scientists to try and discover the true purpose of this signal. Project PANDORA ran for several years but failed to reach an agreed conclusion as to the purpose of this signal, though they did discover that it was possible for the Russians to decode the signal as it bounced back off the window and decipher the conversations taking place inside the room.

10. Always Consider the Alternative

1. Citation 9601, Tape WH6602.01, 9.20 a.m. 1 February 1966. Lyndon Baines Johnson Library and Museum, Austin, Texas. The conversation can be heard at www.whitehousetapes.com.
2. Church Committee Report, p. 218.
3. That the Catholics had a monopoly grip on power was a throwback to the French days. Those who adopted the religion of their colonial masters were rewarded with land and power. The Catholics made up 10 per cent of the population, the Buddhists 70 per cent.
4. Nun Nu Thanh Quang at the Dieu de Pagoda in Hue.
5. State-Saigon Cable 243, 24 August 1963, drafted by Assistant Secretary of State, Roger Hilsman.
6. TOP SECRET EYES ONLY, department of State Memorandum of Conversation.
7. This is a recurrent theme in the White House meetings, 28 August 1963.
8. In an interview for Air University Review January/February 1974, he said that after debate in Washington they decided to

encourage the military to revolt 'on the stupid assumption that they could organize a better government and make more progress against the Viet Cong'.

9. CIA cable, Vietnam station to Director, 5 October 1963, quoted Church Committee Report, p. 220.

10. There is a further reason for CIA caution here. According to Lodge, the Vietnamese plotters were worried that there were elements in the US military who were sympathetic to Diem and his brother and they would pass these plans across. See Cablegram from Lodge to McGeorge Bundy, 30 October 1963, paragraph 6, Pentagon Papers, p. 233.

11. Cable McCone to CIA station 6 October 1963, quoted Church Committee Report, p. 221.

12. Church Committee Report, p. 222, footnote 1.

13. Cablegram from Lodge to McGeorge Bundy, 30 October 1963, paragraph 10, Pentagon Papers, p. 234.

14. Cablegram from McGeorge Bundy to Lodge, October 30 1963, Pentagon Papers pp. 236–7.

15. Pentagon Papers, p. 238 Lodge's Last Talk with Diem, 4.30 p.m. 1 November.

16. Cable from McGeorge Bundy to Lodge, 30 October 1963, Pentagon Papers, p. 237.

17. Church Committee Report, p. 223.

18. Telegram sent to Washington by Ambassador Lodge, 8.45 a.m., 2 November 1963.

19. Church Committee Report, footnote 1, p. 223.

20. Hersh, Seymour, *The Dark Side of Camelot*, New York 1997, p. 417.

21. Citation 9601, Tape WH6602.01, 9.20 a.m. 1 February 1966. Lyndon Baines Johnson Library and Museum, Austin, Texas. The conversation can be heard at www.whitehousetapes.com.

22. This figure was admitted by William Colby.

23. Quoted in Ranelagh p. 439.

24. Hersh, Seymour, *The Dark Side of Camelot*, p. 418.

25. CIA memo 2 November 1963, information as at 07.00 hours, paragraph 4.

26. Thompson was working for BRIAM, the British Advisory Mission, and his dispatches, masterpieces of top-quality military intelligence, can be read at the Public Archives in Kew, south London.

27. Church Committee Report, pp. 324–5.

28. 17–138 CE.

29. 38–161 CE.
30. *Daily Telegraph* 22 June 2004. The weapon is on display at the Vienna Museum of Military History along with the open-topped car in which they were travelling.
31. According to the official record of the District Court: 'Nedeljko Cabrinovic confessed that he was the first of the conspirators to hurl a bomb against the archduke's carriage, which missed its mark and which on exploding injured only the occupants of the carriage following the archducal motor car. Gavrilo Princip confessed that he fired two shots from a Browning pistol against the archducal motor car, by which the Archduke Franz Ferdinand and the Duchess Sophie of Hohenberg received fatal wounds. Both perpetrators confess that the act was done with intent to murder.'
32. This is measured in gold transfers. At 1914 prices, the deficits are: Germany £125m, Austria/Hungary £55m, UK £42m, France £25m, Italy £19m, the Balkans £8m. The beneficiaries are: the USA £278m, Japan £183m, Spain £84m, Argentina £50m, Holland £41m, Switzerland £12m, Sweden and Uruguay £10m and Norway £4m – which left Europe crippled with debt as they both spent their gold reserves and borrowed heavily to pay for this most futile of wars.
33. Transmitted by Thames TV on 28 April 1988. At the time the media split into two camps. Thames TV made a documentary, *Death On the Rock*, which argued that the SAS used excessive force and should have arrested them. The *Sunday Times* and the *Sun* took the opposite view and ran a campaign supporting the SAS, in particular attacking the memory and integrity of Carmen Proetta, the star witness in the television programme.
34. It was (and remains) an article of faith among Republicans that the British ran a shoot-to-kill operation against them from the early 1970s. In particular the IRA claims that the British government used the SAS – and subsequently Protestant paramilitaries – to do their dirty work. The IRA are correct in their claims though wrong in the specifics. Many I have spoken to on the British side concede privately that there was a shoot-to-kill policy but it was not the SAS who were the principal gunmen.
35. £38,700 less 37,731 French Francs which had already been paid in legal aid.
36. At the time Gerry Adams and Martin McGuinness came to the negotiating table with the British, the IRA had suffered huge losses of men and material over the previous twelve months. The

paramilitaries were substantially weakened making Adams' case for a political settlement all the more compelling.

37. There is no doubt that this was a senior IRA active service unit (ASU). McCann had been convicted and sentenced to two years for possession of explosives. Farrell had been convicted and sentenced to fourteen years for causing explosions. During her time in jail she was the leader of the IRA prisoners. According to British Arniy Intelligence, Savage was a senior IRA member and an expert bomb maker. When they were buried in the IRA plot at Milltown, Michael Stone, a Protestant paramilitary, attacked the crowd with grenades, killing three. *An Phoblacht*, the Irish republican newspaper, described them as volunteers.

38. The following account was put together from the official law reports, internal documents and SAS sources.

39. At the inquest there was a dispute among the experts about the aerial. At that time, the IRA used an ICOM IC2 transmitter, the size of an ordinary commercial walkie talkie. Over the years, the Provisional bomb makers had had a lot of trouble with spurious signals (some of them generated by the British army) which had resulted in bombs being detonated early. To counter this they had developed encoders and decoders but these required a good clean signal. The SAS soldiers shot the IRA members dead because they were told this was 'a button job' but this was not true. This device needed three switches not one. An on/off switch for the power, an on/off switch for the encoder and a third switch to transmit. The only way that this could have been a button job is if all the switches had been on but the IRA would not have done this as the batteries would have run down quickly. There was a further common sense reason why this could not have been a button job. Tripping over, being nudged in a crowd would all be enough to trigger the bomb.

40. All Al Qaeda suspects are told to allege torture and mistreatment regardless of how they are treated and this is commonplace for all terrorist groups.

41. Quoted in Thomas, Hugh, *Doppelgangers*, London 1995. The opening chapter has an excellent summary of Hitler's medical condition.

42. Kilzer, Louis, *Hitler's Traitor*, USA 2000. This brilliant book by a double Pulitzer prize winner makes a very convincing case for Bormann being a Russian spy, using the code name 'Werther'.

43. Kilzer, Louis, *Hitler's Traitor*, USA 2000, p. 200. Knowing the German plans, the Russians waited for and completely

outnumbered the Germans, with 1.3 million troops and 3,444 tanks against the Wehrmacht's 900,000 troops and 2,700 tanks. The Germans were smashed, lost the war on the eastern front and began the slow pullback. For the Wehrmacht it was all over.

44. Hosmer, Stephen T., *Operations Against Enemy Leaders*, USAF/RAND Corporation, 2001, p. 34.

11. The Unbroken Chain – From Sadat to the World Trade Centre

1. He got this nickname because he was a compulsive kleptomaniac.
2. House of Commons, 27 February 1945.
3. One of the others was Nokrashy Pasha, another one who was then assassinated himself.
4. Simonne Lacouture, Jean, *Egypt in Transition*, New York 1950, p. 140.
5. Carlson, John Roy, *Cairo to Damascus*, New York 1951, pp. 90–1. Carlson is a highly controversial figure, much hated as a sensationalist and alleged FBI agent. All that may be true but these quotes are in character of much that al-Banna believed and expressed elsewhere.
6. On the record interview in 2003.
7. The source for this is a British intelligence officer who liaised with the Egyptians. For obvious reasons, his identity must remain confidential.
8. Personal interview in Cairo.
9. The related concept is *din moser*, which is the duty to kill a Jew who intends to turn a Jew over to non-Jewish authorities.
10. To the fury of the Egyptian Intelligence Service, Rahman was acquitted having run the defence that he had only been asked a theoretical question and did not realize that he was being asked about Sadat. His subsequent actions show that the court got it wrong.
11. For an excellent account of Qutb and his significance see Gilles Kepel's book, *Revenge of God*, Polity Press, Cambridge 1994.
12. Casey was appointed as DCI, Director of Central Intelligence on 28 January 1981 and retired 29 January 1987. He was a key figure in the Thatcher–Reagan relationship that defined the 1980s, spending a lot of time with Mrs Thatcher, often meeting her for one-to-one conversations.
13. 17 March 1979.
14. He said recently that it would be easy to overthrow the Mubarak regime in Egypt, the problem was that there were not enough

Islamic fundamentalists in the Egyptian military to run the country after a *coup d'état* but this remains their medium term target.

Epilogue

1. Fineman, Daniel, *A Special Relationship: The United States and Military Government in Thailand 1947–1958*, Honolulu 1997, p. 216.
2. Phao was married to the daughter of one of the colonels who helped install Field Marshall Plaek Phibunsongkhram as the military dictator who controlled Thailand.
3. Fineman, p. 134. Phao's police officers assassinated four MPs.
4. The US Ambassador in Thailand was John Peurifoy – his previous posting was as the US Ambassador who worked closely with the CIA and the US State Department in the *coup d'état* against the democratically elected government of Jacobo Arbenz Guzmán in Guatemala. See Chapter One.
5. Church Committee Report, pp. 38–9.
6. CIA cable from Station Officer to Director, 11 October 1960. Church Committee Report, footnote p. 42.
7. Church Committee Report, p. 41.
8. Mulroney says he has no memory of this man.
9. Church Committee Report, p. 182.
10. Church Committee Report, footnote p. 38.

INDEX